Public Pensions

Public Pensions

Gender and Civic Service in the States, 1850–1937

Susan M. Sterett

CORNELL UNIVERSITY PRESS

Ithaca and London

First published 2003 by Cornell University Press

Printed in the United States of America

Library of Congress Cataloging-in-Publication Data

Sterett, Susan Marie.
   Public pensions : gender and civic service in the states, 1850–1937 / Susan M. Sterett.
      p. cm.
Includes bibliographical references and index.
   ISBN 0-8014-3984-1 (cloth : alk. paper)
1. State governments—Officials and employees—Pensions—United States—History.   2. Local officials and employees—Pensions—United States—History.   I. Title.
   JK2474.S74 2003
   331.25′29135173′09034—dc21

                              2003002040

Cornell University Press strives to use environmentally responsible suppliers and materials to the fullest extent possible in the publishing of its books. Such materials include vegetable-based, low-VOC inks and acid-free papers that are recycled, totally chlorine-free, or partly composed of nonwood fibers. For further information, visit our website at www.cornellpress.cornell.edu.

Cloth printing   10 9 8 7 6 5 4 3 2 1

For Maya
who thinks writing about firefighters and mothers is cool-wow

Contents

Acknowledgments

This book began with a hunch, and I am grateful for the education that allowed that hunch. At the University of California, Berkeley, Harry Scheiber taught us about the significance of federalism to the American economy. In addition, Martin Shapiro taught me to take for granted that public law scholars should care about administrative law; I would otherwise not have paid attention to controversies over governance of bureaucracy in the states. The reading I did with both made me think that the exciting new social welfare scholarship emerging from the mid-1980s onward missed something by not attending to litigation in the states. In the Cornell University law library I had the pleasure of first tracking down old state court decisions that told me my hunch might lead me somewhere.

There had been an explosion of scholarship on the social welfare state, and I found myself conversing in my head with feminist scholars whose work on social welfare inspired me. I am grateful to the transformation in the scholarship of the welfare state brought by the historians, sociologists, and political scientists whose studies I engage in this book. Without their work, I never would have thought to ask the questions I did.

For comments on early drafts, conversation, ideas, editing, reference to sources, and suggestions about how to deal with frustration, I am grateful to Bonnie Adrian, Elizabeth Chambliss, Jane Collins, Lisa Conant, Marianne Constable, Howard Gillman, Linda Gordon, Mark Graber, Hendrik Hartog, Karen Orren, Grey Osterud, Lucy Salyer, Susan Schulten, Theda Skocpol, Jack Tweedie, Jeremy Waldron, and the readers for Cornell University Press. I have also benefited from responses to material I have presented at conferences of the Law and Society Association and of the American Political Science Association and at the University of Edinburgh, Queen Mary and Westfield Colleges of the University of London, the University of Denver, and Syracuse University. Archivists at the law firm of Fennemore, Craig in Phoenix and at the Arizona, New Hampshire, and Pennsylvania state archives guided me to relevant parts of their collections. A Henry Phillips Award from the American Philosophical Society provided financial assistance. The University of Denver has provided financial support and leave, and its Rosenberry Fund paid for permission to reprint the illustrations. I thank Pat Sterling, who copyedited the manuscript, and Sheri Englund and Louise E. Robbins at Cornell University Press, who shepherded me through the book publication process.

Without the reliable and excellent care provided for my daughter by the workers at the Schlessman YMCA and the Park Hill United Methodist Children's Center in Denver, I would never have been able to find time to work on the manuscript. Andrea Morgan, Tom Russell, Aida and Danny Morgan-Russell, and Nick, Rae, and Chloe Morgan filled in to help me finish.

Maya Sterett has taught me the work of mothering, admiration of public service, and the significance of books. She has also agreed to take responsibility for remaining problems in the text.

Public Pensions

CHAPTER ONE

Social Welfare in the States

My daughter treasures the red plastic firehats and badges our nearby firehouse gives her when she visits. The men let her climb onto the truck, try on their real firehats, and see the boots and uniforms standing ready for use. All the symbols of power are there for a small child: trucks, hats, uniforms, bells, and lights. Like many American children, she loves seeing the trucks screaming down the street; she likes to announce that they are going to put out fires. As young children, many Americans first envision government power as the power of firefighters. We cannot as easily see or describe what many other government officials do; I can only rarely get students to care about what a disability claims decision-maker does. Firemen do something we can see: they rescue people from damaged buildings and automobile accidents, and they put out fires. Even other visible government officials aren't quite as magical. Police also perform visible service, but they are less idealized because they bring trouble for some, though cities have tried to build support for police by bringing the police into the community. Teachers and social workers don't have uniforms, and presidents are far away. Firefighters are government at our service.

Until September 11, 2001, we were content to be grateful for the work of firefighters and gently amused at the awe in which many children held them. The attack on the World Trade Center brought the awe that many had grown up with into newspapers, magazines, and popular tributes for the hundreds who died. Even the New York City police, under public disapprobation after the assault on Abner Louima and the death of Amidou Diallo, soared in public esteem.[1] Overnight, police and firefighters became national heroes, celebrated throughout American culture. What had long been an adorable trait of young children—that they could imagine no more heroic and noble profession than that of firefighter— blossomed into shared national honor. The syndicated comic strip *Heart of the City* by Mark Tatulli ran a drawing on Veterans' Day in which veterans and a small girl salute a fireman and a policeman who together struggle with a ladder amidst rubble (see figure 1).

Despite our affection and admiration for firemen, however, the service of citizenship has been thought of within political theory as military service.[2] Public culture affirms that citizens owe military service to their country. We have a day to

HEART OF THE CITY   *BY MARK TATULLI*

NOVEMBER 11, 2001
VETERANS DAY

Figure 1. Heart of the City. © 2001 Mark Tatulli. Dist. by UNIVERSAL PRESS SYNDI-
CATE. Reprinted with permission. All rights reserved.

honor veterans, not a day to honor police officers and firefighters. Yet in the nineteenth century the service of citizenship included fighting fires; men served local
governments, not just the national government. Because the attack on the World
Trade Center had to invoke a response from local government, we renewed the
meaning of local government service as significant to citizenship. *Heart of the City*
stated an American sentiment with simple eloquence: on Veterans' Day those we
usually honor turned to honor the firefighters and police officers of New York.

The tragedy in New York revived a theme in American life: the *service* in public service, most especially in dangerous public service, and its significance in
local as well as national government. In responding to an attack on the nation by
doing their civilian, municipal jobs, firefighters and police officers performed
service equivalent to that of the military. A photograph that has become a sym-
bol of American tenacity enacted that connection: three firefighters raise an
American flag in the rubble of the World Trade Center, echoing a famous photograph from World War II of U.S. Marines raising the flag on the Japanese island
of Iwo Jima.[3]

We have acknowledged the service the military provides through benefits such
as pensions and preferences in hiring. Similarly, firefighters, police, and their families receive municipal pensions for retirement or for injuries that occur while they
serve. Payments to injured firemen and their families have a legal history, one that
courts then used to evaluate payments to other civil servants. The legal history of
payments to those who had *served* developed alongside prohibitions against public payments to those who had merely *worked*. In contrast with both, the courts

allowed local governments to grant charitable payments to some of those who were regarded as intrinsically *dependent*. In the early twentieth century, that history shaped what was possible when the states considered payments to poor mothers, to men injured at work, and to the elderly.

Judges, then, policed the boundaries of service and charity; what was excluded from both was ordinary labor. Farmers or mill workers had neither served nor were helpless; states and localities could not subsidize them. Distinctions between public and private today focus on the employer. In the nineteenth century the nature of the service rather than of the employer determined whether something was service or not. Firemen in the early nineteenth century were almost all volunteers, but they were in public service.

Little of this history has appeared in scholars' analyses of social welfare. The heart of this book concerns the ways state courts changed and yet continued to insist upon distinctions between service, work, and charity, between dependence and independence. They did so as legislatures instituted new programs against aspects of which taxpayers and county commissioners brought lawsuits. Beneficiaries also sued to make reluctant officials pay. In the course of this litigation, courts continued to state the concern for the dependence of the poor that had long been a part of the law. State and local governments raised much of their money with property taxes, and not everyone was eager to pay them. Suing was one way people could try to stop taxation. The long political struggles over an income tax in the United States may constitute "the great tax wars," in Steven R. Weisman's words, but skirmishes over taxes in the states and localities have also been frequent. Some have occurred in court, and some of those court cases concerned payments to public servants, the poor, and the disabled.[4]

The public service that firefighters, police, and other civil servants have performed means that the money they receive is never discussed as government charity, or welfare, as we pejoratively call public assistance. Nor do government pensions for those who have worked in jobs covered by public insurance, or for their families, raise any concerns in public debate that the money will create dependence among the recipients. They have earned the money. The public service that firefighters do marks them as independent, no matter that they get government payments.

In contrast, when we pay people out of pity, we worry about their dependence on public money. Law, both common and statutory, has treated poor mothers as necessarily dependent and therefore pitiable at best. In the early twentieth century some advocates for poor women argued that like soldiers, mothers performed public service; they did so by raising children. Statutes, though, seldom recognized poor mothers as anything other than dependent. In recent years, public policy has eliminated even the concept that charity is appropriate for poor mothers.

In 1996 the Personal Responsibility Act required that poor parents, most often mothers, who gain payments from the state must work; work is to cure the dependence that payments from the state create.[5] In 2002 the George W. Bush administration supported the expansion of work requirements but chose not to expand the availability of job training or of child care.

Placing firefighters alongside mothers on public assistance highlights a distinction that many Americans take for granted but that some scholars have pointed out as a puzzle.[6] It is not only that we recognize public service and now work as worthy of public benefit. The meaning of public payments does not just depend on whether one gets assistance after working; having a spouse or parent who worked can be enough. Families who gain public benefits through the service or work of a wage earner are seldom the targets of public concern as dependents. Many of the families who tragically lost wage-earning husbands, fathers, or mothers in the attacks on the World Trade Center will receive municipal pensions or federal assistance, charitable donations from a shocked United States, and payments from a national compensation fund. Americans are deeply sympathetic concerning the losses they have suffered and the difficulties for mothers of raising children after a father has died.[7] But the terms we apply to what people do and the state payments they get—service, work; charity, pensions; dependence, independence—were embedded in *state* constitutional law in the United States long before the New Deal's 1935 Social Security Act. In nineteenth-century law, dangerous service in localities merited pensions. As states expanded pensions, litigation redefined service, and by the time of the New Deal, ordinary wage labor also merited reward. Childbearing and child rearing, however, still marked dependence and merited, if anything, only charity; they were seen neither as service nor as noticeably dangerous. How were these ideas embedded in law? And how did they change?

State constitutional and common law and state courts' accessibility to litigants made it difficult to institute *national* social welfare payments. Because so much of governing happens in the states, the state constitutional governance of pensions is significant in its own right, but it also had implications for interpreting the national Constitution. Once Roosevelt signed the Social Security Act in 1935, and corporate lawyers challenged the programs toward which employers were required to pay taxes—unemployment insurance and old age social security—it was state constitutional debates concerning public payments that provided the groundwork for explaining why the programs were indeed constitutional. Remembering that the United States is federal leads us to state disputes over firemen, police, and poor mothers. Those disputes in turn shaped meanings within the national Constitution.

The shifting meanings of service and independence in American life make up the framework that shapes the rest of this book. Early twentieth-century debates over social welfare and constitutional interpretation brought new problems, inviting the courts to rethink old principles.

From Service to Work

In the early United States, service signified independence, a valuable quality in a republic. In contrast, pitiable people who could not care for themselves merited charity. An initial meaning of independence included not working for a wage; laboring was regarded as nothing more than wage slavery. The abolitionist movement and the Civil War changed those meanings dramatically, as Amy Dru Stanley has explained.[8] But these meanings shaped the constitutional law governing firefighting and charity in the nineteenth century.

In the antebellum United States, cities celebrated municipal fire services and fire departments. Firemen were *volunteers* and thus merited reward as did soldiers. Cities paid firemen not because they had served the nation but because they had served the locality. After the Civil War, services became paid and professional in cities, making service less evident in public culture; in law, though, service began to include paid *dangerous* service. Then nineteenth-century intellectuals began to celebrate all work as public service, and we recognize the importance of work today, not least by tying public benefits to it. The public acclaim that firefighters and police earned after September 11 powerfully demonstrated that we no longer require that service be voluntary to merit honor. In the early twentieth century, as public court battles successfully justified labor as service, states expanded payments to include workmen's compensation. Until the New Deal, though, state courts were unwilling to allow legislatures to mandate payments to the elderly or to poor women as rewards for service.

State court cases illuminate the historical significance of federalism in American citizenship. The demands of the nation for military service usually draw attention in any analysis of the service of citizenship.[9] In the nineteenth century, however, the localities always needed men ready to fight fires, whereas the national state made only sporadic demands. Taking military service as the exemplar of the service of citizenship ignores the federal structure of the United States. In the nineteenth century, foreign nations and domestic rebels were not the only enemies, and wars were not the only dangers. Fires threatened the tightly packed cities, and early in the century, volunteering to fight fires was a local service of citizenship. In return for that service, states provided for charitable homes or relief payments for volunteer firemen long before the Civil War. Volunteers had answered a call, taking time from their families and risking their lives for the common good.

Once state and local governments began to *employ* firemen (and policemen and teachers), service no longer looked so distinct from work. Police worked as police in order to support themselves. Were police then like farmers or steelworkers, who worked in a market economy to support their families? If so, would not any payment beyond an agreed salary encroach on their independence, constitute theft from the public treasury, and violate state constitutional presumptions against class legislation against (i.e., laws that benefit one class of people at the expense of another)? If police were more like soldiers, however, then they had served the public good and deserved compensation beyond their wages. States thus expanded pensions to include paid firemen and police, then teachers and other civil servants. When local officials refused to pay, judges had to decide whether dangerousness had been essential to service after all.

To demand military service or firefighting from citizens is to demand that citizens recognize obligations to the polity that are beyond the daily demands of working for a living. Not until the late nineteenth century did work become a public obligation for men (and for African American women), one that the state was willing to enforce through vagrancy statutes and labor contracts. Intellectuals argued that consenting to an employer paralleled consenting to government, making the labor contract parallel the political contract. Just as a free man consented to being governed, an employed man was free because he had consented to an employer. Thus, working for an employer became both necessary public service and the hallmark of freedom—or so intellectuals who had never labored long hours in a steel mill or at a sewing machine argued. Citizens owed their country labor; professionals would take care of the firefighting that had once been voluntary service.[10] Working Americans resisted the idea that freedom included "wage slavery"; freedom implied that one could opt out. But by the late nineteenth century, contract was seen as so important to a well-ordered society that state legislatures enacted laws requiring that people labor.[11] If men were to receive the benefit of being part of the polity, they ought to return something of value, not just service but wage labor. Isomorphism between the political contract and the employer–employee contract made working a public obligation rather than something one did only to pay for food, shelter, and amusement.

Pensions paid in old age or to compensate injury or illness have been called part of the social rights of citizenship, or a marker of belonging, to use T. H. Marshall's term. The United States has tied pensions to work and service rather than to simply belonging, but such payments first emerged from local governance, not from the central state that gained Marshall's attention.[12]

Into the messy variability of local pensions administered in the late nineteenth century entered economists, social workers, and political scientists with new ideas about how to ensure that workers and their families would be protected in case of disaster.

The New Social Welfare

From the late nineteenth century onward, progressive reformers educated in Europe concerning the possibilities of a social welfare state—including I. M. Rubinow, Edward Devine, and Abraham Epstein—proposed that states provide pensions for people who, through no fault of their own, were unable to support themselves: injured, ill, and disabled workers; unemployed workers; and the elderly. They called these programs social insurance, for they would require both workers and employers to contribute to funds that would insure workers against disasters or debility. Social insurance would provide state payments to all employees, not only to those who had served the state through either voluntarism or public employment.

The most vigorous advocates were often men attuned to the risks of the workplace for workingmen and the families who needed to depend on them.[13] They believed that the need for these programs rested in transformations in industrial capitalism, which led to frequent injury. Moreover, many workers were employed at low wages in an economy prone to frequent financial crises, recessions, and depressions that could plunge people into desperate poverty. Paying those unable to work and saying they had *earned* payments departed dramatically from paying people because they were pitiable, or investigating whether their injuries were their fault, or assuming that their unemployment resulted from laziness.[14] According to social insurance advocates, men hurt or unemployed within industrial capitalism had earned payments; they were not dependent. Like the social theorists who believed that the wage-labor contract paralleled political freedom, Devine and Rubinow argued that men injured or in poverty who had served their country in industry *deserved* payment.

Mothers were particularly vulnerable. Maternal responsibilities made working for wages difficult, though some took low-paid work they could do at home, such as needlework or rolling cigars or taking in boarders (which charity workers believed put women at risk of sexual immorality). Those who found employment in factories or offices had to arrange some way to care for their children. The fortunate could rely on a neighbor or an adult family member; others put children in the care of older siblings, or left them to the streets, or placed them in orphanages for what the mothers hoped would be a short stint. Social insurance advocates believed that the programs they wanted would protect mothers by paying them if their husbands died. Women whose husbands disappeared, however, or whose children's fathers had never been husbands, would not be eligible for social insurance. Women who had lived and worked with poor women in urban settlement houses were aware of such problems.

The prominence of such women as Florence Kelley, Julia Lathrop, Edith Abbott, and Sophonisba Breckinridge, and their attentiveness to the harms that urban industrialism posed for women and children, have led scholars to call the politics of the Progressive Era maternalist.[15] Activist women argued that social insurance for male workers was not enough. Breckinridge argued for equal wages for women. Lathrop and others argued that mothers themselves should receive payments to compensate their publicly valuable work of raising children (although the casework methods of social workers and charity workers led most to believe that the recipients required close supervision, since they were unlikely to understand budgets or how to run a household).[16] Some activists, including charity workers, believed that the individual morals and choices of poor women were the problem.[17] Middle-class clubwomen across the country enthusiastically supported payments for poor mothers, and after 1909, these mothers' pensions spread throughout the states. Because states often allowed counties to choose whether to implement the pensions, however, even though the idea changed the way public welfare workers saw motherhood, in many counties it meant very little change for the poor women themselves.

Rubinow and Devine believed that payments to mothers were glorified poor relief, making poor women dependent on the state. Legally, married women were dependents of men, and nothing about their proper legal dependency implied that they had earned mothers' pensions, whatever advocates thought. Although women's rights activists bitterly protested the enforced legal dependency of married women, Rubinow, Devine, and Epstein saw no reason to change it.[18] If men as workers and husbands could get more secure payments when they were ill or injured, they could better protect women from needing poor relief.

During the nineteenth century, women were believed incapable of being full legal citizens because of their intrinsically dependent nature. There were some changes in women's rights through the century: married women gained the right to hold property from the 1840s, the right to their wages from the 1870s, and the right to vote in state elections from the 1890s.[19] The judges who interpreted these rights, however, often believed it was not possible to transform a woman's dependence on her husband.[20] She should not earn wages that were separate from household money, and the judges often interpreted wage statutes narrowly to maintain the legal fiction of unity. (Enforcing unity may not always have been bad news for married women; a woman separating from her husband could use the law to try to extract money from him, since she was properly dependent on him.) Despite the changes in statutory, common, and constitutional law over time, women's status in family law as dependents remained remarkably consistent until after the New Deal.[21]

The ideas of Devine and Rubinow, Kelley and Breckinridge, and others shaped the social welfare debates and policies of the day. One scholarly debate about those ideas concerns whether payments to poor women were first instituted as mothers' pensions in the United States because of the work they did in raising children or simply because they were intrinsically dependent. Theda Skocpol has argued that advocates meant to enact payments for mothering as service but that implementation derailed the program. Linda Gordon has argued that the separation of social work from social insurance grounded payments from the beginning in pity.[22] But recognizing law as part of the political structure of the United States means that it was not only social workers and social insurance advocates and their legislative opponents who shaped policy; so did railroads and other businesses, cranky taxpayers and county commissioners who took their complaints to court. Litigation continued the old distinction between those who served and those who did not, and in law, mothers did not. Further, debates about service involved discussion of local pensions for civil servants as well as for poor women or the elderly or injured. The United States was very different politically from any country in Europe, and its political structure shaped what was possible.

Theda Skocpol has attended to the significance of the political structure. Her explication addresses the uneasy perceptions of the American state held by American reformist elites. The United States had no reliable bureaucracy that could distribute pensions according to criteria to be set by legislatures, and that lack of administrative state capacity, she has argued, made it unlikely that social insurance policies would work as happily as they did in Europe. The United States did distribute some national social welfare payments: national military pensions throughout the nineteenth century honored the service veterans had performed and could have provided a stepping-stone to broader social welfare payments. They did not, according to Skocpol, because American elites in the late nineteenth century held those pensions in contempt as being distributed widely with little regard to tying payment to actual service rendered.[23] Still, those pensions have provided fruitful grounds for research concerning what it means to earn pensions, and, since veterans' family members could also receive them, how the national government defined families.[24]

If we include the significance of federalism and state constitutional law in understanding political structure, however, as I argue we must, national military pensions are not clear precursors to national social insurance. National military pensions were *constitutionally* distinctive: the national government could spend this money only because it had the constitutional power to conduct war. Since states and localities did most of the governing, they were the ones with the power to distribute money for more than military service; men fought fires locally, and the dependent and pitiable were local responsibilities. National welfare payments would require a change in constitutional thinking, and that came about through the practices of litigation in *state* courts and through argument and advocacy in *state* bureaucracies. Analysis of social welfare must include law not only as a *structure* but as a *site of contest*. Litigation in specific cases contested the meanings that common-law categories contained for public payments.

Litigation was both a structure and a site of contest for state social insurance programs. Following pensions for civil servants, states began to enact workmen's compensation, or payments to those who had been injured on the job. A few states enacted old age pensions, beginning with Arizona in 1914. They tried to justify these payments by explaining that the elderly in poorhouses and receiving county relief payments had labored long and hard building their country; they had thus not only worked but served. When this argument succeeded in the legislature, however, it failed in court: state courts held the programs unconstitutional in every state that enacted mandatory old age pensions before the New Deal.

Ann Shola Orloff has analyzed the conditions for the political success or failure of old age pensions in three countries, including the United States. Like Skocpol, she grounds her explanation in the U.S. structure of governance. The national government had no reliable bureaucracy that would distribute pensions through rules rather than through patronage. Yet the national civil service retirement pensions enacted in 1920 raised the question of general old age retirement pensions; indeed, Orloff argues that they made other pensions possible.[25] Since American governance was chiefly local, though, municipal pensions are the more relevant comparison, and cities had been distributing money to retired firemen for years. Those pensions were not simple precursors to old age pensions; rather, they fit into the complex web of constitutional governance in the states that controlled charity and rewards for service. The structure of governance that draws the attention of Skocpol and Orloff should include constitutional litigation and contests over statutory interpretation in the states. It also should include the programs the courts affirmed, such as payments for civil servants. Focusing only on what they denied, mandatory and generous old age pensions and mothers' pensions, does not explain why they denied those programs.

The debates of those who thought so systematically about the labor market and how to address the human costs it imposed have made us accustomed to treating general old age pensions, worker's compensation, and payments to poor mothers as social welfare. I. M. Rubinow, Edith Abbott, Sophonisba Breckinridge, and E. T. Devine, well aware of locally administered poor relief, wanted to design programs that would be on a wholly new footing. But localities had paid some men not on the basis of poor relief but because they had served. The category of service and what it meant in the states influenced a whole set of payments: to firemen's charities, then to men who raised money to buy substitutes for Civil War service, then to firemen, policemen, and teachers for disability or the incapacity that old age brought. Each was distinct from general old age pensions, for they rewarded public service, which remained distinct *in law* from the ordinary labor of farmers and independent workers until the New Deal brought old age social security.

Even as the national government took responsibility for social welfare in 1935, federalism remained crucial in the shape that programs took, as Suzanne Mettler has argued. The 1935 Social Security Act differentiated between payments as a result of workforce participation and charitable relief for the desperate poor. Programs divided recipients into those who gained more generous federal-level payments and those who, not gaining payments through employment, were left to state programs and state administration. Mettler calls this a division of the welfare state into an "upper tier" and a "lower tier."[26] Pensions for the elderly were separated from payments to poor women who were raising children, enacted as Aid to Dependent Children (ADC) and left largely to the payment and administration of the states.

Even in national payments to the elderly, Congress distinguished between kinds of work; not all labor was deemed valuable enough to deserve pensions. The work of many women and African American men—domestic labor, clerical work, teaching, nursing, and agricultural labor—was initially excluded from the provisions for old age social security.[27] Such exclusion meant that few African Americans and white women could participate as workers in the "upper tier" of the American social welfare state.[28] The federalism that Mettler argues shaped the tiers also fits with what scholars have called a two-track welfare state.[29] That term distinguishes between programs that make payments which Americans believe claimants have earned, such as old age social security, and programs that make payments which most Americans believe claimants have not earned—in particular, Aid to Families with Dependent Children, transformed in 1996 to Temporary Assistance to Needy Families.[30] The federal government both enshrined and transformed the distinctions that state courts had made between earning and charity. Mothers' payments continued to be a matter of charity. In contrast, though no state court had previously been willing to recognize the lifetime labor of the elderly as service meriting reward, the Social Security Act granted them pensions as entitlement. Although the state courts had held that not all labor was service, the debates that that distinction had forced laid the groundwork for acceptance of labor *as* service after the New Deal, with some states enacting constitutional amendments to ward off previous problems.

Among those trying to create a world in which mothers did not work for wages,

Rubinow and Devine believed that insurance for working men would protect the wives and children. Impatient with the unreality of that vision, Kelley and Lathrop believed that the women should get money on their own account. Today, most mothers are also waged workers. Government payments that aspire to keep women at home with their children make little sense to the many parents who daily juggle the demands of workforce and family, and indeed, the new policies are designed to limit the choices the poor can make.[31] The social rights of citizenship in the United States now require work of virtually everyone but children (and some who have access to another's wage, whether through marriage or inheritance). Criticizing work requirements, Frances Fox Piven has pointed out that requiring recipients of public assistance to work for their checks is likely to hurt low-wage workers: they may be replaced by "workfare" recipients because workfare pays less than the minimum wage. To keep the wages of other low-wage workers down, an employer faced with a tight job market can turn to the more employable of those on public assistance.[32] The value placed on waged work that emerged in the late nineteenth century has made even receiving charity require work.

Litigation tends to conserve the categories written into the law. In the nineteenth and early twentieth centuries, the state courts did indeed try to maintain boundaries between service, work, and charity. Yet state court judges also agreed to expanded definitions of those who had earned payments—until legislatures tried to expand "service" to include all the elderly and poor mothers. How could judges insist on consistency and yet agree to new meanings?

Constitutionalism, the Common Law, and Litigants

Cases challenging pensions or demanding them from local governments did not appear in state courts only because someone cared about maintaining some grand constitutional principle requiring that people serve before getting a public payment. Taxpayers who did not want to pay additional taxes (whether or not they cared about the principle), county commissioners who did not want to cede control to the states, and policemen denied a pension by the city all sued under the long-standing doctrine that limited taxing and spending to a public purpose. Litigation relies on rules rather than opinion polls, making it possible to challenge programs long after cases that first articulated the relevant doctrine seem outdated to economists and political scientists and even state commissions. Litigants had to mobilize the public purpose doctrine, and state commissions had to interpret it. When they did, they ensured that the doctrine persisted.

Persistence of the public purpose doctrine frustrated legal reformers because it allowed state judges to strike down programs designed to help working people—

even though some judges approved remarkable innovations such as regulating child labor in the states and limiting the hours that women could work. Legal scholars struggled to understand judges' decisions. Believing that something in the world outside the law books shaped decisions, in 1908 Louis Brandeis and Josephine Goldmark provided evidence of the harm to women caused by long hours at work to try to persuade the U.S. Supreme Court that it should allow states to limit the hours women work. From their "sociological jurisprudence" and from the work of others, including scholars at Columbia University and Yale Law School, came legal realism.[33]

Legal scholars joined the ferment of reform extolling the virtues of a generous social welfare state. A few believed that the new state about which Rubinow, Devine, Lathrop, and Breckinridge wrote so passionately required new tools and a new focus for scholarship. Frank Goodnow, who was a professor both of law and of political science at Columbia University, urged that law in a new social welfare state would require tools more sophisticated than holding governments accountable by approving programs or striking them down as unconstitutional (the practice that had exasperated Progressive lawyers such as Louis Brandeis). Rather, as governments took on new tasks, safeguarding rights would require proper procedures in administration. Thus, the real concern for scholars ought to be administrative law, which encompassed all the organization of public administration. Goodnow's comparative study of administrative law, published in 1893, noted the historical contingency of local government organization.[34] If organization was contingent, it was not constitutionally required. Governments could be reorganized to serve public purposes, and European states might offer some lessons for Americans in how to do it. His colleague Ernst Freund agreed. Freund moved from Columbia to the University of Chicago, also teaching both law and political science. He trained Sophonisba Breckinridge, the sociologist who helped to found the Chicago School of Social Work.[35] For Freund and Goodnow and their students, understanding social welfare rested in knowing the administration of the law.

Goodnow and Freund were right: if rights matter in a regulatory and welfare state, it is in the workings and the supervision of administration. Yet the historical debate concerning the welfare state centers on just how much legislation the courts did or did not hold unconstitutional, not on how they interpreted the many statutes they held to be constitutional. Goodnow's and Freund's crucial point was that the two shade into each other: once programs are established, if we care about rights, we had best care about how statutes are interpreted. This book suggests bridging the gap between constitutional and statutory scholarship by integrating Goodnow's and Freund's scholarship on social welfare into discussions of constitutionality. Examining how courts supervised the interpretation of statutes reveals meanings of dependence and independence just as the constitutional cases do.

How could Freund and Goodnow believe in the importance of law and legal consistency, yet admit the possibility of new powers? Goodnow's answer was to incorporate all the organization of governance into his study of law. Freund emphasized the importance of historical context. To argue that judges truly use the categories they claim to rely on yet also acknowledge legal change is a problem for any analysis of transformation within the courts.

Alarmed that some legal realists had become too dismissive of the importance of rules to judges, Roscoe Pound tried to answer the question of how legal reasoning could allow both change and stability. In 1938, Pound, who had coined the term "sociological jurisprudence," wrote against those who were skeptical that rules mattered. He argued that legal scholars must attend to the "gradual shaping of obstinate traditional precepts and doctrines through the need of applying them to new economic conditions." Reapplying doctrine did indeed "reshap[e] ideals of the legal order."[36]

The practical use of those "obstinate traditional precepts" is what kept litigation as consistent as it was. Believing that legal principles ought to be consistent and sustained over time, practitioners, including judges, acted as though they were. Pound insisted on those precepts just after the United States Supreme Court had been under attack as a politically motivated group of men bent on preventing any government from doing anything about the Depression. Certain that judges could not just do whatever they wanted to, he cited the "constraint of professional opinion" and "the toughness, as Maitland calls it, of a taught tradition."[37] Legal frameworks that embed language from a given period make that language available for later litigants who see new ways of using a doctrine. For example, Pennsylvania corporations unwilling to pay taxes for old age pensions argued that the pensions violated the requirement that spending had to be for a public purpose. Those who had drafted the public purpose language decades before had intended it to stop payments to railroads. Litigants can force courts to confront old language, even if a wider public does not care at all.[38] In challenging pensions, state commissioners and taxpayers mobilized the law for their own purposes, but what they mobilized included "obstinate traditional precepts."

Precepts that are too obstinate become divorced from the changing world they govern, but if they are not obstinate at all, precepts do not matter. The historian G. Edward White has argued that federal judges in the late nineteenth century believed that they were to enforce consistent constitutional demands, fitting new facts into unchanging principles. He calls this delineation of right and wrong actions for government "boundary pricking." A judge could find it difficult to determine *how* a new situation fit, but changing the principle itself was never the answer.[39] In the matter of public spending, later courts treated mid-nineteenth-century cases concerning payments to firemen's charities as relevant to pensions for teachers or all the working elderly.

Acting as though they never departed from the past allowed legal officials to treat law as though rules provided certainty. In contrast, scholars ranging from legal reformers to critical legal theorists have time and again pointed out the indeterminacy in legal reasoning. Law is indeterminate because legal officials want to leave possibilities open for the future, because they redefine categories over time, and because litigants construct facts to invoke some legal rules and not others.[40] Why, then, study the deployment of law in social life, if people interpret it strategically? Indeterminate is not the same as meaningless, and legal interpreters do often converge on what the law requires. Agreeing on the questions that states must answer—How is something service? Are certain people dependent enough to qualify for charity?—is convergence. In addition, some officials' words matter more than others; if litigation threatens, judges can induce other state officials to take them seriously.[41]

With regard to pensions, acting as though new situations fit into old principles became increasingly difficult as state courts successively ratified new pensions, except mandatory mothers' pensions and mandatory old age pensions. Old distinctions between service and independent work made no sense in a world where large organizations offered pensions to employees and localities offered pensions to teachers. Thus commissions studying old age pensions emphasized indeterminacy in the law, whereas courts emphasized consistency. To the commissions, decisions allowing civil service pensions should have allowed old age pensions as well. To courts, they did not. Yet work and service were no longer categories that courts could persuasively maintain. They certainly tried: courts struck down states' old age pensions in 1916, 1923, and 1932 despite support for them from legislatures and commissions. In doing so, however, they sparked constitutional amendments or, in some states, opinions from the attorneys general that reinterpreted state constitutional provisions in order to hold the new programs constitutional. When the Great Depression and the New Deal finally brought national old age pensions, state commissions and litigation in the courts before 1935 had laid the groundwork for fitting new pensions into constitutional categories.

For a long time, the Progressive Era perspective on judging triumphed in characterizing the age: judges erected a barrier against an emergent regulatory state. More recent scholarship has argued that if judges were trying to halt changes in the state, they were doing so out of firm convictions about correct methods of governance which had long been part of the common law; they were not inventing new categories.[42] Extending earlier precedent into new tasks that states and localities were undertaking, courts insisted that their ongoing supervision of the purposes legislatures found for spending was appropriate. Not until after 1937 did legislatures finally win the concession that determining what counted as an appropriate object of spending was a legislative rather than a judicial task.[43]

In their efforts to determine who had served, who deserved charity, and who was independent, state courts emphasized "the common good," a consideration that persisted through the early twentieth century. Concern for the common good pervaded nineteenth-century constitutionalism—perhaps surprising, given how often we think that American constitutionalism has to do with individual rights.[44] Indeed, William Novak sees concern for the common good as the touchstone for antebellum courts, which grounded their view of the common good in the common law, not in constitutional law. He argues that shifting to constitutional reasoning after Reconstruction emphasized individual rights, not the common good of the common law.[45]

This book demonstrates that pensions do not match that map; rather, reasoning from the common good suffused the law of pensions and charitable payment both before *and* after the Civil War. After the Civil War, legislatures changed the way they provided money: they paid individuals rather than collectivities. As a result, courts judged whether states could pay individuals, but they still considered the common good. Early decisions were made under constitutions, and later constitutional cases drew on the common law. Indeed, one problem that state pensions encountered in the courts was exactly that they attempted to depart from English poor law, read in the state courts as one way of interpreting what constitutional law required.[46] Constitutions and the common law were both believed to demonstrate right principles of governing.

With their commitment to governing according to the past, courts provide one layer in the governance of the United States that Karen Orren and Stephen Skowronek have called "patterned anarchy": multiple institutions with conflicting commitments make decisions; no one institution has final authority; and how the legislatures, courts, and, in this instance, administrators embed meaning shapes ongoing, unsettled politics.[47]

Taking the "toughness of the taught tradition" as significant in governing payments from the 1850s to the 1920s requires making sense of what, indeed, the constitutional requirements were. The constitutional challenges in the states from railroad lawyers, financially strapped county commissioners, and dependents of dead policemen and firemen all contributed to changes in the national constitutional context for social welfare. Central to that development were both state constitutional change and state judges' assessments of service, work, and charity. The following chapters tell the stories, overlapping in time, of how litigation changed the meanings of service and dependence. Chapter two explains the public purpose doctrine, the primary principle governing spending in the nineteenth century. Chapter three shows how courts applied it in cases regarding payments for firemen and for the conscription of soldiers before 1876. Chapter four traces how courts moved from recognizing collective obligation to rewarding individual service in military pensions after Reconstruction. Chapter five then follows the public purpose doctrine as it began to apply to civil servants. Chapter six shows how taxpayers were able to sue and ensure that motherhood would not be considered service once state legislatures instituted mothers' pensions. Chapter seven examines disability payments in the form of workers' compensation and pensions for the blind. Chapter eight recounts how states that considered mandatory pensions for the elderly were stopped because no state court would allow them. Finally, because the New Deal limited the importance of the public purpose doctrine, the book's conclusion explains its final collapse.

CHAPTER TWO

Independence and Dependence under the Public Purpose Doctrine

S tate courts supervised spending for veterans, police, firemen, and mothers well into the twentieth century because they had supervised subsidies to businesses and payments to poor people throughout the nineteenth century. To supervise both state regulation and spending, the courts used the doctrine of public purpose, a doctrine that had a long history. States had three inalienable powers: the power to tax; the police power, or power to regulate in the public interest; and the power of eminent domain, the power to take land in the public interest.[1] Much of the scholarship concerning public purpose addresses the nineteenth-century rulings on the state's inalienable police power: its ability to regulate everything from grain elevators to polygamy.[2] The public purpose doctrine also governed the power to spend money for certain people, for corporations, and for charity. Neglecting that meaning of the doctrine has allowed scholars of social welfare to neglect the significance of law in governing social welfare.

Under the public purpose doctrine, states could spend money for charity, which appropriately went to those who were intrinsically dependent; for businesses that courts were willing to say were of general public benefit; or for people who had served the state by providing a general public benefit related to the obligations of citizenship. Embedded in the doctrine of public purpose was concern with profoundly American questions of what it meant to be free and independent. Understanding pension payments to firemen, police, and the elderly requires first outlining the principles that unified charitable spending with spending for businesses and individuals.

Courts had two related concerns. First, as Howard Gillman has explicated police-powers jurisprudence, both American law and American political ideology had followed some commitment to equality since the nation's founding. That required striking down any special privileges that legislatures granted unless they served a public purpose: that is, the general welfare. To grant special privileges outside that limit would be to enact "class legislation," as the courts termed it.[3]

Equality, however, was premised on independence, which implied a natural inequality, or dependence, of some classes of people, especially women, children, and those disabled by injury or age. Legislating for their support would not privilege a class of people who ought to be treated equally; instead, it might serve a public purpose. Independence and dependence were fundamental ways of thinking about freedom and labor in the American republic. Determining who deserved charity required determining who was independent and who was not.

As political historians have extensively documented, independence once meant being a producer or a property holder. Independence required working for one's self, producing enough to exchange for all the goods a family needed. For farmers, of course, a natural disaster could make the difference between being independent in that antebellum sense and being desperately poor—although still independent in law. Still, the version of labor, in which men were organized as heads of families in a nation of small republics was crucial to a Jeffersonian understanding of a free citizenry.[4] But the small producers' sense of independence was always in jeopardy, both because slaves also sometimes possessed the skills of artisans and mechanics and because manual labor did not always gain respect. Scholars have demonstrated the continuity between cultural beliefs in the independence of labor and legal decision-making concerning the police powers of the states.[5] An independent worker could not receive public payments, courts often insisted—even after the Civil War, when meanings of independence were changing as industrial capitalism transformed the economy into one of large organizations rather than small producers.

Yet labor conditions were actually very closely constrained by legal conditions.[6] During the nineteenth century, workers were not entitled to rely upon regular practices such as dinner breaks. Worse, they could not recover wages for work already completed when employers discharged them—which made it difficult for workers to change jobs or move.[7] Indeed, before the Civil War, the legal powers of an employer provided a powerful reason to count employment as dependence rather than freedom. Because the lived reality of freedom for many white workers was thus tightly constrained, the contrast of slavery made freedom seem more real.

After the Civil War, political economists and labor organizations worried about what changes in the American economy meant for the independence of labor. By 1870, two-thirds of American workers were employees; even in agricultural states, about half the labor force worked for others.[8] The abolition of slavery made it impossible to define the freedom to labor as whatever slavery was not, (though blackness could still be defined as subservience, which implied dependence). For political economists, freedom became the freedom to sell one's labor in the market. Contracting represented self-governance. Parties to a contract were equal at law, whatever the social inequalities between them. Wage labor therefore no longer meant dependence but rather independence.[9]

To the former slaves, freedom still meant the Jeffersonian ideal: to be an independent farmer and producer of goods, under the direct supervision of no one.[10] The initial promise of forty acres and a mule acknowledged that meaning of independence for freedmen, but it was not the policy that the Freedmen's Bureau followed; instead, it forced both men and women into labor contracts. Bureau officials worried that freedmen were unaccustomed to selling their labor and might not do it willingly. Whites feared that blacks would be idle rather than industrious once they were no longer enslaved.

Although political economists redefined independence to mean freely selling one's labor on the market, the vagaries of employment even for white male workers made the distinction between dependence and independence perilously tenuous. Unreliable machinery or bad judgment by a tired coworker could lead to a debilitating workplace injury that would transform a person's independence to dependence. In the industrial North the depression of the 1870s led many men who had been wage earners to beg on the streets.[11] Diagnosing the problem as shiftlessness, Massachusetts joined other states in making it a crime to beg.[12] Leaders in charity work approved, despite recognizing the structural causes of unemployment. The emergent profession of philanthropy saw unemployed young urban men as willfully lazy, placing themselves outside the boundaries of contract: if they had opted out of the benefits of the independence of the American worker, they had opted out of the benefits of choosing an employer.[13]

The freedom in wage labor rested in being able to bargain without restrictions over the conditions of employment. However much that definition did not capture the experience of laboring in large organizations, in law the ability to contract was freedom. Courts were to reinforce that freedom by ensuring that laborers had "liberty of contract" unencumbered by legal restrictions. States could therefore not regulate the hours men could work or the wages they were paid. Because women and children were intrinsically dependent, however, states *could* regulate for them; as dependents, they had no freedom of contract to lose.

Since legislatures always retained the power to regulate for the public good, they could also regulate privately owned businesses that were "public in use," to quote an 1877 decision from the United States Supreme Court.[14] Regulating or subsidizing such businesses, especially railroads, benefited the whole public. Subsidizing charities that served the general welfare, such as orphanages, also satisfied public purpose requirements, as did spending for the intrinsically dependent. Spending for an independent laborer or for a private business, however, would undermine the independence of American labor and the fundamental equality of Americans. These legal concepts were reflected in political debates over independence and dependence and subsequent court rulings.

How could charities or privately owned businesses be "public in use"? A "private" business was regarded as quasi-public both because corporations had public charters and because of the service that they provided. Karen Orren has therefore interpreted early nineteenth century cases concerning businesses as cases concerning public service. For example, *Dartmouth College v. Woodward,* which reached the United States Supreme Court in 1819, treated business as akin to a service. The trustees of the college sued the state of New Hampshire for interfering with their property rights in the college by changing the terms of their state charter. The Supreme Court held that the legislature could not change the terms of the charter; doing so would violate the U.S. Constitution's prohibition on impairing contracts. Yet the state always retained its ability to regulate for the benefit of the general public, since its police power was inalienable. Dartmouth College's charter was a contract, but on the other hand the college remained subordinate to the sovereign legislature. As Orren has argued, legislators "were closer to a period when most activities were characterized by subordination rather than autonomy, compensation as well as profits."[15]

Treating private organizations as quasi-public because they provided a service also governed grants of money to charities that benefited either the dependent poor or those who "served" in the early nineteenth-century sense.

"Benefit or Convenience to the Public"

Legislatures could tax and spend only for a public purpose, and in the nineteenth century, courts determined what that meant. Courts developed the public purpose doctrine as it governed taxation and spending in the review of state programs benefiting businesses as well as in the review of payments to charities. State legislatures distributed grants, monopolies, and tax exemptions to businesses. State constitutions and courts tried to limit these "gifts."

The prohibition of special privileges—that is, spending for private benefit other than compensation for service—was often part of the states' initial constitutions, as Howard Gillman has shown in discussing the importance of public purpose in American governance of police powers. For example, the Virginia Declaration of Rights and the Massachusetts Bill of Rights prohibited privileges except for public services. After 1818, new states required that taxes be uniform; those clauses also implicitly included prohibitions on special privileges.[16] After the 1830s, virtually all state constitutions provided for uniform and equal taxation.[17] Reform of state constitutions from the 1850s onward further extended efforts to limit state taxing power.[18] Treaties by the leading commentators and jurists Thomas Cooley (1868) and John Dillon (1872) consolidated the law of taxation and stated as a universal principle the requirement of equality and uniformity to protect against confiscation, as Cooley called illegitimate taxation.[19] Along the way, judges had the opportunity to apply these provisions to many regulations, subsidies, and taxes in the states, further elaborating the public-purpose requirement.

Both courts and commentators saw the prohibition of spending for anything other than a public purpose as part of the general law.[20] The concept of the general law depended on a theory of both constitutional and statutory interpretation: general law stated right principles that were to govern for all time, principles not dependent on the peculiarities of particular constitutional provisions. Many judges shared this perspective on what has been called the "declaratory" theory of law, or the belief that the job of judges is to declare the law as it is, though legislatures and even other judges might possibly misinterpret it.[21] Because a prohibition on spending for other than a public purpose was part of the general law, courts grounded the requirement in different states' constitutional provisions. The general law also allowed judges to read constitutional requirements as consistent with the requirements of the common law, or the accretion of judicial decisions over time. After the Civil War, many state courts made the prohibitions much more specific in response to political complaints over spending for both railroads and charities.

Thomas Cooley, who synthesized the law of taxation and the constitutional limits on what states could do, saw the law as something much more general than the particular provisions of state constitutions. He believed that the law should accord with "the common thoughts of men," as he stated in a speech at Harvard in 1886. The common thoughts of men, which could be discerned with proper reflection, clearly would not support the granting of privileges that would elevate one class above another. At the time, his interpretation seemed dramatically different from that of Christopher Columbus Langdell, who became the dean of Harvard Law School in 1870 and thereby was able to build an institution around his approach to legal interpretation. Langdell did not care what the general thoughts of men about the law might be, for those general thoughts could be as wholly wrong as the general thoughts of men about logic might be.[22] The principles were there, according to Langdell, but they could be difficult to discern. Although Cooley approached the problem of interpretation differently, both he and Langdell believed that legal reasoning embodied principles applicable across the boundaries of common law and constitutions.

Widespread local aid to railroads and to charities occasioned many of the changes in constitutional provisions in the middle of the nineteenth century and after the Civil War. Subsidies in the form of bonds would mortgage the future of states and localities. If railroads went bankrupt, localities would have very little to show for their subsidies except debt.[23] Although Cooley and Dillon, leading commentators on public purpose, at first opposed regulation, they thought it wrong to grant subsidies to businesses, including railroads. Both state and federal courts, on the other hand, were allowing subsidies to railroads even while prohibiting them to most other businesses.[24] The Michigan Supreme Court, where Thomas Cooley was a justice in 1870, was one of the few to strike down aid to railroads. Since such aid was unpopular in Michigan (as it was throughout much of the country), the popular press celebrated Cooley's 1870 decision, but legal scholars criticized it as unfounded in law.[25]

Amendments intended to prohibit aid to railroads were sometimes assumed to prohibit aid to charities as well, for they forbade the lending of the state's credit to any corporation *or* a gift to any organization. Twenty-six states had enacted some provision prohibiting aid to private institutions by 1931, when a scholar collected information on the topic.[26] These constitutional amendments emerged in some states from frustration with rampant favoritism: grants to sectarian institutions were useful to politicians who wished to shore up their electoral support.[27] The amendments reflected the concerns of the people of a state or its legislature more than they indicated resolution of a problem, for state and local governments continued to allocate money, as evidenced in court challenges. For example, the Illinois Supreme Court held that a state's or locality's paying less than the full cost of keeping a child in an industrial school hardly aided the institution, so it did not violate the constitutional provision prohibiting aid to institutions.[28] States were still responsible for the dependent poor, so alongside the limits, they often included exceptions that allowed support for dependent children or veterans' homes.

In 1874, New York enacted an anti-gift constitutional provision in response to concern about railroad subsidies and the rapidly expanding aid to charities, deployed effectively for political purposes by Boss Tweed. Yet giving money to the indigent was still seen as fulfilling a public purpose. In 1875, after the amendment came into force, the New York legislature considered who were the legitimate poor. One proposal defined them as "foundlings," "idiots," and the "deaf and dumb," who, at law, could only depend on others.[29] Helplessness would have a claim on charity, as it always had. The New York definition would also have included children of Civil War casualties as dependents of people who had served. Furthermore, *local* (as opposed to state) assistance to private charities was still constitutional, and aid to poorhouses continued to grow.[30]

Subsidies to businesses and payments to individuals raised the same legal issues as New York clarified in case law. In 1876, shortly after the state enacted its anti-gift amendment, Justice Charles J. Folger of its highest court explained public purpose in deciding a taxpayer's complaint regarding a subsidy to a private sawmill in *Weismer v. Village of Douglas*:

It has been accepted in this State as a binding adjudication, that the legislature may tax, or delegate to a political division of the State the power to tax, or may compel that division to tax, to raise money to pay a legal, equitable or moral claim, or to do that toward an individual which proper and expected sense of gratitude for public service ought to prompt, or a feeling of charity (which, in a legal sense, is, perhaps, as used here, no other than a moral obligation) urge. It may also be conceded that that is a public purpose from the attainment of which will flow some benefit or convenience to the public, whether of the whole commonwealth or of a circumscribed community. In this latter case, however, the benefit or convenience must be direct and immediate from the purpose, and not collateral, remote or consequential.[31]

Payments for sawmills, payments for service, payments for charity: Justice Folger delineated the differences. Subsidies to sawmills were prohibited, but New York could pay businesses that provided a "benefit or convenience to the public." Exchange, then, governed the anti-gift provisions in state constitutions: since subsidies to businesses benefiting the public generally served a public purpose, they did not constitute an illegitimate gift.

California's constitution of 1879 provides an excellent example of the anti-gift constitutional provisions:

The Legislature shall have no power to give or to lend, or to authorize the giving, or lending, of the credit of the State . . . in aid of or to any person, association or corporation . . . nor shall it have power to make any gift or authorize the making of any gift of any public money . . . to any individual.[32]

As in other states after the Civil War, California voters were concerned with corporate privilege, particularly the state legislature's generous grants to railroads.[33] Nothing about the new amendments, however, allowed the states to abandon their traditional responsibilities to the dependent poor. California, like other states after the Civil War, was trying to contract legislative power, particularly to curb aid to railroads. The drafters of the new constitution still wished to ensure that aid to veterans would be constitutional. Another section provided that "nothing contained in the Constitution shall prohibit the use of state money or credit, in aiding veterans who served in the military or naval service of the United States in time of war." Further, the section allowed for state support to state institutions for "orphans, or half-orphans, or abandoned children, or children of a father who is incapacitated . . . or aged persons in indigent circumstances . . . [or] needy blind persons."[34] In short, the constitutional provisions affirmed common-law charitable obligations and rewards for service. The dependent classes could still receive charitable payments; the independent could be paid if they had served the state.

The uniform principles such laws embodied allowed the United States Supreme Court to decide a case under the public purpose doctrine in 1874 which, like New York's *Weismer,* limited assistance to businesses—probably much to the relief of the towns that no longer wanted to pay for it. All the Supreme Court needed to ground its decision was the Fourteenth Amendment's clause that prohibits the taking of property without due process of law. The Citizens Savings and Loan Association of Cleveland held bonds that the city of Topeka, Kansas, had issued in order to give money to an ironworks. Topeka would not pay and defended itself by saying that the state had never had the authority to allow it to issue the bonds in the first place; therefore, the bonds were an unconstitutional use of the city's credit. The United States Supreme Court held in *Loan Association v. Topeka* that Topeka was right: the state could not authorize a subsidy to an ironworks:

> To lay with one hand the power of the government on the property of the citi-
> zen and with the other to bestow it upon favored individuals to aid private en-
> terprises and build up private fortunes is none the less a robbery because it is
> done under the forms of law and called taxation. . . . We have established, we
> think beyond cavil that there can be no lawful tax which is not levied for a pub-
> lic purpose.[35]

Topeka could therefore default on its bonds, for its taxes had never been taxes at all. Because an ironworks was not public, taxes to support it were "robbery."

Most judges held that railroads, on the other hand, did merit aid because they served a public purpose.[36] The general public had access to railroads if they could pay the fares, or bought goods that were shipped by rail, and therefore benefited generally from subsidies offered to railroads, according to the courts. Ironically, the public purpose doctrine and the post–Civil War state amendments enacting it were specifically designed to prevent subsidies to businesses and especially railroads. Yet large corporations could get subsidies if their interests could be made to seem those of the public.

Who Was Dependent?

Subsidies to individuals raised a different question. States had long paid the intrinsically dependent; delineating them from the independent was one of the tasks of public purpose jurisprudence and the poor law. White male workers, no matter how poor, were not dependent people. African Americans perhaps were, but the solution was to make them work. Women, children, and men who were disabled, whether through injury or insanity, were considered dependent people.

Some cases contesting payments directly to people or businesses raised constitutional questions as to what was an illegitimate taking of property or an illegitimate gift. Other cases interpreted the statutes only in the states allocating responsibility for the poor. Constitutional questions were not very different from common-law or statutory ones, however; all were part of the unity of right principles for governing which the law stated. Relying on a statute to justify giving money to someone who did not deserve it would inappropriately cross the boundary between public and private purpose. Statutes had to be interpreted carefully lest a township give money to someone who was not genuinely poor. A township that gave away money too readily would be using tax money for something other than a public purpose, moving into the realm of "robbery," which the United States Supreme Court justices had so thoroughly condemned in 1874 in *Loan Association v. Topeka* and which the states prohibited in their own jurisprudence.

The right principles of governing, judges found, were involved in settling conflicts over what it meant to be an independent laborer, which were in turn connected with slavery. A widely cited case came out of Kansas in 1875, decided by Kansas Supreme Court Justice David Brewer, later of the United States Supreme Court. Because Justice Brewer was so thoughtful about the principles of judging, the case is worth exploring in some detail.

Justice Brewer came from an eminent New England family. His father had been a missionary for the Congregational church, and Justice Brewer absorbed his father's serious religious sense. His training at Yale under Theodore Dwight Woolsey confirmed his commitment both to religion and to limits on government. Right principles were all of a piece; the U.S. Constitution properly read was consistent with religion, though the duties of a godly man reached beyond what a government could do.[37] Brewer was a nephew of Stephen Field, who became a state supreme court justice in California in 1857 and a United States Supreme Court justice in 1863.[38] Brewer had trained in law with another uncle, David Dudley Field, a New York lawyer and legal reformer.

Before the Civil War, Brewer, like others within the Congregational church, was an abolitionist. After the war his religious belief in the fundamental moral equality of men led him to oppose racial discrimination.[39] In 1870, he moved to Kansas and gained a seat on the state supreme court, a good place to begin to enforce his vision of freedom. He gained a seat on the United States Supreme Court in 1890, where he opposed discrimination against the Chinese.[40] Like many white abolitionists, Brewer believed that people ought to be able to sell their labor without state restriction. After Reconstruction, that principle would lead him to support the doctrine of "freedom of contract," which restricted the states' ability to regulate the conditions of labor.[41] Because Brewer, like many judges, believed that there were basic right principles for governing, he unhesitatingly interpreted state and federal constitutional provisions as though they stated those correct principles. Even if they were not stated as directly as one might wish, judges could clarify all constitutional provisions in light of the common law.

Justice Brewer's career has received close scrutiny in recent years. His decisions illuminate the subtlety that a commitment to free labor implied in court doctrine: he ruled against legislation favoring laborers while also holding against legislation that discriminated against the Chinese. His belief in right principles allowed him to ignore both Congress and the states, for either might get the law wrong. With the United States Supreme Court, therefore, he crafted a general federal common law that only the federal courts could reliably discern.[42] His commitments had been clear long before he sat on the Supreme Court, however. Particularly in one decision by the Kansas Supreme Court, he read into law his belief in recognition of the stringent legal consequences of the freedom of independent, producer labor.

State ex rel. Griffith v. Osawkee Township (1875) followed an environmental disaster in Kansas. Osawkee Township had offered bonds to buy grain for farmers, who had suffered what the court said was virtually complete crop failure after a grasshopper plague.[43] James Griffith, a taxpayer in the township, sued, claiming that the township had no authority from the state to buy grain for farmers. Justice Brewer held that the payments violated the state constitutional provision allowing payment to those who "may have claims upon and aid of society" and, by implication, disallowing aid to those who did not have such claims.[44] Justice Brewer explained that although the state might have an obligation to the helpless, it could not favor one class of business people over another. As business people, the farmers were independent; legislation to benefit them would be class legislation, not serving a public purpose. "We speak," he wrote, "of the ordinary laborers, mechanics and artisans as poor people, without a thought of describing persons who are other than self-supporting. Indeed, the large majority of our people are poor people, and yet they would feel insulted to be told that they are objects of public charity."[45] The poor he spoke of were self-supporting because they were paid for their work, whether as employees or as small producers.

Farmers might not have been as insulted as Brewer thought, since the locality had determined that self-support in farming was close to impossible that year in Kansas. But for those not working in the service of the state, which farmers were not, the price of being judged independent was ineligibility for payments from the state, because *public* payment constituted an illegitimate threat to independence. Justice Brewer's Christian charity required that he help provide *private* charitable aid to farmers suffering local devastation, and he worked on the Kansas Central Relief Committee, which distributed funds from the East to the farmers.[46] The *business* of farming, however, was not something of general public benefit, so a public subsidy for farming would not serve a public purpose. Not only did Brewer concern himself with being cautious with tax money; he also clearly intended to do his part to preserve the independence of the working poor, which was necessary for citizenship.[47] To Brewer, farmers represented free labor, and the image of labor as not under the direct control or supervision of anyone had long animated the political ideals of a free republic. But it was rapidly losing any basis in the experience of working Americans. The presumption in law that independent labor was something men did continued into the late nineteenth century. Women's labor on a farm was invisible because women legally owed their household and wage labor to their husbands.[48]

In further defining the category of independent workers, Justice Brewer included carpenters and shoemakers, of whom he said: "We have no thought of asserting that because a man is not rich, or even because he has nothing but the proceeds of his daily labor, therefore taxation may be upheld in his behalf. Such taxation would be simply an attempt on the part of the state to equalize the property of its citizens."[49] Legislation equalizing property would violate a right to private property; it would also be class legislation, which had been drawing judges' legal fire throughout the country.

Justice Brewer believed that Kansas workers who were small producers—farmers, carpenters, shoemakers—and wage laborers had the proceeds of their labor, and that constituted independence.[50] On the other hand, "We speak of those whom society must aid, as the dependent classes, not simply because they do depend on society, but because they cannot do otherwise than thus depend."[51] A man capable of working, no matter the difficulties in the economy, was not intrinsically dependent, and only the intrinsically dependent (and those who had performed some service of general benefit to the state, a category of people not present in this particular case) should receive aid. Dependence was a personal characteristic resulting in complete helplessness. Classes of people who shared that characteristic included the blind, the injured, children, and women. Dependence was *not* a problem of economic failure, though. Had it been, the disaster in Kansas would have been enough to make farmers dependent and therefore eligible for aid. Economic dependence flowed not from poverty but from an individual characteristic: "They cannot do otherwise than thus depend," as Justice Brewer put it.[52] His implication that only the intrinsically dependent merited relief had been a long-standing part of poor law, the law governing the relief that townships and counties paid the desperately poor during much of the nineteenth century. Only blindness or injury made men dependent, and the recourse for the dependent was poor relief.

Brewer spoke in public and wrote for public journals more often than any other justice of his time, continuing even into the early twentieth century to outline who deserved charity. In doing so, he relied on an understanding of dependency that had little to do with his cases concerning aid to railroads. In a 1906 article for *Charities and the Commons,* a journal aligned with the social welfare advocates who believed that charity supplied the answers, Brewer distinguished among people who applied for charity. There were the sick and injured, who could not help themselves. There were those who could help themselves "if a door of opportunity be opened." And then there were "professional mendicants."[53] The first two groups deserved help, but the danger that a petitioner might belong to the third group was enough to require investigation of every applicant for charity. To the readers of *Charities and the Commons,* Brewer's 1875 decision in *Osawkee Township* posed no problem, for they favored private charity that closely attended to the moral worth of recipients and ensured that aid did not go to men who *could* work.[54] Indeed, such a decision would simply ensure that deserving people went for assistance to the proper place: to private charitable institutions rather than the public purse.

This Kansas decision and *Loan Association v. Topeka* were the subjects of uneasy discussion among twentieth-century social insurance advocates until the New Deal, and presciently so.[55] When the Pennsylvania Supreme Court in 1925 decided a case challenging the old age pensions that the state legislature had enacted, both advocates and critics and finally the Pennsylvania court itself all addressed Justice Brewer's decision, drawing on his distinctions between dependence and independence. Curiously, *Osawkee Township* was less significant in challenges to aid to farmers in the 1890s: judges in some state courts cited Justice Brewer's unsympathetic treatment of desperate need only to distinguish the case, holding in North Dakota, Nebraska, and Montana that aid to farmers did serve a public purpose and did not undermine independence. Justice Brewer could not have appreciated the difficulty of farming on the frontier, one judge respectfully said.[56] Only the Minnesota Supreme Court also limited aid to those who were on their way to the poorhouse.[57]

Osawkee Township illustrates the connection between business subsidies and payments to individuals. Courts in states without such explicit provisions as those in New York, Pennsylvania, and California built similar spending limits into their interpretations of other state constitutional provisions. These included prohibitions similar to that in the federal Constitution's Fifth Amendment against taking private property without compensation. Justice Brewer, like other judges of his time, would have seen no reason to tie the decision more closely to a particular provision, since legal reasoning concerned right principles, and those right principles were Christian and constitutional.[58]

The United States Supreme Court decision in *Loan Association v. Topeka* (1874) also provided a precedent to support an understanding of general legal principles in any state; Justice Brewer cited it in *Osawkee Township* (1875), and so did Justice Folger in New York's *Weismer* case (1876). Again, the justification for subsidy was a matter of exchange: a state legislature could grant subsidies and exemptions in exchange for benefits to the general public. Distinguishing legitimate from illegitimate spending became pervasive in state courts with or without anti-gift constitutional provisions.[59] This mixed jurisprudence—drawn from the federal Fourteenth Amendment and state equivalents, taxing provisions in constitutions, public purpose provisions, and provisions prohibiting gifts—led to many state and federal court decisions that checked state spending and regulation for all but the dependent poor.[60]

If a desperate farmer was not among the dependent poor, however, who was? The poor law had a long history but varied across the states, so the common law was crucial in answering that question. Counties provided two kinds of assistance: "outdoor relief," or payment to the poor, and "indoor relief," or almshouses in which the needy lived, often whatever the cause of their neediness—unemployment, injury, mental illness, age. Both were subjects of litigation, either because a locality did not want to pay an individual or because someone wished to challenge a payment to a charity. Although constitutions did not state that they enshrined the common law, determining the meaning of constitutional provisions such as public purpose required defining terms, and defining terms required turning to the common law and statutes, once again reinforcing the practice of treating law as of a piece. Since states borrowed from one another and English poor law had governed in the colonies, some principles were evident.[61] The disabled, the elderly, and women and children were eligible for support, but counties and townships were responsible only for poor people who were legally *settled* in their locale, which was not the same as residing there. Figuring out where people were legally settled proved a fruitful source of litigation: townships and counties sued each other, trying to limit their responsibility. For example, a man unable to find work in one county who moved to another to look for work, leaving his family behind, might become injured in the new locality and unable to work. Women were domiciled, or legally resident, where their husbands were legally resident.[62] Which county was responsible for the injured man and for his wife and children? Courts settled disputes between townships or counties by deciding at what point claimants had become paupers within the meaning of the poor law.

States used "settlement" to exclude people likely to become public charges, whether the newcomers were from a neighboring county or state or from a distant country.[63] Poor relief law persisted in most states into the twentieth century; to advocates of national welfare, the lawsuits between counties and townships were wasteful, a reminder of why the federal government should take responsibility.

Seldom did any township dispute that poor people needed support; rather, they disputed who counted as the dependent poor and which locality should support them. Requiring settlement not only led to litigation among localities; it made moving risky for workers, since they would lose the protection provided when a county was legally responsible for them.[64]

With townships wrangling over responsibility, courts had to elucidate meanings of dependence. Poor law was a last resort, and poor law therefore intersected with family law. In common law, if not by state statute, men had a legal obligation to support their families. In the nineteenth century a woman whose husband was alive and able-bodied could not often claim poor relief for herself or their children, for to grant them poor relief would be to exempt a man from his obligations as a husband and father—even if those obligations went unenforced or remained unenforceable because the man had moved far away.

Some locales did grant poor relief to men whose wages were very low, even after the Civil War, although wage-earning had by then come to imply independence. The meanings of independence and dependence shifted slowly and unevenly across institutions. Even in the late nineteenth century, wage-earning could still be seen as dependence: a man's inability to earn enough to support himself and his wife and children could define pauperism. That made poor relief a subsidy for low wages.[65] Before England reformed its poor law in 1834, local poor relief there had also acted as a wage subsidy, and American poor law often built on English practices.[66]

Because a woman was defined as intrinsically dependent, some courts were willing to hold her eligible for poor relief even where a man might not have been. Wages for women were low enough that single women routinely relied on poor relief.[67] Further, a woman whose husband had died could sometimes claim poor relief even if she had some assets. At law, however, even if a wife worked for wages, the courts assumed that her husband was responsible for the support of his immediate family. In many states (though not in Kansas), children were held responsible for their aging parents; only the elderly without families to support them were eligible for county payments.[68]

Two cases from New York illustrate the contrasting approaches taken to men and women in defining "pauper." In 1888 a Mr. Motolario claimed poor relief in Delaware County, New York. He had been working for the Ontario and Western Railway, moving between New York City and Delaware County according to where the railroad needed him. In May, in an accident on the job, he lost his right leg and left foot. Before his injury he had maintained a family in New York City, where his family continued to live whether he was working there or in Delaware County. Delaware County sued New York City, claiming that Motolario was the city's responsibility because he had been legally settled there. In January 1889, however, the court held that before his injury he had not been a dependent person and could not be one until an injury made it completely impossible for him to earn any money; therefore, he was the responsibility of the county in which he was injured, not the one in which he had previously lived.[69]

Two transformations relevant to the poor law made 1889 a late date for this case. First, some states, including New York, were operating both outdoor county relief and poorhouses (indoor relief). Both came under attack for their corruption, and poorhouses were continually reorganized in an effort to improve them. By the late nineteenth century, charity reformers believed that the key to improvement was to devise separate institutions for different kinds of needy people, eventually leaving the poorhouses to the elderly.[70] In midcentury, states that paid outdoor relief found the unending disputes between townships concerning residential settlement, or the problems of people with no settlement, reasons to shift policy toward poorhouses.[71]

Second, Motolario was one of thousands injured while working for the railroads, many of whom sued to hold the railroads responsible, and the legal doctrine governing the responsibility of the railroads had grown extremely complicated in the different states. Cases proliferated; winning or losing depended on the jury and judge one had.[72] Where injured men won, employer liability replaced poor law support for them and for their legal dependents (implying a diminished number of poor law cases in the courts). The terrible option of the poorhouse rather than payment of outdoor relief may even have shaped some juries' considerations of liability.[73]

The second case made the point that if poor men were considered independent as long as they could provide subsistence for their families, single mothers even with some resources could still be regarded as dependent. In 1893, New York's highest court held that a widowed mother of four, Pauline Hanson, was eligible for county poor relief as "an object worthy of public charity." Yet after her husband died, she had sold their farm, including a horse, two cows, and two pigs.[74] A man with that amount of property would not have been eligible for poor relief, but Mrs. Hanson, a widowed mother who had not only lost her husband but had recently given birth, was eligible. In short, a man's claim based on disability was not identical with a woman's claim based on widowhood and childbirth. Rather, a man in difficult circumstances was considered independent unless injured, whereas a widow, even with some resources, was considered dependent.

Like other poor relief cases, Mr. Motolario's and Mrs. Hanson's cases raised questions of statutory and common law rather than constitutional interpretation. The statutory and common-law question of who was a pauper had constitutional implications, however, for to give relief to someone not genuinely a pauper was to spend for something other than a public purpose. Separating constitutional from statutory and common law interpretation misses the continuity in courts' interpretation: a common understanding of independence and dependence colored both *Osawkee Township* and cases involving the poor laws. Women as mothers were the objects of charity in a way that men were not; in poor relief cases, women could gain access to funds, however meager, that able-bodied men could not.[75]

Conclusion: Public and Private Benefit

Constitutional amendments limiting legislative acts after the Civil War have seemed to suggest a new constitutional order in the American states. William Novak has argued that an emphasis on the individual rather than the collectivity emerged. Whereas the antebellum courts relied on the common law and emphasized the common good, constitutional law emphasized the power of the central state.[76] In the regulation of public spending, however, continuity rather than disjuncture between common-law and constitutional reasoning stands out. Post–Civil War amendments to state constitutions echoed both earlier bills of rights and common-law cases interpreting those bills of rights. Constitutional decisions prohibiting gifts turned on both early provisions for equality and long-standing common-law divisions between public and private.[77] Policing the difference between public and private in the courts was important precisely because in many states these domains were blurred. The dependent poor were a public responsibility, yet privately held charities provided for children in New York and other states; many almshouses were operated by private charities as well. Railroads were not publicly owned, yet they resembled public highways and therefore could gain a public subsidy. In the early nineteenth century, firemen were not public employees, but they served a public function; thus, publicly supported charities and almshouses were devoted to their care.

The nineteenth-century division between public and private describes a world that is unfamiliar today, focusing as it did on the nature of the work performed or the nature of dependence rather than on the ownership of the business or the status of an employer. That archaic sense of public and private provided the grounds for reviewing spending programs for charities and individuals until the 1920s, when it disintegrated as a result of the expansion of such programs and the inability of courts to maintain boundaries. State courts, though they continued to rule as though they were applying long-standing principles in law, applied those principles to new programs that the legislatures enacted and, in doing so, changed the law—even while seeming to hold it steady—by gradually eroding the underlying reasoning that justified the distinction between public and private.[78]

Understanding that change requires understanding how the courts applied the doctrine of public purpose to spending for firemen and in support of towns that raised taxes during the Civil War to exempt their men from conscription. Taxpayers reluctant to pay brought lawsuits that allowed the courts to consider what public benefit meant in two important settings for citizenship: fighting fires and meeting a draft. Each in turn proved a precursor to later state spending programs—for veterans, police and other civil servants, mothers, and the elderly.

CHAPTER THREE

Payments to Firemen and Soldiers, 1854–1876

The significance of militarism to citizenship is a commonplace of political theory and political history.[1] Citizens fight for their country. Even though the central principles of a liberal state are freedom from the state and equal rights, the United States has also historically been a self-governing republic, and republican governance requires that citizens serve. Because nation-states have often defined military service as masculine, citizenship has long been congruent with masculinity. Of course, only some men have ever actually fought. Others have been exempt because they were too old or held essential jobs or had dependents or otherwise did not meet the demands of military service. They have no less been citizens.

If all men have been citizens regardless of their actual participation in the military, perhaps those who fought stood for all; they did not represent only themselves and their personal commitment to their country. If so, women could equally be citizens, and citizenship need not require masculinity. Historically, though, that equation has not worked. In the nineteenth-century United States, married women owed no loyalty and therefore no service to a national state; they owed their political loyalty to their husbands. In turn, husbands represented wives in the public sphere.[2] As Rogers Smith describes it, republicanism in the United States "was identified with the material self-reliance and martial virtue that combated political corruption and foreign domination. . . . [Women's] limited military capacities were thought to justify [their dependent status]."[3] Republicanism itself, then, embodied masculinity.

Martial virtue marked citizenship in the *national* state, and only the national state could conduct war. Governing institutions in the United States are layered and multiple, however. Federal and state governments can require different commitments of their citizens, and courts can see those requirements differently from legislatures or town councils. Since the United States is federal, citizenship at the national level need not capture local understandings of citizens' obligations. Before the Civil War the United States was a set of quasi-independent republics, unified by the limited powers of the "general" government of the United States.[4] At that time the local service of citizenship involved fighting fires, not fighting wars, though fighting fires in one's hometown required the same virtue as fighting wars for the United States. A divided government meant that the national government had little responsibility for local problems such as fires, and the service required to fight wars earned the gratitude of the national government, not of the individual states or cities.

Just as the national state had to fight wars, cities had to prevent and fight fires. They used their limited resources to do so; with few employees, they staffed fire-fighting through voluntarism, just as before the Civil War the national government met military demands with volunteers. Those noble men who volunteered to fight fires earned the admiration due active citizens. Local service could satisfy the demands of citizenship that mattered most in people's immediate lives, meriting gratitude as much as did national military service.[5]

With the onset of the Civil War the practice of voluntarism no longer met the demands for service, either local or national. Insurance companies had paid taxes to support firemen's charities; by the 1850s the companies were challenging those taxes in court as part of their effort to extricate themselves from supporting volunteer companies. During the Civil War the national government imposed conscription but allowed men to pay a fee for commutation. When towns raised taxes in order to meet their obligations with money rather than men, taxpayers complained to courts about what they saw as misuse of their tax dollars. Fighting fires might be of general benefit to them, whereas fighting wars concerned local governments not because towns could pursue wars but because they could assist their citizens in meeting obligations to the nation. In cases concerning firemen and Civil War conscription between 1854 and 1871, courts did not focus on the qualities of individual firefighters and soldiers, and judges did not praise the heroism of those who had served. Rather, the courts considered the benefits of the exchange between insurance companies and firemen's charities, or between the towns and the national government.

Taxpayers, whether insurance companies or individuals, could appear in court to complain about support for firemen's charities or payment of fees for military service only because at law, taxpayers had a specific and defensible interest in how localities spent tax dollars. That interest had two components. First, by the 1840s the federal courts had begun to grant corporations rights similar to those of individual citizens.[6] The extent of those rights was an axis of disagreement in the state courts and sometimes the federal courts, providing a fruitful source of litigation. Second, as the eminent treatise writer John Dillon put it in the second edition of his *Law of Municipal Corporations* (1873), "the city corporation holds its moneys for the corporators, the inhabitants of the city, to be expended for legitimate corporate purposes." Seventeen years later, he expanded on the point, explaining that taxpayers were like stockholders in a private corporation.[7] No clear definition of public and private corporations was evident, though courts expended considerable thought in delineating the two.[8] Suits by taxpayers against municipalities were similar to suits by stockholders against a corporation: each corporation could spend money only in accordance with its charter and in the interests of the stockholders. But the two corporations were not identical; municipal corporations' public duties, such as supporting the poor, had no exact equivalent in private corporation law. The responsibility to spend for a public purpose, then, or not to take property without just compensation, was a limit on what states and their subsidiaries—countries, towns, and cities—could do. That limit was enforceable through lawsuits.

Once legislatures could define what serves a public purpose, the entire question of spending for a public purpose was no longer justiciable. In the nineteenth century, though, the courts provided one more place for disgruntled taxpayers to dispute the expenditure of public funds. Understandings of exchange were embedded in the law concerning the taxes that fire insurance companies paid and the money that towns paid to exempt their citizens from military service. Insurance companies tried to remake the antebellum law that allowed municipalities to charge them a specific tax. Taxpayers in towns that paid to exempt their men from the draft during the Civil War protested in court that meeting the national obligations of citizens was not the business of a township. Together, the payments and the challenges to them illuminate the significance of exchange and federalism in public service.

Fire, Firemen, and Insurance

Fire was a topic of pressing concern in crowded cities before the Civil War. Wooden buildings, smokers, accumulated trash, and the production and storing of gunpowder all promised danger. State legislatures therefore enacted statutes allowing officials to condemn buildings and prohibiting the manufacture of gunpowder. Limiting fires meant authorizing cities to punish people who stored gunpowder, to tear down condemned structures, and to prohibit building new ones of wood; courts dismissed rights of private property in attempts to prevent a fire from ripping through an urban neighborhood.[9]

Fighting fires connoted the same heroism as military service, without war's horror of obligatory killing. Well-off men—the financially independent—served in the early nineteenth century. As honorable men who did honorable work, they volunteered to defend their towns from devastation, thus meeting the finest aspirations of citizenship. Men regarded firefighting in volunteer companies as the service of citizenship.[10] Urban producer elites constituted the membership, though when a fire broke out they would rely on workers to help. In New York the laborers who became firemen in the 1820s and 1830s still represented independence because they were journeymen shipbuilders and carpenters and other craftsmen—work that was not wage labor.[11]

In other cities, volunteer fire companies included men both in white-collar occupations and in the independent laboring trades. Many held property, the antebellum mark of an independent citizen. If men who held a variety of paid occupations fought fires together, the service of citizenship could unify rather than divide them.[12]

One might suppose that recognizing service as the basis of citizenship would promise inclusion by race as well, but the antebellum culture of firefighting was a culture of urban white workingmen's clubs; white men served together, and the common representations of firemen did not include even free blacks. Camaraderie included the rowdiness for which the public came to know firemen; firefighting companies were well known for fighting each other rather than fires.[13] Firefighting companies also entertained themselves and others by competing in minstrel shows, which excluded men by race. Performances in blackface made fun of both aristocrats and slaves, playing to distinctions between those groups and the working audience.[14] Black culture represented joy and play, in contrast with the supposed sobriety of white working culture (a sobriety belied by the firemen's clubs), yet minstrel shows treated black culture as low and contemptible.[15] Members of the white working class distinguished between themselves and black laborers. Moreover, since many understood blacks to be intrinsically dependent, white laborers in New York opposed abolition before the Civil War.[16] Prominent wealthy advocates of abolition in New York did little to convince white crafts workers that abolition was right. Associating free labor with service to the state, as firefighting did, excluded black Americans as a matter of course, just as American political life did.[17]

However much firemen's companies were clubs, they also promised to control the fires that always threatened. Cities that relied on volunteers tried to support firemen's charities. New York City suffered a great fire in 1835, with losses that ruined fourteen of New York's twenty-five insurance companies.[18] In 1837 the New York legislature required that insurance companies incorporated under the laws of any other state pay into the New York state treasury a tax amounting to 2 percent of all premiums, for the support of firemen's charities to compensate men for fighting fires—or so the states justified the provisions, though that tax would also, of course, favor in-state insurance companies. Subsequent laws had the insurance companies pay the tax directly to the volunteer fire department, not even passing through the public treasury for appearance's sake. Other cities around the country followed suit. Some also exempted firemen from military service. Like the firemen themselves, cities recognized their work as equivalent to the quintessential work of citizenship.

Before the 1850s, fire insurance companies often supported volunteer fire departments beyond paying taxes, for their business depended on the effectiveness of firemen. They rewarded companies who were first to the fire, held banquets, and paid into firemen's charities whatever firemen asked, sometimes thousands of dollars.[19] They also offered rewards for those who discovered fires.[20] Some such offers proved counterproductive: firefighting companies would fight each other, rather than the fire, over a promised reward.

When steam engines became available in the 1850s, they were difficult to operate, requiring trained workers, but promised to save property with fewer men and fewer engines.[21] Between the need for expertise and the desire for more reliable firemen, effective firefighting seemed to require a professional force. Thus, by the 1850s insurance companies were advocating paid, professional firefighters rather than volunteers. Not only would a paid, trained force know how to use steam engines, but the cities would pay for the engines so the insurance companies expected their expenses to drop.

Only insurance companies incorporated in a "foreign" state were taxed to support firemen's companies. Such targeted taxation—which raised money for the firemen's charities while giving a competitive advantage to local insurance companies[22]—was wholly consistent with the organization of politics in the early and middle nineteenth century. It seemed obvious that those who stood to benefit most from public policies should pay for them. Since a good fire department would limit insurance companies' losses, legislatures could conclude that the insurance companies should pay.

That these taxes were imposed only on companies from outside the particular states, however, placed a burden on interstate commerce, at least according to the insurance companies, making it difficult to build a national business.

In the 1850s, corporations began to sue to dismantle barriers to interstate commerce. A famous interstate commerce case decided in 1851 by the United States Supreme Court, *Cooley v. Board of Wardens,* concerned the power of the states to impose a tax on ships that did not use a local pilot in the harbor; the tax itself paid a pension to the local pilots and their dependents. The question was whether the regulation constituted too great a burden on interstate commerce in violation of the federal Constitution. The Supreme Court concluded that some subject matter was local, including the regulation of pilots. But differential taxes and licensing schemes were the subject of litigation that made its way to the United States Supreme Court between 1875 and 1890 as businesses increasingly operated in a national economy, for state regulation impeded smooth expansion.[23]

Between 1854 and 1862, targeted taxation for the benefit of firemen's charities was subject to a flurry of challenges in the states. Insurance companies challenged the taxes in New York, Chicago, Philadelphia, New Orleans, and Milwaukee, arguing that taxing corporations from out of state violated the privileges and immunities clause and takings clauses in state constitutions.[24] The courts looked coldly at the taxes and at firefighting itself, never praising the service the men had performed. That romanticism was left to the popular culture and, ironically, to the cases that emerged after Reconstruction, when firemen in cities were paid for their work. (In the eyes of firemen themselves, wages diminished the nobility of service, but the courts then celebrated service; see chapter five.)[25] In the 1850s, though, state courts resolved that states *could* tax the insurance companies, not because the service was noble but because the insurance companies benefited from firefighting. Conceptions of public and private benefit shaped their decisions.

In 1854, New York's Court of Common Pleas, the state's general jurisdiction court, decided a complaint concerning New York's tax on foreign insurance companies. The New York City fire department sued John S. Noble because the Insurance Company of the State of Pennsylvania refused to pay. In a companion case with identical arguments, the fire department also sued James Wright, an agent for the Reliance Mutual Insurance Company of Philadelphia and the Insurance Company of North America. In both cases the companies claimed that the tax was an unconstitutional taking of property for a private purpose because it benefited a private corporation, the fire department. The companies also claimed that the tax violated the U.S. Constitution's privileges and immunities clause, which on a common interpretation guaranteed that all could equally pursue the ordinary trades.[26]

The volunteer fire department used the tax for its widows and orphans fund; years later, in 1887, Augustine E. Costello published an adulatory history of the Fire Department of New York.[27] To illustrate his discussion of the constitutional challenge, he chose to emphasize the heroic work of the fire department and the nobility of its charity (figure 2). In one illustration, a fireman hails a woman and child alone in a window, perhaps after a hearse has passed by. An angel bearing the shield of the fund stands over a man fallen in the line of duty. Finally, the fund is a lifeboat for a woman stranded in the middle of the ocean, holding a baby and a small child. Without the lifeboat, she has no means to care for her family. Just two pages later, Costello's next illustration for the court case brought home even further that firemen protect women and children left without their men (figure 3). Here, the fireman showers coins over a woman with three children. He is in uniform and draws the coins from his firehat to show that the money results not from his personal benevolence but from the benevolence of firemen. The fire insurance companies that paid the tax do not appear in either illustration.

A NOBLE CHARITY.

Figure 2. A Noble Charity. From Augustine E. Costello's *Our Firemen: A History of the New York Fire Department, Volunteer and Paid* (1888), 707. Negative # 75250. Collection of the New-York Historical Society. Reproduced with permission.

The legal arguments were much less touching, ignoring what the fire department did or did not do for widows and orphans. William A. Hardenbrook and William Curtis Noyes, the lawyers for the Reliance Mutual Insurance Company, argued that the firemen's charity was private and therefore no taxes could flow to it:

> Instead of collecting or applying the money exacted to any public burden, or as their shares in any such public burden, [the tax legislation] gives it to a private corporation for its own uses, not to a public purpose. That it may possibly go to a private charitable purpose can make no difference; for the support of the "indigent or disabled firemen" is not a public use any more than that of "indigent or disabled" persons of any other class.[28]

Was the fire department private? It was not a chartered municipal corporation, but if supporting firemen was deemed a public function, the charter did not matter. The direct benefit the insurance company received from the firemen meant that it should pay, even if the charity was not public.

John Reynolds, the lawyer for the fire department, took the latter tack. He conceded that the firemen and their charity were private but that

> there is no more appropriate source from which to draw this tax for the benefit of disabled firemen, than from those who make profit by dealing in insurance. They receive in fact the benefit of the service of the firemen, and if disabled while in service it is entirely equitable, that the insurance companies should be taxed for their benefit.[29]

BEFRIENDING THE WIDOWS AND ORPHANS.

Figure 3. Befriending the Widows and Orphans. From Augustine E. Costello's *Our Firemen: A History of the New York Fire Department, Volunteer and Paid* (1888), 709. Negative # 75251. Collection of the New-York Historical Society. Reproduced with permission.

Mr. Reynolds and the firemen won more than they requested: the court held that the charity was public:

> There can be no doubt that the plaintiffs are the representatives of a public charity well worthy of support, and entitled to the favor of the public, even if it cannot be said of it that such an appropriation is the applying of moneys to the public use.

If the tax may be imposed for the benefit of the department, I see no reason why it may not be payable at once to them instead of passing through the state treasury for that purpose.[30]

The court did not resolve the question of how public the charity was; it was a "public charity" but not quite a "public use." Nevertheless, the state or city could most assuredly require the insurance companies, as the main beneficiaries of fire departments, to pay. Private exchange publicly enforced, more than collective responsibility, colored the legal interpretation of support for the fire department.

Both the court and contemporary commentators spent more attention on the question of whether the tax unconstitutionally discriminated between citizens of different states than on the question of what constituted the public. Although federal and some state law had begun to treat corporations as citizens, not all states did, and whether corporations had the rights of citizens was a matter for debate. The New York court would not grant corporations the rights of citizens. Rather, it held that since the statute discriminated between corporations that were incorporated in New York and those that were not—a wholly different matter from discriminating among citizens—the statute did not violate any privileges and immunities.[31]

The case report following the decision notes that "these cases, affecting a business of increasing magnitude, have elicited so much attention, not only here but in different sections of the Union," that commentary on the decision was justified.[32] That commentary reveals the axes of disagreement concerning what "public" meant and whether a corporation was a citizen.

Mark Skinner, a former justice of the Illinois Supreme Court, disagreed with the New York court: The fire department, he said,

is in no sense a public corporation, much less a political one, in the sense in which city and town corporations are; and cannot, therefore, claim any such rights or powers as are sometimes granted to such corporations. It is purely private, both in its constitution and the ends for which it was created.[33]

Moreover, a state should have to treat foreign corporations as it did domestic ones; both should share in the privileges and immunities of citizens—or so believed the midcentury defenders of corporations.

No less a legal light than Daniel Webster also wrote against the decision. He had built his flamboyant national reputation by defending corporations and defending national power against that of the states; his tearful defense in 1818 of Dartmouth College against the state of New Hampshire before the United States Supreme Court is legendary.[34] Even a firemen's charity could not persuade Webster to temper his fervor for national power and the citizenship of corporations.

His long battle for corporate privilege was not fully resolved in corporations' favor, however, until after the Civil War. In a prescient note, the state court reporter introducing the commentary after the decision noted that the problem of taxation of foreign corporations would persist until the United States Supreme Court settled it.[35]

Cases continued to appear as states and localities tried both to raise money and to protect their insurance companies. In 1852, Illinois enacted a provision, similar to New York's, for charities for volunteer firemen: tax revenues from insurance payments made to companies incorporated outside Illinois would go to injured members of the private firemen's association. It was soon challenged as a violation of public purpose requirements, but in 1859 the Illinois Supreme Court upheld the tax as serving a public purpose. Like the New York court, the Illinois court explained that the benefits the insurance companies enjoyed allowed the state and city to require them to pay:

> The legislature . . . thought proper to divert this fund to the direct endowment of this charity, which was instituted for those, who should be disabled while in a service, the general effect of which, is for the direct benefit of the underwriters, and to what source therefore could they more properly look, than to those in whose service, the objects of this charity would receive the injuries, entitling them to the benefits of the charity?[36]

Both the Illinois and the New York justices were uncertain whether the status of the fire department as public or private even mattered. All that localities had to do was ensure that those who benefited paid the taxes—which would seem to deny any sense of public, collective responsibility. Insurance companies benefited from firemen, so insurance companies should pay for them.

The Illinois court, however, concluded that the charity was public not because a fire department was incorporated, as a public corporation would be, but because it served a public function, like that of poor relief. Therefore, the legislature could appropriate money to the firemen's charity "as much as the institution for the blind."[37] The firemen's charity could get money because it benefited *disabled* firemen, just as a charity for the blind did. By the time any fireman claimed money, at law he was a dependent person.[38]

What sense of "public" did these decisions embody? Political and legal historians have made two opposing arguments concerning the place of public interest in the antebellum era. The form that taxation took is part of what historian Robin Einhorn has called the segmented politics of the time. Insurance companies are only one illustration of the principle that those benefiting from municipal services were the ones who should pay. She has argued that dividing responsibility so narrowly denied any concept of a shared interest among all the citizens of a city. In contrast, William Novak's 1996 analysis of state regulation follows historians who have argued that state legislatures and cities used the tools at hand to pursue a broad sense of public interest, subsuming private property rights. Those tools included targeted taxation and conditions placed for the common good on licenses and individual corporate charters.[39]

Targeted taxation allowed states and cities to provide public services despite their limited resources. City governments in the mid-nineteenth century had no reliable civil service. Without extensive state infrastructure, accomplishing public purposes required attaching conditions to the use of private property and rewarding the much admired volunteers, amateurs, private businesses, and mixed enterprises that provided what we now call public services.[40] That the courts supervised targeted taxation and spending for charities reconciles the different characterizations of the period offered by historians. Governance required taxation for the benefit of all, but individual organizations—those upon whom the primary benefit of collective goods fell—could be the agents required to serve that public purpose or to provide a public service. Thus, the insurance companies lost in principle in their attempts to dismantle discriminatory state taxation, although in similar cases they did win meager victories in Philadelphia and Louisiana. There, courts required that the state or city redraft the legislation to tie the benefit more closely to the tax and to ensure that the money at least pass through the public treasury.

The United States Supreme Court, the court of last resort, in 1869 decided a case in which frustrated insurance companies claimed that the taxes violated the privileges and immunities clause of Article 4 of the Constitution. Since only citizens were guaranteed those privileges and immunities, their case depended on the Supreme Court's holding that insurance companies were citizens. But Justice Stephen Field wrote for the Court that "corporations are not citizens within [Article 4's] meaning." Furthermore, Field explained, insurance was not commerce: insurance companies issued contracts, and those contracts were not "subjects of trade."[41]

In states that saw insurance companies as having special obligations, the companies had to pay, not the local government. Perhaps, we might think, the localness of fighting fires dictated that particularly unsentimental approach to what courts would later see as service; fighting fires did not call up loyalties to the republic, however much it could substitute for military service. Even in the cases concerning military service during the Civil War, however, courts were not certain that military service was anything more than an obligation that localities owed by statute to the national government. They could pay because meeting collective obligations required paying, not because states and towns owed honor to those who had fought for the national government.

Fighting: Local and National Obligations

In 1837, Alexis de Tocqueville noted that the United States was unlikely ever to impose conscription; compulsion fit too badly with "the notions and habits of the people."[42] Bounties filled the army with paid recruits instead, though their numbers were unlikely to be enough to fight an all-consuming war. The Civil War was that war. When it became clear that the Union could not fight successfully without more soldiers than voluntarism and paid bounties could provide, Congress passed the Conscription Act of 1863, which set quotas of soldiers. Acknowledging both the common practice of paying bounties and the mistrust of compulsion that Tocqueville had observed, however, until July of 1864 the statute provided for commutation, or buying one's way out of service, for $300. It did so in order to limit the price of substitutes, which might otherwise cost whatever the market would bear.[43] The $300 fee represented a workingman's salary for a year, making it a real burden but one that did not require risking life. Although Congress eliminated commutation in 1864, the statutes still allowed conscripts to purchase substitutes.

The imposition of quotas reinforced the local meaning of the war for Americans. Many men who volunteered early, in both the Confederacy and the Union, wrote passionate letters home about the ideals of the nation and freedom that animated their service. They served in companies composed of men from their hometowns, which in turn formed regiments of men from neighboring towns.[44] Men may have fought for the grand issues of liberty or the Constitution or states' rights, but they did so with men who were their neighbors, with whom they shared the labor of farming as much as they did the ideals of liberty. Consequently, losses in a battle could decimate the men of one township.

Since conscription came just as popular belief in the ideals of the war were fading, many men bitterly resisted it, most notoriously in New York City in 1863. The fees one could pay to get out of service made it a "rich man's war and poor man's fight," to quote the popular slogan from the South.[45] The immigrant German and Irish poor objected not only to the draft but to fighting a war for the benefit of blacks, which is how they saw it.[46] Tweed's Tammany Hall responded by floating municipal bonds to buy the loyalty of the white urban working class by paying the fees to exempt the poor from service; those who were better off paid their own fees. Raising money collectively to pay commutation fees or to buy substitutes made the war less a poor man's fight. New York's Board of Supervisors also exempted from conscription police, firemen, militia, and poor men with families.[47] Newspapers around the country reported New York's draft riots, and those riots provided some of the motive for other towns to raise money to fill their conscript quotes with substitutes.

Immediately after Congress enacted the Conscription Act, many localities raised tax dollars to pay commutation fees or to buy substitutes, thus saving many of the men of their town from personal service in the war. If a town would raise the money for substitutes, then even those who could never afford to buy a substitute could escape conscription. The substitutes were men eighteen and nineteen years old or immigrants, two groups not subject to conscription.[48]

Towns struggling with the high cost of meeting quotas sometimes tried unsuccessfully to gain relief from their state legislature. Towns desperate to meet their quotas without sending off their own men even sent recruiters to Canada. Officials also pressed men to form associations to contribute to the funds for substitutes, promising to pay the associations back, but often found that the promise to pay was easier to make than the payment itself.[49]

Buying substitutes brought substantial debt to towns, and lawsuits added to their burdens. First, taxpayers challenged towns' efforts to raise funds for recruits as an unconstitutional use of tax money. Second, if a town reneged on the promise it had made to repay associations that had hurriedly raised money, their disappointed members would sometimes sue. Town officials then found it convenient to remember they had never had the constitutional power to pay out the money.[50]

These cases, since they depended on the anger of a taxpayer or the reluctance of a town, were scattered but widespread. Towns or the state itself faced court challenges during and shortly after the Civil War in seventeen of the twenty-two states in the Union subject to the conscription quotas. The other five were border states filled with secessionists and draft evaders: Delaware, Kansas, Kentucky, Missouri, and West Virginia. Men in those states could probably find easier ways to escape the draft than to prevail upon their towns to raise money to buy substitutes. Republican or Democrat, men did not want to die, and many throughout the Union evaded the three drafts imposed after 1863, but the border states had the highest rates of illegal evasion.[51] Men who were not inclined to evade the draft illegally could gain exemptions by reason of health or family responsibilities. Corruption in the administration of the draft could also save them. Widespread resistance to conscription, both principled and pragmatic, may have provided some counties and townships with no need to raise money collectively to save their men from the draft.[52]

In the seventeen states where taxpayers did sue during and immediately after the Civil War, state supreme courts held the payments to be constitutional. The courts cited each other, building a common law concerning public purpose and payments to soldiers. As they decided the cases, state court judges had to consider both what towns owed the national government and what they owed the individuals who met their national obligations. Appellate cases concerning bounties reveal concerns about citizenship and its obligations, the responsibilities of towns, and the place of women as citizens.

A case from Woodbury, Connecticut, an agricultural village near Hartford, illustrates towns' and taxpayers' quarrels over paying the costs of meeting quotas. Under the 1863 Conscription Act, Woodbury's quote was thirty-two men. The town resolved to raise $200 per man in order to buy substitutes. Constitutionally, was the town illegitimately helping individual men to escape their burdens, or helping the town as a whole to meet its obligation? Military service could be something the unfortunate men who fell within the draft requirements owed but no one else did. Alternatively, the men who were drafted were the agents most useful to the general government in conducting a war, and conducting the war served the general interest. In the latter interpretation, those men who were drafted served for all. In the former, the military obligations of citizenship were accidental and personal, of no general benefit.

Charles Booth argued for individual obligation when he and others sued to prevent Woodbury from paying for substitutes. He claimed that the town unconstitutionally took property without compensation when it levied taxes to buy substitutes for those drafted and that it "thereby unlawfully undertook to transfer the individual liability of each person drafted by the United States, to widows, orphans and non-military subjects, as well as to those liable in their own persons to do military duty in behalf of the United States." Property was being taken unjustifiably, for "the liability to military service in defense of the country is wholly a personal liability."[53] Service was not a liability of general public benefit, according to the taxpaying men of Woodbury who sued, but fell on particular members of the community. Conscription was a "personal liability"; therefore, the men subject to the draft could not ask their town to pay for them. "Nonmilitary subjects" would gain nothing in return for their tax dollars, for they did not owe service.

According to Booth, widows and orphans were a particular subcategory of those liable for taxes but not for military service, because unlike married women and children with fathers, they had no men who represented them. Married women and the children of military subjects *would* benefit from the tax if their husbands and fathers thereby gained an exemption from service, but since widows and orphans were not under the governance of a man, they received no benefit from paying a tax to keep men at home. Using the tax money of widows and orphans to pay for substitutes thus constituted a taking. Widows and orphans were in a liminal state. They owed no personal obligations and, not being citizens, were not subjects of the general government or of the town, yet they were certainly inhabitants and possibly taxpayers.[54] Widows thus served Booth's arguments, but married women did not.

The lawyers for the Town of Woodbury responded that the citizens of the town—that is, the men—shared an interest in preserving the Union, whether or not they were personally subject to conscription. Men over forty-five, who were exempt from conscription, had "an equal interest in the stability of our institutions," and those subject to the draft served the interests of all. Unlike other citizens, the men subject to the draft owed "service, either personal, by substitute, or the commutation."[55] Although that obligation fell on the men under forty-five because they were best able to fight, the interests they were serving were not simply their own, and neither would a town be pursuing only young men's interests by paying their commutation fees. The town excluded women and children when explaining who had an interest in governance, for they received benefits and owed obligations via husbands and fathers. The lawyers for the town ignored widows and orphans, since they did not fit into any helpful category.[56]

The Connecticut Supreme Court accepted that the power to conduct a war was a national power and no business of state or local governments. Judge Thomas Belden Butler wrote that

> the state government, as such, is under no obligation to aid the general government in such an exercise of its powers. . . . By what principle then can the legislative branch of the state government be justified in taxing the people of the state, or authorizing their taxation by towns, to confer gratuities upon persons drafted by the United States?[57]

Fighting in the army satisfied a man's obligations to the general government, not to his state. Since towns were creatures of the state, they could do only what states would allow them to do, and men could owe to their town only what they owed to their state. Even though the burden of quotas fell on townships, the obligations actually fell on individual men, for towns were not subsidiaries of the national government. Having held that wars concerned the "general" government, the court immediately acknowledged a general interest in the pursuit of the war and went on to say that taxing to pay the bounties could serve the general public benefit, both by promoting efficient service and by sharing the burden of military service among all citizens. As citizens of the United States, not of their separate states, conscriptees owed some duties to the national or general government. In fact, said the court, the obligation to serve in the military preceded the Conscription Act:

> Every citizen is bound to take up arms when necessary in defence of his government, not as a matter of strict law, but as an incident of citizenship; and the selection of a class only, of a certain age . . . is . . . not based on any peculiar or special obligation resting upon the class.[58]

Booth lost. His interpretation of what military service meant was wrong; the interests of the class of men subject to conscription were the interests of the whole.[59] All men, not only the men subject to conscription, shared in the obliga-tion to support the general government. All men and women, including widows and orphans, would benefit by saving the men of the town. As the Pennsylvania Supreme Court put it in a similar case, "The able-bodied were enrolled, not be-cause they only owe military service, but because they were most fit to perform it."[60] Military service was a general obligation of citizenship, and the nation could choose to share the burden among all citizens. Although a state had *no* obligation to assist the national government in serving its purposes of conducting a war, a lo-cality could aid its citizens in meeting *their* obligation to the national govern-ment. When a locality did so, the state was helping citizens meet their individual obligations, not the federal government in pursuing its war.[61] In an era in which courts were using the public purpose doctrine to prohibit class legislation, able-bodied men eligible to serve in the military constituted a universal class. Their in-terests were significant enough to be a measure of the public welfare. Even escap-ing service was of public benefit because of the importance of men—that is, citizens—to the life of the community. In the vivid language of the court, men were "the bone and sinew of industry, the largest source of revenue, the mainstay of families."[62]

A town could raise money to meet its *collective* obligations, however, not the personal and private obligation of any one citizen.[63] Such payments were not im-plicit in the exchange of citizenship: service for protection. Without positive leg-islation authorizing payments, no one could claim them. Still less could the state pay the fee for any one individual who had bought his own way out of the draft. Rather than regarding towns simply as collections of individuals, the courts con-sistently tried to distinguish public from private in supervising bounties. As the Pennsylvania court said in 1870, "The public received the benefit, and it is just and right that the public money should pay for it."[64] Everyone had "an interest in the stability of institutions," the interest for which the Union pursued the war. The obligations of service were obligations all men had, even if only some were drafted.[65] Towns could assist groups of men in meeting those collective obliga-tions.

Townships could pay not only for service but also for *exempting* local citizens from service. Conscription had long been considered wrong in the United States, as Tocqueville had noted. To balance voluntarism with the need for bodies, the general government could define service to include its purchase. Militarism, not service, was crucial to defining national obligations. Although in later years the service to the nation would be remembered and the purchase of it forgotten, in the turmoil of conscription the baseline of citizenship did not rest in actually fighting.

As the war ended, the treatise writers took over the job of smoothing the rough edges of controversies. Thomas Cooley addressed payments from states and towns in both his 1868 *Treatise on the Constitutional Limitations on the Legislative Powers of States* and his 1876 volume on taxation, both published shortly after the Civil War and the early rash of pension cases. In his 1868 volume he struggled with the obligations of state and federal citizenship:

> The duty of national defence . . . rests upon the national authorities. This much is conceded, though in a qualified degree, also, and subordinate to the national government, a like duty rests upon the State governments, which may employ the means and services of their citizens for the purpose. But it is no part of the duty of a township, city or county, as such to raise men or money for warlike operations.[66]

At the same time, because the national government required localities to produce men for the military, taxation to provide substitutes or meet the obligation in some other way could satisfy public purpose requirements.[67] In 1876 Cooley added the much more adamant statement that "under the general grant of municipal powers, [towns] are without authority to impose upon their people any burden by way of taxation for any such purpose."[68] That statement would have surprised the officials of Woodbury, who had received judicial approval for such taxes.

Conclusion: Obligations to the Nations and the State

Cooley reconciled state and national obligations by making a fine distinction: localities could not fight a war, but they could aid their citizens in meeting their obligations to the national defense. Patriotism to the nation formed no part of state citizenship. Although the line between taxing for purposes of war, which states could not do, and taxing to assist citizens in meeting national obligations, which states could do, was difficult to discern, Cooley and many state court judges relied on it. That distinction between the different obligations provides a partial accounting of why, in these cases, the courts and, for that matter, Cooley provided very little heartfelt discussion of patriotism and danger as justifications for payments to citizens. His blunt denial of the power of a state to raise money for war contrasted with his view of the federal government's power to tax to distribute pensions. Pensions, he noted, could be useful in "inciting others to self-denying, faithful and courageous services in the future."[69] He praised the quality of people who served in the military, but for the purposes of national, not state, pensions.

Federalism and exchange more than honor for individual service dominated the cases concerning payments in the states and localities for both firemen and soldiers. In the earliest cases judges did not praise the service, bravery, or courage of those fighting fires or fighting wars. Questions of state and national obligation, of responsibilities from one collectivity to the other, predominated. Those collectivities were either the states and the national government or the fire insurance companies and the fire departments. Later in the century, when states and localities tried to enact payments to individual veterans, once again the courts had two choices. Either they could stay with the doctrine concerning collective responsibility, or they could abandon it to celebrate individual service. The independence of the state systems allowed courts to settle the problem as they would.

More states remained skeptical about the virtue of payments to veterans than they did to firemen and, later, other civil servants. The next two chapters explore each in turn. As a cult of masculinity emerged in Western countries in the late nineteenth century, a celebration of individual heroism moved from the popular culture into the courts, but more readily for firemen than for veterans in the states.[70] Retroactive bounties for veterans would not induce anyone to serve, so they could not assist in pursuing a war. What, then, could they be other than a transfer from taxpayers to a private group, or theft?

In the American federal system, which divides responsibilities between state and federal government, there is often no one clear hierarchy of governance. As Russell Hanson put it in discussing the creation of social welfare in a federal state, "even a nominal chain of command often does not exist."[71] In the nineteenth century the federal government could order citizens to comply with their national obligations—something the state courts readily acknowledged—but could not order the states to comply with obligations they did not have. Should states wish to assist their citizens in meeting their separate obligations, they could. Policing obligations in the courts required policing the boundaries between federal and state responsibilities: what the state could do with regard to its citizens' national obligations. Judicial analysis was not passionate about the virtues of military service. Up through the years of Civil War, though militarism had been central in defining republican citizenship, that citizenship was membership in the nation, not the states.

CHAPTER FOUR

Military Pensions in the Courts, 1877–1923

Those who fought at the beginning of the Civil War had volunteered. The letters they left behind have told us that Union men fought for the ideal of liberty they believed the Union represented; Confederate soldiers believed they fought for state sovereignty, or to expel the Union invaders, or for the principles of the American Revolution as white southerners saw them—all of which involved fighting for slavery.[1] As the war dragged on, other men fought because they had been drafted and had not taken one of the many routes for escaping conscription. After the war the memory of the depth of its horror faded, leaving the heroism that military service represented as a reason to expand the pensions that the federal government had long granted to soldiers.

In a federal polity, federal pensions implied little about what state and local governments owed or even could pay veterans. The states and their creatures, the towns, had not conducted the war and had no power to conduct a war. The Civil War years had brought taxpayer squabbles over paying to meet town quotas and thereby escape conscription—hardly the stuff of public honor or memory. Once they had finished with such payments, though, what could towns or states possibly owe to veterans? If military service represented nationhood, why should any taxpayer from Acton, Massachusetts, or Orange County, New York, have to support soldiers outside of poor relief? Those questions surfaced every time a town tried to pay its veterans, and they reappeared after World War I.

The experience of the Civil War transformed the public world that followed; militarism became the language of both disputes and celebrations. The North saw the emergence of a cult of celebration of the Civil War. White southerners shared nostalgic sorrow for what they called the Lost Cause, a white supremacist longing for the world of racial subordination that slavery represented.[2] Memory of the war also colored labor politics. Labor activists argued that employers should recognize the sacrifice of the workers who had gone to war by granting them a greater portion of the value of production. Employers often answered activists with state militias.[3] Given the significance of the Civil War in American life and the subsequent pervasiveness of militarism, state court judges had to wonder whether what had once been national service had become local and state service as well. By the early twentieth century every possible social welfare payment would be called a pension, drawing on analogies between military service and labor. National and state pensions raised different questions, though, and how courts treated those questions shifted between the period following Reconstruction and World War I. National military pensions raised no constitutional problems at all, since military service clearly promoted a national purpose, and federal courts so held when they had the opportunity. National officials allocating pensions to veterans and their dependents recognized and policed appropriate familial relations of dependency (less often recognizing the service that women provided to the military).

State pensions were more of a problem. After Reconstruction and until World War I, because state courts in the Northeast reached different conclusions concerning whether national service merited state reward, new litigants could protest state payments. Southern state courts, adjudicating disputes among localities over the little cash available for education and poor relief, limited the claims of veterans. What a man owed his country and what his country might generously pay in return had little to do with what a state might pay him. Not until after World War I did increasing numbers of state courts, again facing questions of state aid, begin to collapse the distinction between state and national obligations, agreeing that members of grateful nations might live in grateful states.

The payment of pensions contributed to a sense that there was a nation-state that embodied the will of a unified people and merited citizens' service. Public celebration of military service rested uneasily alongside federalism and the separation of state from national citizenship, which persisted in the nineteenth century in court cases. Decisions were inconsistent across states; given the ordinary practice of citing one another, the disarray indicates the lack of consensus concerning the place of national service in local governance. That legal disarray moved toward consensus after World War I, though continuing erratic attention to legal standards allowed one threat in New York to reverberate throughout the country.

The shift went largely unacknowledged in the state courts. Courts write history as though they are doing what they have always done: simply following what clear legal principles require. As Roscoe Pound had it in his 1938 commentary, legal categories change as litigants invoke "obstinate traditional precepts" in new circumstances.[4] If judges are not following clear legal principles, they are not abiding by their institutional obligation to follow the law, or so lawyers and judges would argue. By the time cases concerning benefits for veterans came up just after World War I, judges could blithely dismiss alternative views, ignoring the legal controversy that persisted in a dwindling number of states. Rewards for the duties of citizenship recognized the obligations of citizenship, and state and nation recognized both after the First World War.

What went unsaid in the case law was the unfulfilled promise that equal male citizenship held for racial minorities. The United States had claimed to fight the "Great War" for democracy. Not only did the hypocrisy of such a claim provide immigrants and African Americans grounds for objecting to the war, however difficult war fever made that objection;[5] The injustice that persisted after the war in race riots, lynching, discrimination, and segregation stood out in stark relief against the military service men had done for the country.[6] Judges might debate state and national citizenship and service, but Mexican American men in Texas and African American men across the country found the unfulfilled promise of military service to be a catalyst for protest and political organizing.

State and National Citizenship

In the early nineteenth century, courts and other governing institutions treated the states as separate from each other, each an independent republic, though governed by a somewhat shared common law.[7] The Civil War shifted the focus of governance from the states to the national government. The Civil War amendments to the Constitution—the Thirteenth prohibiting slavery; the Fourteenth guaranteeing equal protection, due process of law, and respect for the privileges and immunities of citizens in the states; the Fifteenth affirming the right to vote regardless of race—promised a national state, not a state of independent republics. The national government would reach into the states and guarantee rights; the United States would be a national republic of rights, equality, and citizen loyalty to the nation. That promise was an "America that never was," as Rogers Smith has said, borrowing from Langston Hughes, for after Reconstruction ended in 1876, the national government—including the Supreme Court— abandoned black Americans to the racial hierarchy and terror of the South.[8] For white Americans, directly tying individuals to the national government via rights characterized governance after Reconstruction.[9] If the states became less significant as independent governments, service to the nation could be the same as service to the state.

The tension between state and national citizenship had been debated concerning the Fourteenth Amendment's privileges and immunities clause, which stated that no citizen of the United States could be denied the privileges and immunities of a citizen of any one of the states. Antebellum cases and political debate had acknowledged a state citizenship with natural rights and obligations separate from those of national citizenship. The United States Supreme Court in the 1873 *Slaughterhouse Cases* quickly put that idea to rest, refusing to protect common-law privileges and immunities; the rights and obligations of state citizenship were up to the states to determine. In other cases the Supreme Court also refused to nationalize the rights of citizenship, allowing the states to decide whether women could vote and virtually gutting the efforts Congress made to protect black Americans from the viciousness of the Ku Klux Klan and the governments of the southern states.[10] The federal courts, however, did hold that the due process clause of the Fourteenth Amendment embodied national rights of citizenship—most notoriously, freedom of contract. White men were free to form labor contracts, allowing the courts, for example, to strike down legislation that protected unions, on the grounds that it interfered with men's freedom of contract. The courts also held that there was a general federal common law that they had an obligation to enforce.[11]

What would national rights for citizens mean for the tie between state and citizen? Would the increasing power of what had been called the general government mean that the state became identical with it? The Civil War amendments and judges' interpretations of them pulled in different directions: the amendments nationalized the rights of citizenship, whereas courts' interpretations placed the states at the center. State cases involving military pensions demonstrated similar conflict: legislatures might grant pensions, but state courts could remain skeptical that any state payment should go to veterans other than the poor relief available to all the desperate poor in each township.

Women and Erasing Service

Sometimes military service has seemed to provide the only possible common purpose for citizens, the only thing that raises their sights beyond the immediate petty concerns that divide them from their neighbors. The hope that it might bind all together, though, has had its own exclusions: if militarism required masculinity, nothing that women did could count as service. Noting the significance of gender to military pensions, though, requires noting how much that contemporary assumption excluded during the Civil War.

Women were largely excluded from the official rolls of the military, which in turn meant that when national pensions payments expanded dramatically, women not related to a veteran had no access either to pensions or to the preferences in civil service hiring that men had. Women were excluded from the army yet participated in capacities officially unrecognized. Some women actually served as soldiers by disguising their sex.[12] Others, following the camps, cooked and cleaned or were nurses or spies—or prostitutes.[13] The federal government recognized their contributions only reluctantly; Harriet Tubman had served as a spy for the Union, but it took thirty years for her to get a pension for her work.[14] Women who tended to injured men were themselves at risk and suffered as well the psychological trauma of exposure to violent death.[15]

When women were admitted to the military during World War II, they were allowed to make up only 1 percent of the armed services. Even then, white women who enlisted did not seem entirely respectable to their communities; they were released from family supervision, and rumors abounded about their free behavior with men.[16] Sex segregation in the military did grant some sexual freedom, allowing women to explore lesbianism as well. The meanings of service for women differed according to race, however. Whereas white women might wish to enlist to serve their country (while also gaining freedom from family), black women saw service as working for racial equality in addition to serving their country.[17]

Engendering war as masculine required much more than ignoring the services women performed in the field. It required seeing battle as dangerous slaughter as well as the protection of lives from attackers, particularly the lives of vulnerable women and children. Fighting a war had to be active, rather than passive, and therefore masculine. Proving one's manhood has always been central to the romance of war, and the Civil War held that meaning, crucial for African American men.[18] Part of the trauma of war, however, has been that soldiers could do so very little about their circumstances. That helplessness in impossible circumstances also characterized poor women's lives on the home front. War work often involved providing for soldiers, just as home domestic work did. What required bravery was not action, the expected adventure, so much as the utter helplessness of being in battle with too few supplies. Men in battle were often in a highly feminized position. Frequently helpless, when they could do something, that something was often providing goods for one another.[19] Soldiers during the Civil War were what contemporaries called "shook over hell": that is, suffering from what psychiatrists described during World War I as shell shock, during World War II as battle fatigue, and now as post-traumatic stress disorder.[20]

Looking at quintessentially feminine work—childbearing—brings out further ironies in the effort to distinguish between men's and women's risks. Childbearing, the work that made women depend on men, was itself tremendously dangerous; many women died or suffered severe injuries, particularly before the 1870s when doctors began to accept that cleanliness could reduce the risk of infection and death. Before that, women's lifetime risk of death in childbirth was 8 percent. Even as late as the 1930s, childbirth resulted in 4.5 deaths per thousand births in New York City.[21] Yet in the allotment of public pensions, men's place in the danger of either war or home life counted, whereas women's seldom did. Even for men, however, that was clearly true only with regard to national pensions.

National Military Pensions: Necessary and Proper

Military pensions were a part of English governance even before the American Revolution. Thereafter, when pensions were first instituted in the United States, many criticized them as exactly the sort of English practice the American national state should avoid. The national government allotted pensions first to indigent officers; after the War of 1812, soldiers too received them.[22] Then Congress eliminated the requirement that recipients be indigent, so national pensions no longer resembled locally administered poor relief. Each new pension statute required only an expansion of what had come before. The federal power to conduct war, as stated in the Constitution, allowed those pensions; the states did not share that power.

National Civil War pensions were first legislated as promises in a desperate effort to draw more men into the military: between 1862 and 1866, Congress expanded pensions first to widows, mothers, and children, then to fathers, sisters, and brothers of soldiers who died during the war. These pensions were an attempt to allay men's concern that they would leave families behind to starve if they joined up and were killed.[23] The honor ascribed to military pensions for dependents did not exempt families from scrutiny concerning whether they really were a family, questions made pressing by the administrative and legislative expansion of such payments. In 1862, when the Bureau of Pensions under authorization from Congress included more family members and increased payments for widows and orphans, claimants had to document their family ties—no small feat in an era without regular records. Marriage documents could be unclear, and some states recognized common-law marriages, which by definition had no formal ceremony or paperwork.[24] The problem was compounded for former slaves who had served in the military and tried to claim pensions. Since masters had seldom provided for formal weddings (which would have acknowledged an autonomy that directly contradicted slavery), anyone married under slavery was unlikely to have any evidence of marriage beyond swearing to having lived together for a long time.

In policing what would count as a fraudulent or legitimate claim, the Bureau of Pensions had to decide, as the historian Megan McClintock put it, "What, indeed, was a marriage?" If the bureau recognized informal arrangements as marriages—as it virtually had to, given desultory recordkeeping—drawing a line between marriage and an illegitimate affair could be excruciatingly close to arbitrary.[25] For the women claiming pensions, that arbitrary line-drawing meant a great deal: federal pensions for wives and mothers of the Civil War dead eased financial reliance on relatives.[26] Parents who claimed pensions had to prove that they had been dependent on their sons, and evidence for that might be elusive as well. The Bureau of Pensions first accepted testimony from employers, neighbors, and friends concerning how a young man spent his pay; after 1873 it accepted a young man's demonstrated intention to support his parents.[27] The bureau made the bulk of these decisions concerning who would be paid; Congress handled individuals' complaints about being denied a pension.

Women whose husbands, fathers, and brothers had enlisted had access to military benefits as a result of the sacrifices they had made in losing their men to the war: that is, men's service created dependents' desert. Congress accompanied the piecemeal expansion in general bills with special bills granting pensions to individuals, making the pensions widespread and very popular but also subject to criticism by those who saw them as tied to nothing more than political favoritism. By 1910 about 18 percent of all Americans over age sixty-five were receiving federal military pensions, among them the veterans themselves and their dependents.[28]

During the nineteenth century, more was at stake in military pensions than provision for the widows and children. Agents, including lawyers, who made claims on dependents' behalf and could bring claims to court often collected substantial fees. In fact, they made so much from the claims that in the 1890 statute expanding pension benefits to family members, Congress also limited the fees that attorneys could collect to $10; bringing a case to the federal court suddenly became much less lucrative.[29] Before that, some cases came before the federal district courts and courts of appeals. Claimants sometimes thought their agents' fees were too high, occasioning disputes in court between pensioners and their lawyers, or prosecutions for embezzlement by the federal government. The Supreme Court itself decided a few cases concerning agents who kept the whole pension as a fee after procuring it ostensibly for a client.

Congress's morass of special and general laws expanding pensions created room for dispute concerning how much anyone could claim.[30] Taxpayers themselves could not bring suit over federal pensions, as they could to challenge local spending. Localities, with the powers that the states had granted them in their constitutions were corporations, albeit public ones, and taxpayers could defend in court their stake in how those corporations spent their tax dollars. But only the agents and the federal government policing them could raise questions about pensions and their beneficiaries. Claimants could complain within the Bureau of Pensions, and they did; until the late nineteenth century, Congress also acted as a court of appeal, addressing constituents' claims for pensions via either bills that expanded eligibility or private bills. Because Congress and then the Court of Claims listened to the plaints of those who wanted federal pensions, the cases left to the federal general jurisdiction courts before the late nineteenth century were those in which the government prosecuted agents, though on occasion they also adjudicated claims among quarreling family members.[31]

Agents argued creatively to keep fees or pensions, sometimes amounting to the substantial sum of $500—more than a laborer could earn in a year. The federal courts held that the pensions belonged to the claimants rather than the agents, despite any promise otherwise. For example, when Allen Cotton claimed a pension after his mother's death, based on his father's service in the Revolutionary War, nieces and nephews argued that as her grandchildren, they deserved part of it. He answered that the statute provided for children, not grandchildren. He lost: the United States Supreme Court decided to interpret the statute generously and include "grandchildren" within "children."[32] Judges treated such cases as requiring matter-of-fact interpretation of a statute rather than raising large questions of constitutional interpretation.

When one guardian raised the Constitution as a block to his ward's getting a pension, though, the United States Supreme Court addressed it. William Williamson's parents had died after the Civil War, and he was entitled to a pension based on his father's military service. His guardian, a Mr. Hall, obtained the $500 pension from the government but did not pass it on to his ward. The federal government prosecuted Hall for embezzlement. Hall defended himself by arguing that he could be prosecuted only under state law, if at all. He also argued that Congress was reaching beyond its powers by enacting that spending statute; spending for the benefit of individuals was a "municipal," or local, purpose.

In *United States v. Hall* (1878), Justice Nathan Clifford answered the claim by treating pensions as almost self-evidently constitutional, ratified by long practice. Justice Clifford pointed out that Congress could not only declare war but enact laws "necessary and proper" to carry its declaration of war into effect:

> Bounties may be offered to promote enlistments, and pensions to the wounded and disabled may be promised as like inducements. Past services may also be compensated, and pensions may also be granted to those who were wounded, disabled, or otherwise rendered invalids while in the public service, even in cases where no prior promise was made or antecedent inducement held out.[33]

Since pensions had long been accepted in the United States, long-standing practice itself affirmed their constitutionality.[34] That was enough of an answer to the question; there was no need to argue further that Congress could also provide for soldiers' children, even though they themselves had not fought.

Scholarship on military pensions has focused on federal pensions, taking for granted the division of responsibility that made pensions one of the few constitutionally legitimate federal programs that gave money to individuals.[35] Military pensions during the nineteenth century evoked the importance of that federal system. Before the Civil War the significant privileges and immunities that citizens held were based on their state citizenship; state sovereignty delineated much of government responsibility.[36] Only the federal government's ability to conduct war allowed it to pay the pensions. Only the treatment of the money as a matter of statutory right, opening opportunistic agents to prosecution for fraud and the government to claims from those denied the funds, made the constitutional basis of the programs visible in court.

Social insurance advocates disliked federal military pensions as they existed in the late nineteenth century because they were often not tightly tied to service.[37] They seemed limitless, with Congress continually tempted to extend them and to enact special bills granting pensions to particular men and their dependents, including those who probably did not merit pensions and possibly excluding some who did. Pensions thus represented unprincipled, corrupt, and unreliable public spending. Local pensions were even less tied to service, since local governments did not conduct wars.

Past Services, Rendered Where?

States, however, did also pay pensions to soldiers, even though, unlike the federal government, they could not conduct a war. As the distinctive significance of state citizenship faded, northeastern state courts remained skeptical of the virtues of such pensions; they were still concerned about exactly what states as such could possibly owe to the support of the general government's wars. The payments localities had made during the war, when they were doing all they could to meet their conscription quotas without decimating their population of young men, differed from pensions paid after the Civil War. Those payments could not possibly induce men to serve or meet a collective obligation to the national government. In deciding what to make of state and local pensions when taxpayers challenged them or legislators asked for judicial opinions, state court judges tried to determine the respective obligations of state and national citizenship.

After Reconstruction, Massachusetts, New York, and Connecticut state courts all held that giving a "bounty" to veterans retroactively or to those who had bought their way out of service was not valid because it represented spending for a private rather than a public purpose.[38] The Massachusetts Supreme Court addressed pensions and preferences for veterans in civil service employment seven times between 1885 and 1912.[39] It repeatedly refused to allow any state or local pensions or benefits.

In 1887, the Massachusetts legislature granted veterans a preference for civil service jobs by giving them a bonus in points on a civil service exam; in 1895 the state tried an absolute preference, ranking all veterans more highly than all nonveterans. The Massachusetts Supreme Court immediately struck down the absolute preference; the justices were skeptical that wartime service provided skills needed in the civil service. No other reason for a preference would be constitutional.[40]

When towns, scattered throughout the state, offered payments at their discretion, judges were still doubtful that military service continued to be useful to a locale after the war was over. Taxes from towns had kept their men out of Civil War service by paying commutation fees or purchasing substitutes; retroactive payments, judges noted, could hardly accomplish that public purpose, induce volunteers to serve, or support their families.

The Massachusetts Supreme Court first struck down town payments in 1885. The state legislature had enabled the town of Acton to raise taxes to pay pensions to men who had reenlisted in a regiment the town had raised for the Civil War. Adelbert Mead, a local taxpayer in Acton, thought the taxes were wrong and took the town to court. The state supreme court agreed with him: paying soldiers for services long past and rendered to the national government rather than the locality was not the proper business of the town:

> The object for which the town of Acton has raised this money is private, and not public. The town has made no promise to these soldiers, and is not under any obligation to pay them any bounties. The purpose is not to repay any sums advanced them as an inducement to enlist. The bounty to be paid cannot be regarded in the light of compensation for services rendered; for their services as soldiers were not rendered to the town, and the town had nothing to do with their compensation. The war has been over for many years, and the payment of these bounties cannot encourage enlistments, or in any way affect the public service, or promote the public welfare. The direct primary object is to benefit individuals, and not the public. In any view we can take of the statute, the payments it contemplates are mere gratuities or gifts to individuals.[41]

Paying individual veterans benefited them, not the town as a whole. Without an eye to the future—without encouraging men to enlist—bounties had no public purpose at all. Honoring men for past service was a rhetorical device used to justify giving taxpayers' money away.

Mead's case was far from the end of the story in Massachusetts, although the rest of the cases turned from complaints about local taxes to consideration of state policy. Unlike most state supreme courts, the highest court in Massachusetts provided advisory opinions, allowing members of the state legislature to continue legislative politics by requesting such opinions repeatedly.

The Massachusetts justices were asked to reconsider military pensions again in 1900, 1905, and 1906, which in Massachusetts was a time of extensive official discussion of new social spending programs such as old age pensions, in addition to expansion of military pensions.[42] Each time the court issued an opinion in response to a state statute expanding military pensions, the justices were divided, making the decisions vulnerable to a change in personnel. Was it for the legislature or the courts to determine what constituted a public purpose? In 1900 the Massachusetts court first decided that *Mead v. Acton* had reached too far; what was for the public benefit was for the legislature to determine.[43] Just four years later the justices accorded with the Civil War–era cases from Pennsylvania and Connecticut, reminding the legislature that the legitimate public purpose for the states in paying pensions had been to help the localities meet their conscription obligations to the national government. Granting bounties so many years after the war could not possibly induce service, particularly since the legislature was granting bounties only to those who had not received a bounty previously.

> The object of the act . . . is not to give rewards in recognition of valuable services, and thus to promote loyalty and patriotism, but to equalize bounties given to induce enlistments in a particular military service many years ago.[44]

Since towns had individually raised finds for this purpose during the Civil War, the payments had of course varied, and equalizing payments when they could do nothing other than put cash in people's pockets was not a public purpose. Thanking someone for service long completed would not facilitate getting anyone to serve. Yet in 1912 the court finally advised the legislature in response to its most recent legislation that payments to volunteers who had not received a bounty *would* serve a public purpose.[45] A change in personnel in the court and persistence on the part of the legislature had allowed the state to reward service long past.

The Massachusetts court also addressed preferences shown to veterans in public employment. Initially, the state supreme court did not find such preferences any more appealing than it did bounties. In 1896 it struck down an absolute preference that exempted veterans wholly from the civil service exam.[46] When the state legislature immediately returned to the question and required veterans to take the exam but then provided them with a preference if they passed, the justices advised that they would uphold the preference because the question of what counted as a public purpose was a matter for the legislature to determine, even though the justices themselves were divided. Those who opposed the preference saw civil service reform as a way to stop patronage in public employment. Service in the military might be useful, but it did not necessarily define who was best qualified for a civilian job; it should lead to preference only if that conveyed an ongoing benefit to the public.[47] Further, military service was only one type of public service; the Massachusetts justices in 1900 noted that civil service might also merit reward.[48] Military service was not distinctive, a particularly important point to make in

1900 when states were expanding the civil employment of police and teachers and, in turn, considering pensions for them.

While the Massachusetts legislature and supreme court fenced over pensions and preferences, the state also seriously discussed general old age pensions, which advocates saw as analogous to pensions for the military but administered without favoritism. If military pensions were unconstitutional, it would be difficult to see how old age pensions could possibly pass muster. Nevertheless, between 1903 and 1906 the state legislature considered a number of general old age pension bills. In 1907, just after its attempts to expand military pensions, the state appointed a commission to study old age pensions; the commission reported in 1910 that general old age pensions would be unconstitutional because they did not reward service (see chapter eight). Nothing about the justices' opinions regarding military pensions and preferences suggested that more general old age pensions would be constitutional. If they were not constitutional in Massachusetts, they were unlikely to be elsewhere, since courts borrowed from one another, and Massachusetts was a "gateway" for discussion of social welfare programs in the United States.[49]

Locally paid pensions had no friends among judges in New York, either. Under state law, counties in New York could provide pensions to anyone who had either served or bought his way out of service; the state courts had been willing to concede that bounties were legitimate when paid to get someone to serve during the Civil War.[50] Payments thirty-five years later were different. The bonds used to pay bounties during the Civil War were still being paid off from taxes as late as 1897.[51] That indebtedness would not have cheered the fiscal conservatives who dominated New York's corporate legal world.

In 1899, William D. Guthrie, a nationally prominent conservative attorney, represented Hudson Bush, a taxpayer in Orange County who did not want to pay for pensions. Guthrie was a railroad attorney and a partner in New York's leading corporate law firm, which later became Cravath, Swaine and Moore.[52] When he was not reorganizing railroads, he crusaded in the courts against taxes and government regulation. Bounties for soldiers were just one more excuse for wrongheaded and unconstitutional taxation, from his point of view.

Just before Guthrie took the case against soldiers' pensions in *Bush v. County of Orange,* he published a book on the Fourteenth Amendment, based on lectures he had given at Yale. In it he argued that the amendment properly understood prohibited most of the social welfare legislation under consideration in the states because such laws either violated the due process clause or took property without compensation.[53] Guthrie briefed and argued some of the legendary cases of this period before the United States Supreme Court: the 1895 case striking down income taxes, the 1903 case challenging the regulation of lotteries, and in 1925 the

Oregon case requiring parents to send their children to public schools rather than private religious schools.[54] He believed that constitutional principles were eternal and that criticizing them was immoral.[55]

Guthrie distinguished *Bush* from townships' taxation cases during the Civil War, using Thomas Cooley to reinforce his point. Guthrie linked the pensions to public purpose cases addressing businesses, including *Loan Association v. Topeka,* the United States Supreme Court's 1874 decision in a Kansas case. If federal constitutional law was not enough, Guthrie could rely on New York's anti-gift amendment from 1874. The lawyers for Orange County tried instead to rely only on the line of military pension cases that supported subsidies from towns. Those, of course, had been payments during the war to raise an army, a wholly different matter from money paid thirty-five years later. Guthrie's effort to link the military cases with the business subsidy cases proved successful. New York's highest court held the pensions to be unconstitutional:

> The fact that a majority of the taxpayers requested the supervisors to levy the tax is of no importance. Majorities, however potent in many respects, have no power to impose taxes upon the minority for the purpose of raising money to be devoted to gifts or gratuities to individuals.[56]

Majorities had floated bonds that had required years of taxation to pay off. In law, local taxes were not collective payments for officials to spend as they determined to be in the public interest; they came instead from money belonging to individual taxpayers, who might not be able to muster a majority of voters. Majorities had to be curbed and the principles of constitutionalism maintained. That argument provided a framework for resisting later constitutional change enabling pensions.

The judges deciding these cases held that a bounty given after service would not promote the public purpose of encouraging people to enlist. Pensions certainly would not meet the state's obligation, because Americans moved so much after the Civil War that their service might have been rendered "some other state," as the Connecticut Supreme Court put it, sharing the skepticism of the judges in Massachusetts and New York.[57] The courts held that the state must really be *inducing* service to the state rather than using such service as a post hoc rationalization. Tying service to locale would ensure that spending did not reach beyond a real reward for service.

What State? Service in the South

In parades, citizens might well celebrate militarism and the nobility of those who had died or were maimed in the war, but that celebration could easily fall by the wayside when any state or locality had to pay for it. Fighting for the Union should not have earned any gratitude from the state, or so the Massachusetts Supreme Court held until 1912. In northeastern states that doubt could readily have been an expression of the widespread disgust with federal military pensions as they spread to so many Americans throughout the nineteenth century. As military pensions joined the list of programs for which localities were responsible, including poor relief and education, the difficult practicalities of sharing the limited funds raised through local taxes could subsume either the celebration of war or principled dislike of pensions.

That is just what happened in the southern states, where state and county officials tried to avoid paying pensions. The South celebrated its own version of militarism. After Reconstruction ended in 1877, the region developed state policies antithetical to any commitment to the equality that the Civil War amendments were supposed to ensure. White southerners developed a cult of the Lost Cause, embodying racial superiority and the concomitant principle of state sovereignty that they had hoped for.[58] Decisions by the United States Supreme Court gutted the powers of Congress to enforce equality even had it wanted to, allowing the southern states to reinvent forced labor and governance by racial hierarchy and terror.[59]

If any states would treat service to the local state as equivalent to service to the national state, one would have expected them to be the southern states. Yet they were the least likely to issue soldiers' pensions and paid the least money for them; they did not institute pensions for Confederate soldiers until after Reconstruction, when the federal government stopped supervising the South.[60] Taxpayers' complaints, however, came out of southern states quite late, reaching into 1912 and 1913. State-authorized county relief for soldiers took money directly out of the budget for education and poor relief for those who had not been soldiers. When facing trade-offs, county supervisors and judges no longer saw military service as obviously meriting financial reward above all else that localities had to pay for from their meager taxes.

North Carolina, Georgia, South Carolina, West Virginia, and Kentucky all provided for veterans who had been disabled during the war and for soldiers' widows. County commissioners, boards of education, county clerks, and state comptrollers general all found themselves in a tangle over money. In all but one of those states the courts were unwilling to order state or county officials actually to pay money to soldiers.[61]

The one victory for veterans in the South was a nostalgia-soaked decision from Kentucky, which had not seceded from the Union. James Harp applied for a pension based on his Civil War service for the Confederate army, as provided for by the state statute governing pensions. He received a warrant, and he asked the state's auditor, Henry M. Bosworth, to pay it. Auditors had no more reason to wish to pay tax money for social welfare than did county commissioners, and Bosworth claimed that the pension did not serve a public purpose. Chief Justice J. P. Hobson, writing for the court, pointed out with some irritation that auditors were ministerial officials, and Bosworth should simply do his legal duty rather than question it. Precisely because he was a ministerial official, however, Bosworth probably had not refused the pension on his own initiative. The state attorney general represented him in court, so Bosworth was probably under instructions from the governor's office, which suggests that the state's executive branch did not want to pay the soldiers' pensions that the legislature had authorized.

Whether or not soldiers had served the state proved a particularly awkward question in *Bosworth v. Harp* because the state-authorized pensions would pay Confederate soldiers, who had rebelled against both the national state and the state of Kentucky. Chief Justice Hobson held that paying those veterans served a public purpose because the soldiers had fought for the principle of state sovereignty. Fifty years after the war, he recalled northern criticism of the South, quoting the abolitionists William Lloyd Garrison and Charles Sumner. He also cited the criticism of the Dred Scott case (1857), which had held that black people could never be citizens of the United States. A plea from the lawyer and U.S. congressman Anson Burlingame for an antislavery constitution and an antislavery God had also alarmed Kentucky citizens in the 1850s, Justice Hobson thought. Furthermore, John Brown's 1859 raid on Harpers Ferry had been an effort to "massacre . . . women and children" who were defenseless.[62] Given the terrorism of antislavery, pensions for former Confederate soldiers were legitimate, as Justice Hobson saw it, for men earned pensions by defending helpless women and children. Women had helped to define the Confederacy, as the historian Drew Faust has argued: it was for the virtues of "woman" that men fought, and women served by "shaping national character"; they had also sacrificed their men for the "Cause."[63] In conclusion, Chief Justice Hobson wrote:

> So long as the courage of the battlefield or the risking of one's life for his country is honored and it is the policy of the State to promote the loyalty and patriotism of the people by fostering the martial spirit, such services constitute a reasonable basis for classification. The honor due to the true and the brave is not limited to those who are successful in the struggle.[64]

In dissent, Judge John M. Lassing rather mildly pointed out that fighting for a losing side in a civil war was not service to the state.

Although both southerners and northerners considered service to the Confederacy worthy of greater honor than not having fought at all, the difficulty of actually mustering the money from state and local resources made the honor of that service moot. Raising money for locally paid programs depended on the wealth of the county; poor counties could pay only poorly. As a result, reluctant officials asked courts not to treat military service as though it naturally merited payment before schools or general poor relief. Despite the significance of military service to citizenship, many judges agreed that neither state statutes nor state constitutions had made military service the priority above all others, either in the northeastern states facing cases after Reconstruction or in the cash-strapped southern states.

World War I: Serving the Nation Serves the State?

The belief in social insurance that spread throughout the Western world in the late nineteenth century came in time to transform federal military pensions paid to veterans of World War I. Contributory insurance bureaucratically administered could halt the practices that had so distressed the national critics of military pensions.[65] During World War I, Congress enacted the War Risk Insurance Act, turning the pensions the national government had offered into social insurance. With that act, Congress tried to transform the chaos of military pensions into a predictable system that would compensate all those injured in the war. The act also provided benefits to the family members left behind, both recognizing the loss of earnings that conscription imposed and also trying to soothe those who protested against it.[66] Given a political climate hostile to racial equality after World War I, state officials likely assumed that only white veterans merited pensions, but constitutional politics raised the question once again of whether *states* could authorize pension money at all. The taxpayers and banks that worried about constitutionality were working against the ongoing determination of states to distribute money.

The immediate reaction to the end of the war in the United States was celebration, and the states participated by enacting payments to veterans. The United States had entered late and lost comparatively few men. National leaders, from President Woodrow Wilson to popular commentators, marked the generous service of veterans, eliding conscription by claiming that citizens had "willingly come forward." Literature romanticized the heroic soldier, culminating in Willa Cather's *One of Ours,* which won the Pulitzer Prize in 1923. Since the hero's longing for adventure could no longer be satisfied by the ordeals of the American West, tamed in recent years, war satisfied that need. The rebellious voices critical of the war, such as those of e. e. cummings and William Faulkner, did not represent dominant cultural themes.[67] In the early 1920s, then, the states enacted benefits for veterans in celebration of and gratitude for their service. As taxpayers and county officials objected, the great themes of heroism and skepticism would confront each other in court again.

By that time, national service clearly implied national membership, providing hope for men previously denied it. Members of several groups anticipated that their national service would transform their status. Asians excluded by statute and judicial interpretation from citizenship sometimes gained it through their military service, or at least applied to the Bureau of Naturalization for citizenship based on that service.[68] African Americans had long served in the military yet still faced massive disenfranchisement. Some hoped their military service would encourage white Americans to treat them as equal citizens though others resisted conscription, arguing they did not owe service to a state that treated them so unequally.[69] Even W. E. B. Du Bois, a powerful critic of American racism, argued during World War I that if African Americans served, their position at home would improve. Similarly, in World War II some Japanese Americans volunteered for the army even from the internment camps to demonstrate that they were truly American citizens or ought to be trusted as loyal. The Japanese American Citizens League supported that position and did little to criticize internment.[70]

However contested the racial dimension of citizenship remained, states granted pensions recognizing national service, and once again, taxpayers challenged them. The formal independence of the state court systems resulted in varying decisions concerning whether only the national government should recognize national military service or whether it was something for which states should also show gratitude. By 1912, state court judges had two leading cases, and lines of cases, on which to rely. The two conflicted. After wavering but largely disallowing aid to veterans for some twenty years, the influential Massachusetts Supreme Court justices held that the states *could* pay pensions to veterans. Any court so inclined could read all the Civil War cases concerning town taxation imposed to meet conscription quotas as reaching the same conclusion. Also in 1912, however, the less noticeable Connecticut court had held that states could *not* pay pensions. Most states that saw conflicts in court chose to follow the Massachusetts justices: despite American mobility, service "rendered some other state," as the Connecticut court had put it, could still merit reward. The New York Court of Appeals, that state's highest court, stubbornly continued to hold, though, that service rendered the national government was no business of the state, and the state could not pay for it. Within American federalism, military service might well be worthy but could still be an obligation between national government and individual, not involving the state.

New York's dispute raised problems with aid around the country. Much was at stake: in 1920 the state's electorate had ratified floating $45 million in bonds to pay each soldier $10 for every month served; it joined thirty-five other states that floated bonds to pay bounties. But bankers proved unwilling to bid on them after a lawyer in western New York, Benjamin S. Dean, wrote to the state attorney general that the bonds were unconstitutional. In June 1921 he explained in a letter to the *New York Times:* "If the gift of money by the State of New York to one who has merely performed a duty which he could not avoid to the Government of the United States, and has been duly discharged from that service is not 'merely a private purpose,' what is it?" He cited the United States Supreme Court's 1874 decision in *Loan Association v. Topeka* to support his argument, noting that the Fourteenth Amendment meant that even if a state court supported the bonds, the U.S. Supreme Court could still hold against them.[71]

Dean's letter echoed beliefs in voluntarism as the only service worthy of the name. Voluntarism as a principle of service had not only provided firemen a reason to hold in contempt the new professional forces in the 1850s; it had colored the organization of conscription during the Civil War by allowing people to buy substitutes. Even conscription during World War I had been administered through local officials, who tried to limit the extent to which something so coercive would disrupt American practical beliefs in localism and voluntarism.[72] To Dean, serving because one faced prison if one did not was no kind of service worthy of reward.

After Dean's electrifying letter to the state attorney general, no bank offered any plausible bid on New York's soldiers' bonus bonds. The New York attorney general tried to soothe the banks, saying that it was for states, not taxpayers, to bring cases. But Dean said he could sue as a taxpayer, and Dean was right. His threat to sue was enough to frighten the banks off, whatever the state attorney general said. More than that, according to the *New York Times,* thanks to Dean's threat, banks *across the country* would not bid on bonds the states offered to pay the widely popular soldiers' pensions. Thirty-six states offered those bonds. Could one lawyer from Jamestown, New York, stop them? The Westchester County National Bank finally bid on the bonds only to assist the state attorney general in testing them in court; the bid was low and conditioned upon a favorable ruling on constitutionality.[73] The bank then refused to pay, and the state brought a suit for payment. By special procedure, the case sped to the state appellate division and then to the Court of Appeals.

The Court of Appeals stubbornly continued to distinguish between what was owed to state and to nation. Justice William S. Andrews wrote for the court in *People v. Westchester County National Bank:*

> We know that when the United States declared war it declared it for the whole country; that the government of the state, the government of the United States were equally interested in victory; that while serving the United States our sol-

diers and sailors were also protecting New York. We were all vitally interested in
the war. Defeat spelled unspeakable calamity. Yet the men who gained the victory were not in any respect servants of the state. It did not call them from their
homes or lead them to battle. It did nothing. It exercised no authority. It is said
that our soldiers were taken from homes and occupations and compelled to risk
their lives for inadequate pay while others earned large wages in safety—that the
statute attempts in a small way to distribute more fairly the public burden. It is
all true, but again the state was not the actor. Neither it nor its servants injured
any one. It received no property for which it has not paid.

Nor were services rendered to it in any sense that services were not rendered to
every city in the land.[74]

The state of New York had not conducted the war, even if it had benefited from
victory.

Two justices dissented, including Benjamin Cardozo, who would later sit on
the United States Supreme Court: the states did not have to conduct the war in
order to pay veterans. Justice Cardozo and his co-dissenter relied on decisions
from other states to urge that of course the state could reward soldiers. Nevertheless, bankers were spooked; no cross-state citations could force bids on bonds.

The reporting concerning *People v. Westchester National County Bank* demonstrates that one cannot know how much any case represents practices. That brakes
were put on the bond market around the country does not show in appellate case
reports. The effect of New York's decision on the bond market depended on the
happenstance that a lawyer well versed in old cases decided to write a letter to the
state attorney general, as well as on national networks among bankers and their
lawyers. In contrast to the New York Court of Appeals, which refused to allow the
state to issue bonds, the few other state courts that considered the constitutionality of state programs to pay veterans ratified them. To them, national service had
become worthy of state recognition.[75] Principles of voluntarism and localism persisted well into this much more national period, though, and under long-standing
court decisions the potential for just one taxpayer to bring suit allowed those
principles to endure.

Deciding that service to the nation was service to the state, or that inducing service was the same as rewarding service later, required only the ordinary incremen-
tal steps of legal reasoning, not a reversal of what had come before. Courts simply
erased the underpinnings of the Civil War conscription cases. For example, in
1921 the Washington Supreme Court court held that "if the inducing to enter the
service is a public service, it is difficult to see why the service rendered after such
entry therein is not also a public service."[76] Similarly, the Wisconsin Supreme
Court held that a "bounty" of $10 for every month served, with a minimum of
$50, served a public purpose "as a token of appreciation for the character and

spirit of [the soldiers'] patriotic service." Patriotism, then, did not require voluntary service, as it had seemed to do in the antebellum era. Careful distinctions elaborated over time between inducing and rewarding service went by the wayside. The Wisconsin court reasoned that payment after men had served in the military would "stimulate patriotism," and that was a legitimate public purpose.[77] Both the Wisconsin and the Washington court acknowledged *state* payment for what had once been considered purposes of the *national* government.

In 1922, the year after New York's decision, the California Supreme Court, as though there was no controversy whatsoever, held in a direction precisely opposite that of the New York court: "Legislation having for its purpose the giving of a benefit to soldiers who have served their country in time of war is uniformly recognized as the application of public money for a public purpose."[78] That bland statement ignored the work of William Guthrie in New York dating from 1899 and the more recent and nationally prominent New York argument over bonds.

The constitutional controversy over pensions concerned the distinction between national and local citizenship, which the California court simply ignored or assumed to be insignificant. For its justices, the rights and obligations of state citizenship had become part of those of national citizenship. Spending that retroactively rewarded service would not at all serve the purpose Thomas Cooley and the state courts had deemed legitimate in the 1870s: helping citizens meet their national obligation. The one purpose that had been peculiar to the national government—conducting a war—had in most states become appropriate to the states and localities as well, alongside charity and reward for more ordinary civil service.

War service was public service; the California court did not generalize to civil service or wage labor (though by the time it decided the case, even the United States Supreme Court had held that industrial labor could be regarded as service for the purposes of workmen's compensation). Later in the same opinion it distinguished reward for military service from aid that had been held unconstitutional in other states, distinctions the California Supreme Court cited approvingly. It even held that bounties were not compensation, neatly avoiding California's anti-gift constitutional provision, which prohibited compensation to public servants after they had completed their service.[79]

Although state courts came to grant willingly that the heroism of military service required gratitude, gratitude did not extend to granting citizenship. Military officials had made it clear during World War I that all citizens owed military service, but serving did not make one a citizen, however important militarism had been in political theory and history. The naturalization statute dating from 1870 allowed white people and those of African descent to become citizens, and in 1918, Congress granted citizenship to alien soldiers. What would that mean for Asian soldiers, neither white nor black? Many men applied to the Bureau of Naturalization for citizenship, explaining that the bureau should treat them as white because they had served in the military, and in fact the bureau often did grant naturalization based on military service.[80]

The United States Supreme Court, however, focused on the meaning of "white." Popular and scientific understandings contradicted each other: popular understanding held that people from India were not white; scientific understanding held that people from India were white but that people from East Asia were not. The Court wavered, excluding people on both understandings: Asian people could not become citizens, despite military service.[81]

Conclusion: Recognizing Nation and State

The legal justification for pensions for veterans, that they were enacted in order to induce people to fight in wars, did not hold up very well where states or localities enacted pensions after the war was over. Nor were state and local pensions a very obvious way to reward service if local governments were responsible only for local service, such as firefighting. Nevertheless, most state courts proved willing to change the law by slowly abandoning earlier understandings of what made legislation legal or not.

The constitutional governance of state-paid military pensions represented a transformation in a federal state. If one owed military service only to the national state, rewards from local governments outside of poor relief would seem to obviate the divisions of responsibility in a national polity. The state courts had provided a cautious counterstory to the celebration of military service.

Just as military experience colored so much of public life in the late nineteenth and early twentieth centuries, it colored the law of social insurance. The ferment in the states concerning social welfare provided reason for lawyers to pay renewed attention to military pensions. In 1920 and 1921, the reporters of the *American Law Reports* (*ALR*), the compendium of state law, tried valiantly to keep up with the variable court decisions. *ALR* published three articles on state military pensions, each provoked by one of the cases coming out of the states.[82] The articles noted that states recognized military service, but that *People v. Westchester Bank* probably would have widespread effects. Still, one reporter argued, the case probably was limited to the peculiarity of floating bonds rather than applying more broadly to the issue of paying for bounties out of tax dollars.[83] Between the end of Reconstruction and the 1920s state decisions, service to the national military changed, according to the courts, from something owed only to the national government, and therefore only for the national government to reward, to something the states might reward as well. To say "not in New York," though, does not quite capture the significance of state variability within a national economy, since the one case froze bids by bankers around the country.

The articles in *ALR* on military pensions were just a few among many or similar subjects; significant cases from the states occasioned articles between 1916 and 1924 on mothers' pensions, old age pensions, and civil service pensions. The states, aided by the *ALR*, were building an American law of social welfare centered on service and charity.

In the late nineteenth and early twentieth centuries, states were hiring police, teachers, and other civil servants. They would also get pensions, and frustrated taxpayers, claimants, and city officials would also object to decisions about those payments. Courts think through analogies; the celebration of militarism, alongside the persistent state doctrine concerning public purpose, meant that the constitutionality of the new programs would depend upon the judicial history of military pensions. Just as the courts had eroded the requirement that states recognize service only to their state, courts would begin by relying on the military analogy and only gradually erode it as the basis for pensions.

CHAPTER FIVE

Civil Service Pensions, 1883–1924

On the grounds of the Texas state capitol in Austin are four large sculptures erected between 1891 and 1907. One monument remembers the Alamo with a bronze figure of a Texan holding a rifle. Two commemorate those who fought for the Confederacy during the Civil War: one of these features a soldier on a rearing horse in the midst of battle; the other—Jefferson Davis watching over bronze figures representing the infantry, cavalry, artillery, and navy—honors those who fought "animated by the spirit of 1776." Directly opposite stands the fourth sculpture: a fireman in uniform looking into the distance, holding a lantern in his right hand and cradling a small child in his left arm; the State Firemen's Association of Texas erected it in 1896 to commemorate volunteer firefighters. Each of the four sits atop a large granite base and towers over the path leading up a long lawn to the capitol entrance.

These monuments evoke the virtues of public service. They remember those who fought and died, but they evoke heroism rather than grief. The soldiers are alive and engaged in battle; the fireman is solemn and protective.

Since military service has long been at the heart of the obligations of citizenship, the placement of the fireman's monument with the war memorials suggests an analogy between firemen and soldiers: firemen also perform the ultimate duty, risking their lives to save others. This martial image of the fireman was common during the nineteenth century. For example, a monument in Greenwood Cemetery in New York City, erected in 1848, shows a fireman clutching a child in one arm and carrying a trumpet—used to sound an alarm—in the other; when A. E. Costello published his awestruck history of the New York Fire Department in 1887, he printed a drawing of the memorial (figure 4).[1] Communities depended on their local firemen, who rescued their most precious and vulnerable citizens, the memorial tells the viewer. Although some men surely needed rescuing from fires as well, this image of men protecting the intrinsically dependent elided any man's need for rescue. A fireman stood for all men, doing a man's job of rescuing the helpless from disaster.

Firefighting was thus the moral equivalent of military service. Firemen were never enlisted in the service of the nation, however, not even the Republic of Texas. Firemen served the locality. Initially, they were volunteers; by the 1890s, in

FIREMEN'S MONUMENT.
[Greenwood Cemetery.]

Figure 4. Firemen's Monument, Greenwood Cemetery, New York City. From Augustine E. Costello's *Our Firemen: A History of the New York Fire Department, Volunteer and Paid* (1888), 714. Negative # 75252. Collection of the New-York Historical Society. Reproduced with permission.

the larger cities, they were paid municipal employees. The service that the Texas monument evokes is service worthy of citizenship, given the meanings attributed to military service by the war memorials. Yet firemen served their town or city rather than the nation. Although Americans seldom think of their locality when thinking of the obligations of citizenship today, loyalty to the local community and service to the state were central to citizenship in the nineteenth century.

It is to state and local governments that one must look for the origins of pensions for public servants. The federal government did not institute pensions for civil servants until 1920.[2] By then, most cities and states had set up pensions for firemen and police and for teachers; many had or were considering pension plans for all civil servants. Equally important, then as now, it was state and local governments that organized the day-to-day work of governing: city and town officials were responsible for fighting fires, policing communities, teaching children, building parks, seeing that streets and utilities were constructed and maintained. As late as 1929, states and localities had a total of ten times as many employees, not including educators, as the federal government had.[3]

Legal decisions and public discussions of local and state-level pensions for public employees articulate the assumptions and modes of reasoning through which compensation for a lifetime of service was first granted as a privilege by the sovereign state and then acknowledged as a right earned by civil servants. The gradual and uneven development of these pensions, marked by subtle but significant shifts in definitions of service and obligation and in presumptions about the relationship between the citizen and the state, forms the warp of the story, the long threads that constitute continuity and change over time. The court cases involved form the weft, which weaves back and forth to fill in the fabric; contested matters are the stuff of which history is made, as differing positions are stated, defended, rebutted, won, lost, and reasserted. Any analysis necessarily attends to both warp and weft, for fundamental changes in the culture of public life emerge from the interplay of arguments and interests that constitutes politics in the broadest sense.

Pensions for firemen originated from private interest in the protection of property, not from public interest in saving lives. Insurance companies began making payments to charitable funds for firemen and their families in the 1830s, and cities soon began contributing to these funds as well. When firefighting was professionalized and firemen became municipal employees, individual pensions were part of the bargain. Legal challenges to the payment of pensions to individual firemen elicited justifications that focused on heroism: these men risked their lives to save those of ordinary citizens, and when they died or were worn out in the public service, their wives and children deserved better than public charity. Ironically, this argument evoked the obligations of citizenship at the very time that firefighting had become a paid occupation and ceased to be a duty that citizens assumed voluntarily.

The extension of pensions from firemen and policemen to teachers and then to all civil servants involved subtle but significant shifts in their rationale. A pension system meant that employees received state payments but would not be dependent on the state: they could be proud of their service and of a pension they had earned and their dependents and heirs deserved. In many cities, however, pensions for civil servants came under widespread discussion. Legal debates recognized the differences between firefighting and policing on the one hand and teaching and working in offices on the other. Would the expansion of pensions to so many civil servants mean that firemen's heroism no longer mattered? Teachers and clerks did not routinely run the risk of being killed, maimed, or crippled in the public service, so the analogy to military service was not applicable to them. At each stage the expansion of pension systems was subject to constitutional challenge in the states as the boundaries of "service" shifted in court from voluntarism and danger to include earning a wage.

Pensions for police and firemen became widespread in the early twentieth century; twenty-five states and many municipalities had enacted them by 1913. Teachers' pensions became available in seven large northern cities between 1894 and 1910. States began to institute pensions for teachers in 1908; twenty-one states had established programs by 1927.[4] General civil service pensions followed more slowly. By 1927 they were available in six mid-Atlantic and New England states: Maine, Massachusetts, Connecticut, New York, New Jersey, and Pennsylvania.[5]

Legal challenges to these pensions and public debates about them were numerous and persistent but scattered and local, reflecting the character of pension systems themselves. Only appellate case law considered the issues in a systematic way. The belief among lawyers that even state law established general principles made each appellate case relevant across the states. Constitutionally, each case needed to consider the pensions that had come before. Judges approached those for firemen and policemen with no apparent thought that they might provide an entering wedge for more general pensions.

Policemen and firefighters were regarded as particularly deserving because they risked their lives and the livelihood of their wives and children in order to protect and rescue other citizens. The "bounty of sovereignty"—the power of the state to confer favors on faithful servants—also permitted, but did not require, pensions. Both rationales depended on a distinction between public service—whereby firemen and policemen were servants to the sovereign state—and ordinary employment. Even if generous governments could compensate those who braved danger to fight fires, arrest criminals, or fight wars with pensions, more general pensions might not be constitutional. But the expansion of pensions beyond hazardous occupations began to erode this distinction: Once cities extended pensions to teachers, courts became amenable to expanding the concept of service. Eventually, they moved from the idea of public service to holding that the states could enact pensions just as private employers did, as a way of retaining their employees. In 1924, in a leading case cited in major commentaries, the Michigan Supreme Court upheld a general civil service pension on the basis of this broad justification.[6] Legally, for the purpose of pensions, service had come to include ordinary work, and the government had become an ordinary employer.

Public Service, the Responsibilities of Office, and Administrative Law

The juxtaposition of memorials on the front lawn of the Texas state capitol hardly seems incongruous if risk is placed at the center of the concept of service. The notion of civic duty embodied in the analogy between soldiers and firefighters developed gradually, however, and represented a shift from earlier, more hierarchical conceptions of public service. Compensation for local public servants such as firemen had long been left up to counties and towns. Behind this taken-for-granted stance was a specific concept of public office that was fundamentally different from employment.

Service would first appear to have implied an exchange among equals: a fireman served, and earned a pension in return. That view accords neatly with the central position that contract has held in dominant understandings of American governance. Indeed, during the late nineteenth century a belief that contract was the essence of freedom—that it represented bargains reached among equals in an open market—underlay the belief that freedom of contract paralleled American political freedom.[7] In turn, the model of contract has seemed to capture the limited and hesitant expansion of social welfare rights in the United States: people get what they earn.[8] That explanation, however, misses the distinctive place of public service, which implied subordination. To understand the position of public servants requires an excursion to the now largely unfamiliar ground of the law of public officials. Pensions represented not an exchange between equals but the gratitude of a sovereign state. These two perspectives—one of equality and exchange, the other of sovereignty and subordination—ran in parallel and were not always neatly distinguished. Since public officers gained pensions before ordinary citizens did, the concept of office that justified their pensions deserves explication.

That concept, which was rooted in feudal divisions of responsibility, continued to be relevant as governments took on new tasks during the late nineteenth century. From a progressive lawyer's point of view, adhering to enduring principles in constitutional law *and* accommodating new programs required a delicate balance of accurate historical scholarship with critical reading of those principles. It required Frank Goodnow.

Goodnow was one of the many German-trained academics who found much to admire in the social policies of Europe.[9] From 1891 to 1907 he taught law and political science at Columbia University; in 1903 he became the first president of the American Political Science Association. From 1914 to 1929 he was president of Johns Hopkins University. At Columbia, Goodnow worked with John Burgess of the political science department, Edwin R. A. Seligman of the economics department, and Ernst Freund, a legal scholar who eventually joined the University of Chicago law school. At Chicago, Freund taught law and political science to Sophonisba Breckinridge, who became one of the founders of the Chicago School of Social Work.[10]

In the late nineteenth century, Columbia's economics department was home to many European-trained advocates of social insurance.[11] The environment there facilitated discussion of social reform and the political and constitutional transformations it would require. Although as a constitutional scholar Goodnow believed in the importance of principle, he also believed that principles were flexible enough to accommodate new social welfare programs, of which he was an early advocate.[12] His interest in new government programs led him to urge scholars to study administration, not just the formation of public policy in legislatures.[13] Goodnow thought that as governments assumed new social responsibilities, their organization shaped what was possible. Governments not organized along somewhat centralized, rational bureaucratic lines were less reliable, and he criticized the amateurism that was especially evident in American local governance.[14]

Goodnow, like his colleagues, was eager to define constitutional authority flexibly so that it would accommodate the new tasks that states were undertaking. True constitutional responsibility required administrative accountability. Administrative law had two meanings at the time Goodnow was writing. It could mean simply the study of what administrators did. Alternatively, it could mean external control of what administrators did through legal procedures, from hearings to judicial review of administrative action.[15] Goodnow's 1893 six-book, two-volume treatise, *Comparative Administrative Law: A Comparison of the Administrative Systems, National and Local, of the United States, England, France, and Germany*, started with the first meaning, describing the structure of administration in each of these countries. Goodnow firmly believed that American governments should establish the new social welfare programs that had been implemented in European countries. Pensions, properly drawn from the law of office, were one set of new programs that required administrative accountability.

Frank Goodnow devoted one book of his pathbreaking treatise to the law of office, building from the English and American common-law tradition. He implicitly incorporated the classic commentaries of Sir William Blackstone, the eighteenth-century English legal theorist whose interpretations had guided American judges and legal commentators throughout the nineteenth century. According to Blackstone, who in turn drew from the traditions of feudal law, the relationship between the state and its functionaries was a relation between master and servants, not one of contract.[16] Masters and servants stood in a hierarchical, dependent relationship rather than one founded on an agreement between equals. Hierarchy implied subservience but also mutual obligation: masters were to take care of servants in return for servants' faithfulness. Law, tradition, and obligation circumscribed the roles of each group.

Holding office, then, was distinct from being employed. Even in 1893, when Frank Goodnow wrote in an effort to professionalize public administration and modernize the organization of the state, it was important that he distinguish between public officers and employees, although states and localities might have both. To define "office" he quoted from a United States Supreme Court case, arguing that office "embraces the idea of tenure, duration, emolument, and duties."[17] He noted that office need not include all those elements but had to include at least some of them; otherwise, the worker was an employee. Goodnow concluded:

Thus one who receives no certificate of appointment, takes no oath, has no term or tenure of office, discharges no duties and exercises no powers conferred upon him directly by law, but simply performs such duties as are required of him by the persons employing him and whose responsibility is limited to them, is not an officer, and does not hold an office, although he is employed by public officers and is engaged about public work.[18]

Employment was a contractual relationship not a matter of public duties. In contrast, officers had powers in law; they did not answer the personal demands of an employer. They took public oaths to perform their duties, which was not possible or even imaginable for an employee of U.S. Steel or any other business. Public officials also held office in a way akin to holding property[19]—so much so that they were entitled to compensation even if they could no longer perform the duties of office. Public servants received payment because the positive law had granted it. Yet what the legislature had granted, it could take away.[20] As a master, the state could choose to grant perquisites of office, including pensions, without any grant becoming an enforceable agreement outside positive law. Promises from legislatures bound executive officials, themselves subordinates in a hierarchy, charged with carrying out their legal duties. A hierarchical relationship existed between the state and its servants; bargaining and making a contract did not describe the way servants gained benefits, even in the abstract.

Contracts seemed to respect the fundamental equality of citizens, which explicitly hierarchical relationships—as described in law or through beneficent custom—did not. Contracts were agreements people entered freely; no one, it seemed, would enter a contract if it did not benefit him. The free self-governance essential to contract and to American citizenship could also include compulsion, but that compulsion remained invisible because it was outside the terms of the contract. Agreeing to a job is one kind of agreement when the worker has skills to sell and a number of potential employers. It is quite another sort of agreement when the worker is hungry, has skills developed on, say, a farm which are not applicable to industrial labor, and is seeking a job in an economy with widespread unemployment. Hierarchy could include munificence, and contract could include hard bargains. Hierarchy through the law of office, rather than contract between equals, described most of public service. In the twentieth century however, the notion that public servants deserved pensions because they risked their lives and the well-being of their wives and children in answering the call of public duty shifted to the idea that they received pensions because they were similar to employees of other large organizations.

Long-standing reasoning based in service persisted alongside the ascendant belief in contract among equals. Furthermore, changes in state and local responsibilities came unevenly across the states. The practice of legal reasoning, which requires thinking through already embedded categories, is slow to change, and judges can act from conflicting principles. The separation of powers in the United States allows different institutions to remain committed to their own sets of practices: for example, legislatures can expand spending, while courts can believe they are protecting right principles in channeling that spending. The resulting disorder is explicable in terms of different institutional commitments to reasons and the constitutional status of states as separate sovereigns, but disorder it is.

Hazardous Service and Dependent Wives and Children

The notion of firefighting as an act of citizenship emerged during the early nineteenth century, the heyday of organized volunteer fire companies.[21] This image of self-sacrificing civic service was deliberately carried over as firefighting was professionalized after midcentury. Popular culture had celebrated the manly vigor and democratic virtue of volunteer firemen; urban reformers sought to counter the voluntary system's inefficiency and the disorder it often spawned when fire companies and their juvenile hangers-on fought with other groups of young men, especially immigrants. In 1865, in a pioneering effort at reform, New

York City created the paid Metropolitan Fire Department; other cities placed volunteer fire companies under municipal control by appointing paid officers, providing modern equipment, and imposing bureaucratic regulations.[22]

Similarly, between 1850 and 1870, police in many American cities began to wear uniforms marking their professional status. By 1890, city officials were trying to change police culture. The beat cop had spent his time picking up lost children and homeless people; new approaches to policing emphasized arresting criminals.[23]

The analogy between public service and military service as a judicial rationale for providing pensions to firefighters and policemen was articulated during the 1880s, following the professionalization of these occupations. When cities began to employ police and firemen from whom they expected effective service, they also began to provide pensions for individual employees and their dependents. Professionalism implied regular pensions, which seemed exempt from the rampant favoritism inherent in support for charities. Of course, these jobs were still subject to urban patronage politics.[24] Individual payments to retired or injured police officers provided a direct, tangible benefit that could be used to maintain patronage ties. Therefore, some critics questioned pension schemes because they feared political corruption, but advocates saw pensions as a necessary part of professionalization.

Legal challenges to the payment of individual pensions to firemen and policemen required the state to clarify their basis and elicited justifications that first focused on heroism. Appellate courts and public commentaries on legal decisions spoke of individual courage in the face of danger: through their hazardous service, these men deserved a dignified independence in their disability or old age. Courts and commentators argued further that these men's dependents—their widows, children, and other heirs—also deserved independence rather than public charity.[25] In turn, the men's publicly circumscribed responsibility as fathers meant that their heirs could claim pensions the state had promised. Fatherhood was another role within a hierarchy described by law, not a contract. Courts called fatherhood natural, but they saw many obligations and legal consequences flowing from that natural relationship.

A touchstone case concerning the hazardousness of service was decided in New York in 1883. In *Trustees of Exempt Firemen's Benevolent Fund v. Roome,* the state's Court of Appeals considered a challenge to the tax on private insurers to create a pension fund for volunteer firemen, a tax that the court had upheld in 1854. This time no one questioned the exchange with insurance companies; instead, the new system of payments to individual employees was called into question.[26] Had the firefighters served in a way that earned public gratitude? In holding that payments to individual men, rather than to their charities, was constitutional, the court emphasized firemen's heroism:

> With the growth of the city the number of the firemen increased, and the amount and danger of their service. The old engines[, which] moved with difficulty and [were] cumbrous and rude in construction, gave place to better machines, and the service improved as the demands upon it grew. The dangers of the work were obvious, and a courage and daring which has gone into history began to leave behind it men who were maimed and crippled in the public service, and widows and orphans deprived of their natural protectors and reduced to poverty and want.[27]

That holding was identical with the holdings in the flurry of 1850s cases that such payments were constitutional. The reasoning in *Roome,* however, was new. Rather than emphasizing the benefits to fire insurance companies, the court placed individual firemen and their service to the public at the center. Ironically, it was precisely when firefighting became professionalized that the notion of voluntary, valorous service received a new emphasis in legal reasoning. The judges would have happily endorsed the drawings reprinted in chapter three, celebrating the firemen's widows' and orphans' fund.

The courts lauded the heroism of firemen at the same time as firemen themselves became worried that their self-sacrificing service was being diminished by new firefighting technologies and that they were being degraded to the status of mere employees.[28] As the New York court's 1883 ruling recognized, the introduction of steam engines had changed firefighting. New fire engines required fewer men with greater technical knowledge than the old horse-drawn and hand-pumped engines did. Firefighters feared that such innovations were diminishing their contribution. Volunteers were also contemptuous of the new, paid firefighting force. Tensions were especially high during the transitional period, when paid officers employed by the municipalities were placed in command of volunteer fire companies. By the 1880s, however, fire departments in most large cities had been entirely professionalized, so firemen had to find a new basis for their claim to public gratitude. Since voluntary service of itself would no longer suffice, heroism became the new grounds for firemen's special status. Fire equipment could save property, but saving lives still required individuals to risk their own lives for others. Such heroes might be paid, but that was not sufficient recompense for their service. Facing challenges to pension programs that paid individual employees rather than private charities, the courts relied not on the value of preserving property but on the language of heroism and the duties of citizenship.

The gendered assumptions that underlay this notion of heroic public service become especially clear in the debates that surrounded both proposals for state pensions for individual police and firemen and challenges to widows' and children's inheritance of these men's pensions. Numerous court decisions emphasized the manly qualities that were highlighted in the New York case.[29] Service required traits associated with masculine independence: courage and daring in the face of danger, and risk-taking to protect women and children. Firemen both rescued those whose weakness and vulnerability made them unable to save themselves and supported their own dependent wives and children as fathers and husbands should and as the law obligated them to do. When firefighters lost their lives or were maimed and crippled in the public service, their dependent wives and children should not be left in want. By virtue of these men's service, their dependents deserved more than poor relief, the usual lot of the widows and orphans of disabled breadwinners. Just as pensions preserved masculine independence in old age and disability, so payment from the public purse saved women and children from poverty and want. Firemen and policemen deserved the pensions they received in old age or disability, and their death did not extinguish their dependents' claim. Their widows and orphaned children, like the dependents whom soldiers left behind, deserved support from the state that their husbands and fathers had served so selflessly.

In New Hampshire, a reluctant latecomer to state-paid pensions, participants in constitutional conventions considered the concept of service as it had been articulated in case law and public discussion in other states. The debate illuminates the fundamental questions that arose in many states, as well as the categories and conventions of thought that crossed state boundaries.

In 1912, New Hampshire considered granting pensions for more than one year at a time, which required constitutional revision. The new pensions would be paid by the state rather than the counties. Relief had long been acceptable as a county purpose. Delegates to a constitutional convention again drew on the analogy between fighting fires and fighting wars to justify pensions for men who had risked their lives in public service. One participant stressed the parallel obligations of citizenship to the locality and to the nation:

> I have seen on scores of battlefields the sacrificing heroism of those who are
> today drawing pensions from the general government. I have also seen our firemen contending against the flames on buildings wherein were confined women
> and children, whose lives were in danger, and, if it had not been for the courage
> of those firemen, who took their lives in their hands and entered those buildings
> to rescue the men and women and children who were there surrounded by the
> flames, they would have perished.

He concluded that the firemen's "sacrificing heroism" should be recognized by pensions from the state and local governments: "I hope . . . our cities and towns . . . [will] take care, not as paupers, not in the poorhouse, not in the almshouses, but to provide for taking care of those heroic men who have given up their health and offered their lives in your service and in protecting your property and saving the lives of your wives and children."[30]

Firemen, who "offered their lives in *your* service," did not reduce the citizens to dependence themselves, either by rescuing them or by rescuing their dependent wives and children. Instead, the firemen were subservient to the citizens whose wives and children they saved. Just as men could answer the call to serve during the Civil War by buying a substitute without diminishing their claim to have served, so the masculine citizenry could pay firemen to fight for them, and men would thereby meet their obligation to rescue the lives of women and children.

Another delegate extended the analogy between soldiers and firefighters to police officers:

> There are firemen who are injured in the discharge of their duty. There are po-
> licemen who are injured in the discharge of their duty. There are policemen and
> firemen, and there may be others, who have served their towns and cities long
> and faithfully, and should be granted pensions. . . . A man enters the [police]
> service as a young man, serves twenty-five years, or whatever the limitation may
> be, and at the end of that time is entirely unfitted for further physical, active
> service as a policeman on the force of our large cities, and, if turned out, is actu-
> ally physically unfitted, by reason of old age, to labor further in any other capac-
> ity.[31]

Police and firemen, like soldiers, risked their lives and expended their vital energies in the public service; pensions for them would be a reciprocal recognition of their service, not a matter of charity.

In the 1912 convention, no one spoke *against* pensions for firemen and policemen. Emphasizing a distinction between pensions and charity, another delegate said that a pension was necessary to a superannuated fireman so that "we can keep him from want without his becoming a public charge."[32] Pensions as rewards for service would not create dependence, as many feared that expanded government charity would; rather, pensions would prevent dependence and preserve masculine dignity. Although the constitutional revision of 1912 was not accepted by the state of New Hampshire, the convention unanimously recommended the provision allowing long-term pensions.

A specific conception of masculinity was central to the distinctions made during the early twentieth century between those public employees who deserved pensions and those who did not. Most police pensions were first provided only to the uniformed or "fighting" force, not to the police department's janitors, clerks, and other attendant "civilians." The assumptions underlying this distinction between the fighting force and support staff were made explicit in a 1911 dispute in Illinois over extending pensions to all employees of the police department. Illinois had enacted pensions for police and firemen in 1887.[33] In 1911 the state considered extending its police pensions to the newly appointed police matrons—who worked with juveniles, female victims, suspects, and criminals[34]—and to police telegraph operators, who worked in offices. The *Chicago Tribune* ran an editorial arguing that pensions were a payment for dangerous service, not for sitting in an office: "An attempt is being made in the legislature to amend the police pension law so that it shall take in telegraph operators and some other noncombatant employees of the department. It should be beaten, for it would be an injustice to the men who confront the dangers and endure the hardships of police service."[35] Moreover, state senators argued, expanding pensions to police matrons and telegraph operators was unconstitutional.[36] The legislature's conference committee, responsible for reconciling the house and senate versions of the bill, deadlocked on this question.[37] In June 1911, police telegraph operators filed a mandamus suit in Chicago to try to get the city to pay them.[38] Although the additional pensions were finally enacted, questions of constitutionality and masculinity provided two deeply intertwined grounds for opposing them.

According to the defenders of the public purse who worked at the *Chicago Tribune,* earning a pension should require hazard, or at least a plausible argument that a job could be risky, however peaceful any particular beat cop's life might have been. Their argument, of course, drew on long-standing distinctions in law; law and culturally popular arguments had at least a loose connection. Arguing from hazard would exclude men who were not in uniform; similarly, it could include those women who were in uniform. By 1927 the localities that did provide pensions to the whole uniformed force provided them evenhandedly to men and women in uniform, although police officers were predominantly male.[39] Hazard marked masculinity and service, but not all men held jobs involving the risk of danger in the public service.

The Bounty of Sovereignty

A legislature's choosing to pay civil servants represented what the Illinois Supreme Court called the "bounty springing from the graciousness and appreciation of sovereignty."[40] A pension was not simply a return for service; the legislature could choose not to award pensions, no matter what service a public official had performed. The power to make unilateral decisions distinguishes sovereignty from contract. The legislature as sovereign stated officials' responsibilities as legal duties. The compulsory character of public duties allowed citizens and subordinates to file lawsuits against recalcitrant or negligent officials. Such lawsuits were intended to ensure that officials did what they were ordered to do, a necessary discipline when counties found themselves mandated by the state to spend money they did not want to spend.

Even after the state had enacted pensions, many cities and counties were less than eager to pay them. A leading case on the constitutionality of police pensions followed in Illinois in 1916 when two police officers sued to get the pension statute implemented. Mayor William K. Abbott of Quincy pointed to constitutional limits on spending: sections 19 and 20 of Article 4 of the state constitution contained standard spending limits that prohibited the legislature from paying extra compensation to an official after he had completed his term of service. The mayor pointed out that as the statute stood, an officer who had served only one month after the enactment of the pension and then retired would be eligible, making it clear that the officer was gaining compensation for service already rendered.

The court, however, upheld the pension. Justice Orrin N. Carter quoted John Dillon on municipal corporations and how pensions could benefit them "by encouraging competent employees to remain in the service, and by retiring from the public service those who have become incapacitated from performing the duties as well as they might be performed by younger or more vigorous men. . . . Such pensions generally are not considered donations or gratuities."[41] Carter also quoted Thomas Cooley, the leading nineteenth-century commentator on taxation and constitutional limits:

> The primary object in all such bounties is not the private but the public interest. To show gratitude for meritorious public services in the army and navy by liberal provision for those who have performed them is not only proper in itself, but it may reasonably be expected to have a powerful influence inciting others to self-denying, faithful and courageous services in the future.[42]

The court had to distinguish pensions from gratuities in order to avoid constitutional limits on spending. If the money was a gift, it did not serve a state purpose; if it rewarded people who had served the state, it was not a gift. The court justified the pensions in question by emphasizing the self-sacrificing service that firemen and police, like soldiers and sailors, rendered to the public. Although pensions might legitimately function as an inducement to serve, they also recompensed service that entailed risk and required courage, unlike that expected of other public servants.[43] This condition, which assumed a martial definition of masculine service to the state, made the pensions constitutional.

Judge Carter also ruled that the executive owed payments to the heirs of firemen and police, if the legislature had promised them, as well as to men who had retired. He did not bother to compare pensions to poor relief; poor relief cases were simply not relevant, even though public charity was the primary alternative available to widows and orphans. Pensions promised by the state had characteristics rather of property or entitlement. The peculiarities of sovereignty, however, meant that pensions were an entitlement only if the servant was working under the conditions required by the statutory grant of a pension.

That dependents inherited pensions marked the independence of police and firemen. Dependents could inherit, however, only if the state in its generosity to its servants had had a pension in force while a policeman was serving. In New York the widow of a police officer claimed a pension from the city of Brooklyn on the basis of her deceased husband's service. Because the pension for widows had not been in effect when he died, however, the Court of Appeals held that she was not entitled to it; granting her deceased husband a pension would violate public-purpose requirements, for it would be granting money after the service had been completed.[44] Only when men died while pensions were in effect could their widows and children inherit.

In a 1914 Illinois case concerning whether adoptive children inherited as biological children did, the court ruled that the parental—or, more specifically, paternal—obligation to support dependent children—adopted or not—underlay a child's right to her late father's pension. Bernice Gibbons's mother was dead, killed by her father, who was then sentenced to the state home for the criminally insane. Bernice's mother's parents took her in and legally adopted her. Bernice's grandfather, her adoptive father, had been a policeman. After he and his wife died, Bernice's guardian, Lola Ryan, sued for the pension that would have been Bernice's had Bernice been her grandfather's "natural" child. Cook County lawyers, countering the public image of pensions as protecting widows and orphans, argued that adopted children could not inherit pensions. No one besides these attorneys saw the worthiness of the case, however; they lost in the trial court, in the intermediate appellate court, and in the state supreme court. The supreme court ruled that although pensions were not precisely property, the statute establishing police pensions stated that they were intended to provide for the widows and children of deceased officers:

> The legal consequences and incidents arising from the relation of parent and child are many. . . . They include the right of support, education and care from the parent. . . . Among such legal consequences and incidents are the rights of the children of deceased police officers of certain cities to participate in a pension fund that has been provided by law.[45]

The obligations of a father—a relation not of contract but of kinship—grounded a legal right in a police pension. The courts might refer to fathers as children's natural protectors, but as *Ryan v. Foreman* implied, the relationship was not *simply* a natural one: not only were adopted children treated the same as biological children in this case, but the law described the obligations of parents even should natural feeling fail. Being a parent thus had one of the elements Goodnow listed as a characteristic of office: it included obligations described in law. Household relations were, under Blackstone and in American governance, hierarchical relations of a kind similar to public hierarchies.[46] Just as leaving a pension or property was a way that a man might provide for his family after his death, so providing pensions to the widows and orphans of men who had risked their lives in the public service was a way for the the state to recognize those men's masculine independence and recompense their sacrifice.

No nineteenth-century court held that public service made a moral claim that the state must answer. Pensions were not entitlements of citizenship or rights implicit in civil servants' contracts; they were an explicit grant made to deserving men by the sovereign state. Public servants were still *servants,* subordinate to the government. In 1894 the United States Supreme Court applied this doctrine in a way that limited state employees' claims to pensions. *Pennie v. Reis* was brought on behalf of the heirs of a police officer in California. In 1878, California had enacted a statute granting pensions to the families of police officers who died, but in 1889 the state repealed it. In 1894, when an officer died, his estate claimed a property right in the officer's contribution to an insurance fund that dated from 1878. Such a claim made sense in the context of seeing agreements with the state as contracts, but Justice Stephen Field, writing for the U.S. Supreme Court, held that the officer had only *expected* the money; he had no right to it. If he did not die while the statute was in force, he did not trigger the statute and therefore had no legal claim.[47]

Had Field taken an ordinary contract approach, outside the "bounty of sovereignty," he could have held that the state *owed* the money in payment for service already performed in reliance on the promised pension. In treating the statute as bestowing a benefit that could also be taken away, however, Field held against entitlement to public funds. States *owed* nothing to the beneficiaries even if beneficiaries had undertaken service in the expectation of receiving pensions. State pensions were largesse; the recipient did not earn them. States could have very good reasons to *pay* them, whether to reward the faithful performance of duty, prevent indigence, or induce others into the service; they did not, however, *owe* them. The "bounty of sovereignty" became an entitlement only if clearly so stated in positive law.

Employment in the Public Service

The extension of pensions to teachers and other civil servants required a new rationale and legal justification. Providing pensions to public employees generally, rather than only to those who risked their lives for others, rested on changing conceptions of work as much as on progressive understandings of the state. From the Civil War through the early twentieth century, Americans' ideas about citizenship, property, and labor were fundamentally transformed as working for wages became a mark of freedom and a sufficient condition for citizenship.

Before the Civil War, labor had been something that dependent men did; servants depended on their employers and were subordinate to their authority. In Thomas Jefferson's model of the republic, it was holding property that marked independent citizenship.[48] Voluntary public service complemented property holding. The debate over the abolition of slavery turned on the question of whether selling one's labor could represent freedom.[49] If men without property who worked for wages were independent citizens, then slaves would become free if they could sell their labor. Conservative defenders of slavery argued that industrial workers in the North suffered because their employers *failed* to treat them as dependents; freeing slaves would release masters from any obligation to their servants and reduce freedmen and -women to the degrading conditions of wage labor. If, on the other hand, selling one's labor could signify independence, then citizens without property who exchanged their labor for a wage—whether in industry or agriculture—could also be part of a free republic. Wage labor, not just property holding, would mean real freedom and progress for African Americans.

That idea triumphed after the Civil War. At first, freedmen, who had worked primarily in agriculture, shared the prevalent agrarian view that independence required land ownership. They believed that they had earned a right to the land by making it rich and productive; that enslaved blacks had developed the southern frontier just as free whites had developed the northern and western frontiers under the Northwest Ordinance and the Homestead Act. Yet despite the promise of forty acres and a mule—the basic tools that would enable them to make their independent way in the world—freedom rapidly became reduced to wage labor.[50] The Freedman's Bureau coerced ex-slaves into labor contracts, and federal officials justified that policy by appealing to the freedom of the labor contract.[51] The belief in free labor implicitly transformed paid work from something servants did to something done by independent men.

If citizens were lifelong wage laborers, then how would they maintain their independence in old age and disability? They could not rely upon accumulated property. Pensions both for employees in private industry and for civil servants were widely discussed during the early twentieth century, especially in the *Survey,* the reform-minded journal of the social insurance advocates.[52] Large employers in such industries as railroads, public utilities, and metalworking began to institute pension systems before smaller employers did. These industries were more bureaucratically managed, and pensions were an integral part of new personnel policies. Justifications included retaining workers whose skills were developed through experience and replenishing the unskilled work force with younger, lower-paid workers.[53] Employees in these industries, overwhelmingly male, were expected to remain in the labor force over the long term. Because these industries preferentially distributed jobs on the basis of ethnicity and race, pensions were awarded to white men of native-born or European parentage more often than to men of color or to immigrants. Even in large industries, however, few unskilled laborers received retirement pensions.[54]

As states began to organize the civil service along bureaucratic lines, new ideas of scientific personnel management made pensions for public employees attractive for the same reasons that private pensions were. Managers wanted a youthful and efficient workforce. Would public employees gain pensions for these same reasons, or did public employees earn pensions because they served? Was public service different from wage labor, and if so, how? The justifications that courts had used to allow pension payments to individual firemen and policemen and their dependents were not applicable to other civil service jobs, for if their jobs did not require masculine heroism or imply the master–servant hierarchy, then civil servants would not deserve pensions. On the other hand, if civil servants earned pensions because they were employees, just like those who worked in private industry, then it was no longer necessary for their jobs to be deemed dangerous and manly, or for them to be regarded as public servants. Working for the government need not connote anything fundamentally different from clerking for U.S. Steel.

Pensions for teachers, the first to follow those for firemen and police, received attention when instituted in postsecondary education. In 1905 the Carnegie Foundation established a pension fund for university professors and instructors, receiving national news coverage and consideration in professional journals. The Carnegie Fund was the predecessor of pension funds for university employees today.[55] It began as a fund to which professors need not contribute, and in which both public and private universities could participate. Henry Pritchett, the president of the Carnegie Foundation, presented pensions as a way of drawing talented men into a low-paid profession.[56] The best science would come from minds freed from the worries of material life, secure that they would enjoy a dignified support in their old age and assured that their widows, too, would be spared dependence. Pensions thus did not represent dependence, but rather prevented it. Moreover, professors performed a public service, which explained why they deserved pensions. As late as 1911, Pritchett argued that some work had a public virtue independent of whether the employer was public or private.[57]

Some observers were uneasy about private money governing choices at public institutions, however. Advocates countered, just as supporters of payments to firefighters' private charities had done in the mid-nineteenth century, that if the function performed was publicly valuable, the public or private status of the employer did not matter.[58]

A significant difference between the college professors whose welfare concerned the Carnegie Foundation and the public school teachers whose pensions were soon being debated by cities and states was that college faculty were predominantly men, whereas schoolteachers were predominantly women. Before the advent of common schools and the spread of universal public education, teaching had been a low-status job for young men and a source of part-time work for clergymen, but as the profession expanded—particularly at the elementary level—it was considered more suitable for women.[59] Advocates of women's education and paid employment sought to enlarge the field by arguing strategically that women's maternal nature made them especially good at instructing young children. By the 1870s, in cities and rural communities alike, teaching was the most prestigious profession open to women—most of them white and native-born; black and immigrant women were excluded from such employment except in segregated, private, and parochial schools.[60]

Public officials believed that women should occupy subordinate positions; men should be the supervisors and principals. Since supervisors usually came up through the ranks, however, women who were distinguished by long service might attain supervisory positions. The United States Commissioner of Education found this enough of a concern in 1892 that he endorsed efforts to draw men into teaching.[61] States and cities could hire women for less than they paid men, making them particularly attractive employees. By the late nineteenth century, teaching had become a predominantly feminine profession.

Teachers' work was similar to that of professors; indeed, if educating youth at low wages made university work a public service, teaching unquestionably qualified. Gender figured prominently in the policy discussion of pensions, though, since enjoying a dignified independence and supporting others were not presumed to be the prerogatives and duties of womanhood as they were of manhood. Nevertheless, pensions for teachers were instituted in three large cities as school systems became organized bureaucratically, reflecting the growing acceptance of pensions as an integral part of personnel management.[62]

In 1894, New York became the first city to enact a pension for teachers. Employees contributed, and public money paid the balance. In 1900 the state legislature granted pensions to thirty-three teachers who had retired before the establishment of the pension system, but two years later the New York Court of Appeals struck them down on the grounds that a pension could not have been what induced these teachers to serve, nor could it have been part of their contract for service. The legislature could be bountiful only when it was serving some public purpose; it could not grant money to just anyone and call that money an earned pension. Granting money to teachers whose service had already ended was nothing more than a gift. Serving a public purpose was crucial if a pension was to be more than a gratuity pure and simple.

Justice Edgar M. Cullen explained why the teachers could not get the pension requested in *Mahon v. Board of Education of the City of New York:*

> No one would assert that as between private individuals there arises any equitable or moral obligation to pay for services more than the stipulated compensation. There was no moral obligation on the city of New York to establish a pension system in favor of teachers. Most of the servants of the state and most of the teachers in public schools enjoy no right to be pensioned for services. The question of establishing a system of pensions is one of policy, not obligation. The legislature might well think that in a large city where teaching is adopted as a calling to be pursued for years, and often for life, it would be wise to provide a system of pensions as an inducement both to service at low wages and also to good conduct in service. But these considerations have no application to the case of officers or employees who are not in service at the time the pension system is established or in force. As to such persons the grant of a pension is a mere gratuity.[63]

Under *Mahon,* teaching was regarded as service, not simply wage labor. The dangers of the job and the needs of dependents were not mentioned in this case; pensions could be constitutional without the foundation of masculinity that had seemed to be so crucial in the cases concerning firefighters and police and in the debate about whether Chicago's police matrons should get pensions. The needs of dependents could figure indirectly: the low wages public servants earned might not allow them to provide for their families in old age. (Of course, as Chicago's teachers would later note, women's dependents were more likely to be elderly relatives than children or husbands.)[64] Courts did not entirely ignore the precedents set by the firemen's cases, however. Instead of regarding pensions as a way of compensating employees for performing dangerous work, courts held that pensions could be awarded to teachers because education was in itself an important public service. They recognized that the salary for teachers was low, that most served for only a short time, and that an efficient school system required experienced teachers; therefore, pensions, which might induce them to stay on, were good policy.[65]

Teachers usually had to contribute to their pensions, whereas firemen and police seldom did. Social insurance advocates believed in employee contributions as one way to distinguish pensions from poor relief: with contributions, pensioners would get something only if they paid something.[66] If the teachers contributed, perhaps dangerous work was not a prerequisite, since the legislature would be spending teachers' money rather than public money. That, however, would imply that the legislature was *taking* teachers' money unconstitutionally. The uncertainty in the law once again allowed different resolutions in different states. Wherever states and localities enacted pensions, though, litigation was possible, whether for illegitimately spending public money or unconstitutionally taking a salary. Teachers challenged those contributions as taking property without due process of law or as imposing something other than uniform taxation, since they were among the few forced to give up part of their salary.

The Court of Appeals in the state of New York implicitly upheld the statute establishing pensions for teachers in its decision in *Mahon.*[67] Detroit and Chicago joined New York in paying pensions to teachers in 1895 and 1896. Pensions for teachers were not obviously constitutional in all states, however. Minneapolis, Toledo, and Cleveland all enacted pensions for teachers in 1900 and 1901, only to have them struck down in court for lack of uniformity (they would have to be applied state-wide), for taking a schoolteacher's property without compensation, or for lack of authorization by the state legislature.[68] Not until 1909 would Minneapolis and other cities enact them again.[69] Whatever the grounds, some teachers did not want contributions deducted from their salaries, and they could sue.

Perhaps it's surprising that teachers and other municipal employees themselves would sue to halt contributions, claiming that deductions by the city were unconstitutional. Contributing to a pension requires trust, however—trust that the money will be there when the person retires. It also requires believing that one will retire (a new concept in the early twentieth century), or that one has dependents one wants to leave the money to. As teachers in Chicago pointed out, women who taught throughout their lives were unlikely to leave behind younger dependents. Contributing to a pension also requires that one can actually afford to defer the income. While the amount deducted by Chicago in 1914—$2 per month out of an $80 paycheck—might not seem like much, if it was difficult to live in Chicago on $80 a month, the deduction could be far too much.[70]

In 1911, a teachers' organization in Michigan commissioned a study of the constitutionality of pensions. Michigan courts had been suspicious of state aid even to the much-hated favorite of the legislature, railroads. If building a transportation system might not count as public enough to merit a subsidy, then teaching might not either.[71] The state attorney general had issued an opinion that teachers' pensions would be unconstitutional on public-purpose grounds.[72] In lobbying for pensions, teachers had to show how their work qualified as state service.

In law, everything is in the analogy. Were teachers' pensions like charity, or were they more like payments to firemen, policemen, and soldiers? States had had long experience with charity. States had also had long experience with pensions in the dangerous services. In lobbying for pensions for teachers in Michigan, H. L. Wilgus argued for the constitutionality of pensions by drawing analogies with military and firemen's pensions, not poor relief cases. He ignored the presumed danger of men's service and the dependence of widows and children, which had been so important in the late nineteenth-century firemen's cases. Wilgus argued instead that pensions for teachers would prevent dependence and represented a fitting recognition of public service. They would be constitutional, he contended, because they would foster education by inducing people to serve. Education was much more than wage labor; it was an important public service.[73] Wilgus did not even try to argue that women would make a lifetime career of teaching or leave needy husbands and children if they died; neither individual heroism nor needy children marked the service of citizenship. His effort contributed to Michigan's instituting a state pension for teachers in 1917.[74]

A 1914 editorial in the *School Review* supporting a particular form of pension for teachers stated with regard to New York City:

> The federal government pensions Grand Army officers more than privates; but the federal pension system is open to the objection that it is too much a reward of merit. Moreover, the privates in the army of New York teachers are the ones who are most likely to wear out in the service. The officers of a city-school system are relieved of some of the wear and tear of daily routine.[75]

This analogy with the military implied that pensions were justified as a recognition for service and maintained pensioners' independence; it distinguished pensions from public payments to the indigent and dependent. Yet the analogy with military service fit awkwardly with the feminine qualities considered so valuable for teaching. Teachers were deemed to resemble privates in an army, not substitute mothers (although both teachers and privates were subordinates). Legal reasoning based on desert evoked an incongruous, masculine image of public servants enlisted in the educational army.

The argument that teachers had earned pensions accorded with the dominant belief that white, native-born people were independent and had earned their pay. This principle was seldom extended to African Americans and new immigrants; instead, their labor was often devalued and their autonomous citizenship continually called into question by native-born whites.[76] White women who earned pensions through their work as teachers were clearly differentiated from the intrinsically dependent classes. African American women taught in public schools for African American children, but of southern cities and states—never generous in their spending—only Virginia instituted pensions for white or black teachers before 1929.[77]

State legislatures and city councils granted pensions separately to additional groups of public employees, awarding them in piecemeal fashion for specific occupations, by local jurisdictions. A 1918 investigation in the state of New York found a chaotic mixture of state, municipal, and county pensions.[78] Court cases were part of the chaos.[79] This gradual, however uneven, expansion of coverage reflected not only increasing political support for pensions but also confidence in an increasingly broad and flexible understanding of public purpose as a constitutional requirement. Pensions were not poor relief or any other kind of charitable gift; they elevated retired public servants above the desperate neediness of recipients of poor relief. Nor did they imply that leaving work in old age merited support as a matter of social citizenship, or of belonging to the polity, apart from the work a person had done. States could grant them only in consideration of service, and those who received them gained payments for themselves and sometimes their dependents as a matter of right in positive law.

By the 1910s, major cities and some states were establishing general pensions for all public employees. Both New York City and the Commonwealth of Massachusetts did so in 1911. New York state courts upheld pensions for civil servants in 1913. At the same time, the National Association of Civil Service Employees was pressing for federal pensions.[80] By then it was vital for those who wished to make the programs acceptable to distinguish civil service pensions from general old age pensions (see chapter eight), which reformers, following European policy debates, were considering by 1910.[81] General pensions not tied to public employment, however, were often regarded as prohibited by constitutional provisions; only those for people who served the public were constitutional. Civil service pensions were designed as compensation that public servants earned through long service, not as a right inherent in their employment contract or as an entitlement of citizenship.

Insight into changing popular definitions of public service comes from the constitutional convention held in New Hampshire in 1920. Delegates to the state's 1912 constitutional convention had debated the justification of pensions for firemen and police. In 1920, delegates considered whether teachers should get pensions and whether the state rather than the localities ought to pay pensions for firemen and police. Pensions for teachers raised the latter issue because teachers were employees of the state, whereas firemen and policemen were employed by municipalities. The state legislature had authorized municipalities to enact pensions (which had to be voted every year) for what were considered dangerous jobs.[82] Many delegates were concerned that teachers' pensions would be an entering wedge into state-paid pensions for firemen and policemen. The 1920 characterization of teachers' work reveals the assumptions made by citizens in a conservative state about the nature of work worthy of recognition as service.

All those who participated in the debate believed they had to compare teachers with firemen. In one such comparison, opponents argued that teachers were women engaged in safe jobs and did not need pensions.

The delegate who opened the debate, however, urged that pensions be awarded to "those faithful women who have served in the towns and cities of our State for so many years on the pittance that we have given them." He contended that women needed pensions precisely because their working lives were gendered, countering the argument that women did not need pensions: "Men engaged in most occupations, after their term of active service is over[,] can do some kind of work. What can a woman, who has been a teacher in the public schools, take up after her time of efficiency has passed?"[83] Another delegate countered: "The majority of the teachers get through when they are in service for five, ten or fifteen years; . . . they get through because they want to get married, which is proper, and rear families."[84] Women, he thought, did not need pensions because their work did not last a lifetime. The reasoning here was circular: if women were deprived of decent wages and pensions, they would certainly need to get married. In the eyes of many early twentieth-century commentators, service alone was not enough to characterize someone as deserving a pension; that person also had to have the obligation to support himself and his dependents, which applied only to men.[85] That many women teachers, like other wage-earning women, were independent and supported themselves and others was irrelevant to the gendered principle that underlay this conclusion.

Opponents of pensions for teachers made the "slippery slope" argument: if we grant pensions to this group, they must be granted to all public servants. For some proponents, that was precisely the virtue of teachers' pensions: granting them would extend *state*-paid pensions to police and firemen, who richly deserved them. One delegate, after pointing out that most private industries provided pensions, appealed to traditional justifications for pensions in dangerous occupations: "A policeman or a fireman, who guard[s] our lives and our property, if injured in the service [should] receiv[e] just compensation to keep [him] out of the poorhouse." A man who risked his life and the livelihood of his wife and children deserved a pension "just as much as though he had fallen on the fields of France," but teachers did not deserve such pensions.[86]

The amendment to the constitution authorizing state-paid pensions for teachers did not pass, and New Hampshire had still not settled the question a decade later. In 1931 the constitutionality of pensions once again became a contentious issue (the state was also considering general old age pensions at that time). Advocates of teachers' pensions seemed to think it necessary to assure legislators that the system would be voluntary and contributory, unlike the compulsory system instituted in Massachusetts and other states. The state would help "teachers who help themselves." The superintendent of the Dover schools tried to allay suspicions that former teachers who did not need the money would take advantage of the generosity of legislators; he argued that only those who had taught for a lifetime would use the pensions, not—as the newspaper paraphrased him—"young girls who expect to get married and young men who teach while marking time for some other kind of work."[87] That teaching was chiefly a feminine occupation would limit the need for pensions, since many women would marry and leave wage labor. Despite these assurances, the teachers' pension bill received a negative report from the appropriations committee and was defeated in a voice vote.[88]

Earlier, in 1924, in the widely publicized case of *Bowler v. Nagel,* the Michigan Supreme Court considered the question of pensions for all civil servants in Detroit. Was all public employment now regarded as service? As one of the only states that had disallowed aid to railroads, Michigan had a restrictive understanding of public purpose.[89] That made demonstrating the constitutionality of civil service pensions especially important.

Rather than focusing on service to the state, the court placed the municipality in the position of a private firm that would want to ensure continuity and faithfulness from its employees:

> While it may be said to be their duty to provide for their enforced retirement by saving a part of their earnings, it is a well-known fact, and one recognized by most advocates of civil service, that as a rule they do not do so. The wages paid them are usually but sufficient to enable them to live confortably [*sic*]. Many calls are made upon their bounty by relatives and friends, whose necessities appeal to them. Unlike the business man whose only thought, as a rule, is the accumulation of wealth, they feel it a duty to respond to such calls. . . . The day is happily past when the employer of labor feels no interest in the future of his employees. The railroads, the United States Steel Corporation, and many other large employers of labor, have come to realize that the establishment of a retiring fund is not only an act of humanity, but in the best interests of the stockholders, and justified as an economic proposition.[90]

Like teachers and university professors, civil servants worked for low wages. Their work, however, was no longer regarded as a public service; it was labor, like the labor of steelworkers and railroad employees. When pensions for firemen were first adjudicated by the courts, service had been central to their public purpose. By 1924 the public employer could pay pensions because it was like any other employer. This shift allowed the courts to treat pensions as a business investment. Men's independence and their support of dependents still colored the court's assumptions: workers earned little more than their families needed, yet they were generous to their friends and relatives. The court used examples from masculine work to justify civil service pensions, in conformity with the prevailing assumption that a man should earn a breadwinner's wage.[91]

Three justices dissented in *Bowler,* arguing that a general municipal pension "outside of the hazardous employments [was] . . . an innovation." Despite the parallel between pensions for general civil service employees and for those in industry, for these justices this similarity represented theft from the public purse. Employers paid pensions; when the employer was the public, pensions came out of public funds and therefore had to satisfy public purpose requirements—for which only the dangerous jobs qualified. Allowing pensions to all public employees would be constitutionally the same as granting them to "boiler makers and dressmakers."[92] To the dissenters, pensions for civil servants were no different from general old age pensions; the public-service element that they saw as a prerequisite had disappeared when occupations that were not dangerous were recompensed with pensions.

But that view no longer prevailed: public employees' pensions continued to pass constitutional muster despite frequent challenges. Nine cities with populations greater than 400,000 implemented general municipal pensions between 1915 and 1926.[93] Courts ruled as though they were limiting what the states could do, yet they largely ratified pensions. Even Justice Stephen J. Field of the United States Supreme Court, who was well known for his caution about giving away public money or public power, did not wholly object to pensions when he had the opportunity to assess them.[94] His 1889 opinion had disallowed pensions only because the state had rescinded them. States were sovereign in their jurisdiction; they could not be bound by previous sessions of the legislature but could always make new law. Even their constitutional inability to impair contracts was subject to their power to regulate in the public interest, a power the states could not forfeit.[95]

Businesses performing public functions had always been subject to further and changing regulation in the early nineteenth century.[96] The reluctance to read contract rights into pensions clearly represented continuity with that tradition. State legislatures could choose to grant *and* to rescind pensions. More important, they could decide to extend them to additional occupations. Each new pension seemed to change the constitutional grounding, usually without any acknowledgment of the change. State courts did set some limits: states could not expand pensions without requiring service as a return. Constitutional requirements certainly slowed the process of change and shaped the possible reforms.[97] The most notable thread in legal decisions, however, was not the limits courts set but their willingness to allow pensions.

That willingness did not come about because courts supported expanding social welfare rights more broadly. Indeed, during the late nineteenth and early twentieth centuries, both state and federal judiciaries were aggressively hostile to many kinds of reform legislation. They struck down many statutes designed to support unions or protect workers from danger, condemning them as class legislation—as unconstitutional protection of what one might now call special interests.[98] They eagerly enjoined unions from striking.[99] Constitutional prohibitions on taking private property seemed to prohibit almost every conceivable municipal and labor reform, including many that were being enacted in Europe and advocated by American progressives.[100] Appellate courts did allow a substantial amount of legislation to stand, and where they did not, they ruled in accord with long-standing categories.[101] Nonetheless, courts struck down some major innovations of the period and had a widespread reputation for doing so, whether commentators supported or deplored the decisions.

Pensions were not an inexplicable pocket of generosity in a judiciary otherwise hostile to legislation in favor of workers. Rather pensions rewarded public service at a time when civic employment was expanding and cultural understandings of labor were shifting. By the late nineteenth century, wage labor had become a central element of American citizenship, at least for men. Citizens were obliged to work; they were not free to be vagrant, and those who did not work were suspect.[102] More than the honor newly accorded to wage labor colored these decisions, however. The firefighters' cases represented continuity with a much older tradition in which performance of public functions merited reward, which the sovereign could grant or not. The courts approved these programs for the very reasons that the Bureau of Labor Statistics found them so difficult to analyze in 1929: they were local, and they recognized a particular form of service. Tied to specific occupations, paid by the localities for which the employees worked, these pensions accorded with long-standing common-law practice. By the late nineteenth century they were also consistent with elites' approval of wage labor.

Conclusion: Social Welfare and Legal Reasoning

Studies of social welfare policy in the United States usually take federal programs as the benchmark. Most scholars focus on explaining the 1935 Social Security Act and its successive revisions, which created as much of a national welfare state as the United States had in the twentieth century. Yet the programs that were instituted in the cities and states and the ideas percolating there enabled advocates to propose well-tested, politically viable policies to the federal government well before the 1930s. In thinking about the development of public pensions, those for firemen, police, teachers, and other civil servants should be taken into account: pensions for these government employees had been instituted, often challenged in court, and sometimes upheld since the late nineteenth century. State and local pensions for firemen and police were common, and by 1920 pensions for teachers were being offered by some large cities and debated in others. The inclusion of pensions provided by state and local governments in the analysis of social welfare policy highlights how closely, and for how long, benefits have been tied to employment. What in other countries is a social right of citizenship is in the United States a return for work.

To Ann Shola Orloff, whose comprehensive analysis of the creation of old age pensions compares policies in Britain, Canada, and the United States, the enactment of national civil service pensions in 1920 marked what was possible concerning broader old age pensions in the United States.[103] Policymaking elites learned from the administration of existing programs what problems they could expect when programs were expanded. Orloff argues that in the United States, concerns about the use of pensions to support patronage marked policymakers' reluctance to support general old age pensions.

Taking local pensions into consideration challenges this account of politicians' reluctance to enact pensions. According to Orloff, federal civil service pensions resulted partly from the replacement of the spoils system by a civil service system that provided security of office. As a result, the bureaucracy aged. Reformers worried that job security provided retirement within the job: all who could drag themselves to their offices would stay employed to hold on to their salary, no matter how little they worked. Building a more efficient service required a retirement system to get rid of unproductive workers, and the civil service system guaranteed that new federal pensions would not be subject to the abuses that had marked the Civil War pension system, which served as the model for all federal pensions.[104]

But that explanation assumes that pensions for government employees were new and that patronage played little part in them. In fact, pensions had been initiated by the cities and towns, which employed most of the civil servants, and patronage persisted there even after the professionalization of fire and police departments and the bureaucratization of municipal services. In the states and cities, payments made by fire insurance firms to volunteer fire companies from the 1830s onward had visibly contributed to rivalry among companies. Professionalization of firefighting controlled that competition but made the appointment of officers subject to political favoritism. In large cities the police were notorious for corruption and their close connections to electoral politics. Reformers hoped that payments to individual firemen and police officers would support a more professional culture among these uniformed services, making them loyal to the city rather than to party bosses.

States in which policymakers were most concerned about corruption, including New York, Massachusetts, and Illinois, were the first to institute individual pensions for firemen and police. The courts upheld them in cases from Chicago, New York, and San Francisco as well. In all these cities, public service employment was tied to ethnic affiliation, political party membership, and electoral support.[105] Within state and local policy, public pensions did not await or accomplish the elimination of corruption. Only if federal policymakers watched the policies in the states and cities with alarm could one say that reluctance came from fear of corruption.

The idea that pension systems would mean the replacement of inefficient, aging men with youthful and vigorous ones appeared in many state court decisions regarding police and firemen. Pensions may or may not have contributed to a more efficient civil service. "Efficiency" was common parlance at the time, applied without any evidence based on actual job performance. When the United States Supreme Court judged federal pensions for railroad employees in 1934, the majority did not find the efficiency argument persuasive. Pensions were supposed to reduce accidents because employed men would be younger and therefore more agile and alert, and the opinion noted that accidents had declined steadily for years. Yet even in this hazardous industry there was no evidence to suggest that older men were less efficient. Dissenters countered that accident rates might have fallen more quickly had the retirement scheme been in place.[106] Efficiency was notoriously difficult to evaluate, however, even where a job was something relatively concrete, such as ensuring that a train run. It was even more difficult to evaluate workers' productivity in the civil service.[107]

Pensions paid directly to employees represented part of the political transformation of the system of special taxes, public service, and segmented politics that had characterized the antebellum era. In the early nineteenth century many cities relied on corporate charters requiring private organizations to perform specific public functions and paid them with funds raised through special taxes. This system applied to firefighting among other functions—such as the provision of water, sanitation, and harbor and road improvements—which were later considered municipal responsibilities. The post–Civil War period was marked by a shift toward more direct ties between individuals and the government. According to William Novak's description of the transformation that took place in the legal and political order after Reconstruction, the states turned away from their antebellum commitment to the common good and focused instead on individual constitutional rights and on ties between the central state and the individual.[108] In his view, neither courts nor legislatures emphasized the collective good. With regard to pensions, the initiative lay with the state legislatures, which took over county charitable relief and payments to individuals; the courts' tendency to stress continuity in legal reasoning made them treat the new programs as though they were the old. In the 1880s, courts held that individual pensions served the common good. In the 1850s, in deciding that localities could pay firemen's charities, states had also relied on an understanding of common good, although it took a more collective form. Courts reasoned from the common law and from constitutional provisions throughout the nineteenth century.

Paying pensions rather than charity to individuals was a necessary step toward enacting more widespread payments to citizens as a matter of right, the hallmark of the Social Security Act of 1935. If state and local civil service pensions are regarded as part of a broad effort to get aged and dependent citizens off poor relief and out of poorhouses, these programs are especially remarkable because the pensions were administered as a statutory right and treated as earned, even though granting them remained a prerogative of sovereignty. Long before the 1935 Social Security Act, public service—not just military service—was being recompensed with pensions by many municipalities and states.

Even if one uses the 1935 Social Security Act as the benchmark for social welfare policy, social rights as a matter of the universal rights of citizenship have never been available in the United States. The more regular benefits have been tied to citizens' employment. Many scholars have noted that socially marginal and vulnerable groups—poor women, people of color, and the elderly who had held jobs not covered by Social Security—have relied primarily on federal programs administered by the states and counties.[109] Those programs have been inadequately funded, and their benefits were once clearly doled out in a racially discriminatory fashion.[110] Women working in covered occupations or, initially more commonly, married to men working in covered occupations gained access to the more reliable federally administered programs.[111] Embedding ideas of family in social welfare rights has been a common practice in all Western industrial states.[112]

As courts acceded to each new round of pensions, they approved of tying them closely to employment; thus, moving to general old age pensions not tied to a specific employer was a large step indeed. Still, if work marked citizenship, what remained was to label all employment as service. Perhaps any work could be of service to the state, regardless of whether the state was the employer. Synthesizing the law from the states between 1917 and 1924, *American Law Reports* published articles about pensions not only for soldiers and civil servants but also for mothers and the elderly.[113] New pensions not tied to state employment could be cast as analogous either with poor relief or with payments for public service. State commissioners studying pensions and proposing constitutional amendments came to recognize all wage labor as service.

CHAPTER SIX

Mothers' Pensions in the Courts, 1911–1923

I ndividual American states, unlike the European nations that provided the model for social welfare programs, had to incorporate questions of constitutionality as they designed programs. By 1910, courts had repeatedly approved payments to soldiers, firemen, police, and, less often, teachers, and pensions for all civil servants were under consideration.

New pensions for public employees invited public officials, including judges, to expand the category of service: as payments for service, such pensions were not the same as poor relief, and they were intended to *prevent* dependence among those who had served the state. The new payments did not constitute dependence, advocates reasoned, because they prevented public servants from relying on poor relief. Who else could be removed from poor relief? they then wondered. In 1909 a White House conference on dependent children added to the list mothers with no man to support them. Perhaps the states could provide payments that would support mothers on a basis different from that of poor relief, preventing desperate women from relinquishing their children to institutions. From this conference emerged discussion of the programs called mothers' pensions. The legal reasoning based in service, however, did little to encourage anyone to think that payments to mothers would be constitutional if they were framed as an entitlement rather than as poor relief. Doubts about the constitutionality of new programs emerged out of an understanding of the constitutional strengths, as well as limitations, of established pensions.

Many scholars have closely attended to the question of why pensions for mothers were and were not adopted.[1] The programs were small and usually remained the option of the counties; it is remarkable that such a limited change has received so much attention. Where proposals would change the practices of poor relief, though—requiring counties to pay *all* single mothers and not just poor ones, or instituting state rather than county control, or *requiring* that the counties fund mothers' pensions—the courts read state constitutional provisions as favoring state control but requiring that only poor women could gain payments. Constitutionality and statutory interpretation shaped what was possible for reformers to achieve.

Questions about the constitutionality of mothers' pensions emerged in taxpayers' and officials' efforts to control their tax dollars. As taxpayers, railroads (or the lawyers who represented them) eager to eliminate the programs entirely sued in the states that adopted these programs early. In some cases, state officials forced reluctant counties to conform to the requirements of the new programs. In court, both opponents and proponents had to address the question of whether the pensions were constitutional. The persistence of categories in law, the "toughness of a taught tradition," as Roscoe Pound wrote, quoting the English historian F. W. Maitland, meant that judges assessed mothers' pensions through the old categories: charity as distinct from service, and the bounty of sovereignty. The basis on which the constitutionality of mothers' pensions was affirmed transformed the principles underlying them and limited their application: legally regarded as poor relief, payments were granted as a matter of charity rather than entitlement, and they were paid only to the indigent, not to all mothers.

Existing charitable relief was irregular and depended on electoral support.[2] County commissioners exercised almost total discretion in administering poor relief. In cities, money for social services had long been allocated to what today would be considered private charities, which were often religious.[3] Reformers, however, intended mothers' pension programs to differ fundamentally from poor relief: pensions would not be at the option of the county but be funded by the state and granted as a matter of legal right, not largesse.

New programs required new powers and organization. Statutory interpretation of how to administer the law properly led to regulation of bureaucracies through their procedures.[4] Although constitutional challenges to the very existence of mothers' pensions did not prevail against means-tested programs, those who challenged the way new bureaucracies exercised their authority could win in court. Constitutional limits were implicit in questions concerning the administration of these programs. For example, how much did supervisors of mothers' pension funds have to act like judges when deciding cases? Could administrators control the interpretation of the law themselves, or should judges oversee them? Constitutional questions became matters of statutory interpretation, informed, according to judges, by an understanding of the constitutionally proper way to do things.

Mothers' pensions met two sets of challenges: whether they were constitutional, and how they should be applied. Because they *were* constitutional as charity, lawyers in the one case in which that was in question limited mothers' pensions to persuade courts they were indeed nothing more than charity. Mothers' pensions, like other new programs, had to fit into old categories. Since most were constitutional as charitable relief, understanding the legal disputes concerning the exercise of administrative powers requires first attending to activists' arguments concerning whether poor mothers were objects of charity or public servants.

"Need and Not Exchange"

During the nineteenth century, children beyond infancy had been regarded not as dependents but rather as contributors to the family economy. Those not old enough to work might be sent to almshouses or orphanages when their parents were permanently or even temporarily unable to care for them.[5] Children who appeared to have been abandoned would, if possible, be discharged to foster care. Those in New York City were sometimes sent to the West, where they provided inexpensive labor on farms, often encountering brutal treatment.[6]

By the early twentieth century, reformers had begun to value the emotional tie between children and their parents. Putting children in institutions interfered with the development of family ties; sending them to western farms did nothing to ensure that anyone would love the children rather than exploit them.[7] Almshouses taught children the skills of criminals, reformers believed. Orphanages were too large to allow for proper supervision, and with hundreds of children to care for, even the most well-meaning workers could not develop a close, affectionate relationship with any one child. The social workers, charity workers, and juvenile court judges—the "child savers"[8]—came to believe that it would be best to keep children with their mothers even if the government had to assume responsibility for supporting them financially. A mother's love was the best way to ensure that they would become healthy citizens.[9]

Monetary county poor relief, an alternative to orphanages or almshouses, was available in some counties but not others. Moreover, by the late nineteenth century, poor relief itself was under attack from several quarters, both for fostering dependence and for not allowing poor women to care for their own children.[10] The emergence of a class of educated women who dedicated themselves to labor activism or charity work accompanied the country's economic transformation to industrial wage labor, leading them also to diagnose the problems of poor relief. Socialist labor activists such as Florence Kelley, social workers, and the white middle-class Federation of Women's Clubs all supported mothers' pensions.[11] For them, relief at the option of the counties left women vulnerable to the whims of ungenerous county commissioners. Poor relief did not invite anyone to do the close work required to rehabilitate and uplift poor women; relief via orphanages or almshouses did not allow children to stay with their mothers, who could provide the best care. Mothers' pension programs, if properly designed, would include the moral evaluation and rehabilitative work a social worker could do.[12] In addition, labor activists thought support for working women should include paying them when they could not work, whether because they were raising children or because they had been injured. Pensions rather than poor relief seemed to solve any problem a charity worker might find; hence, proposals for mothers' pensions diffused remarkably quickly. Forty states enacted them between 1911 and 1920, authorizing monthly support payments to poor single mothers, most often widows.[13] Programs varied; some counties granted money to women who worked and others did not, for example.

These programs did not change outdoor poor relief very much.[14] Many were at the option of the county; where they were not optional, they received meager funding. Most states still allowed county commissioners substantial discretion in administering the programs. In states that made the programs mandatory, earmarked funds out of poor relief, and created state boards to supervise county decisions, counties fought the limits on their discretion, sometimes in court. Eventually, the more conservative wing of those advocating the programs won, giving social workers the authority to investigate and judge the worthiness of recipients—though as a practical matter not all states or counties implemented that requirement.[15]

Some proponents of mothers' pensions praised women's service in raising children as analogous to men's service in the military, both gendered forms of service to the state. Military pensions were by then so widely distributed and the culture of militarism so thoroughly entrenched that the analogy was ready to hand; it could prove useful in court if anyone were to argue that payment to mothers was only transformed poor relief.[16] Denver's Judge Ben Lindsey, who had a national reputation for his innovations in juvenile court and for his concern for the poor, wrote vigorous defenses of mothers' pensions. In 1913, just as the new pensions were taking hold in the states, he drew the analogy between mothers' pensions and soldiers' pensions.[17] Advocates did not succeed in framing mothers' pensions in these terms for the courts, however. In the eyes of legal authorities, any payments to women outside the structure of the patriarchal family must necessarily be based on indigence. Critics and, with few exceptions, the courts to which they appealed continued to regard mothers' pensions as a form of poor relief, consistent with the state's traditional obligation to support the destitute and dependent.

The male economists, lawyers, and sociologists who studied and advocated new social insurance believed that women should gain protection through their husbands' insurance.[18] They ignored or condemned mothers' pensions because they were not social insurance for workers but rather nothing more than old-fashioned charity. E. T. Devine led these critics. He worked with the American Association for Labor Legislation (AALL)—the organizational home for the social insurance perspective, which promoted measures protecting labours—and became the first director of the New York School of Philanthropy in 1904. In 1913 he wrote to oppose mothers' pensions in the *American Labor Legislation Review,* arguing that for widows, insurance was "a means of meeting their own share of the risk in more manageable installments." The risk they ran was that their laboring husbands might die or become disabled or unemployed; therefore, it was fair to ask that social insurance premiums come out of their husbands' paychecks. Payments to widows ought to take the form of insurance, not a giveaway that made no reference to thrift. In short, Devine vehemently opposed mothers' pensions as a foolish approach of "sentimental reformers."[19]

The advocates for mothers' pensions were less concerned that aid look like insurance. Insurance would not protect women who were unmarried or whose husbands had long since disappeared. Nor would it take account of the independent service that women performed for the world by raising children, service that social workers and women's club members thought it important to recognize.

Proponents of both social insurance and mothers' pensions framed the payments that people should receive as a return for their service to the public. But Devine countered the argument that mothers' pensions *were* a return for service—just as soldiers' pensions were—by arguing that mothers' pensions were only revamped poor relief: "Need and not exchange is its basis," whereas pensions for soldiers were

> deferred payment for service already rendered, and have no reference to the resources or needs of the individual. Mothers' pensions are described as an act of simple justice, but I venture to say that no one has really ever voted for them or paid his share of taxes to provide for them as an act of justice in any other sense than that in which the bringing up of the foundling, the care of the indigent sick, or the rescue of a victim of drink from his own appetites, are justice.[20]

Devine's analogies were to traditional poor relief programs based in need, which focused on supporting dependency rather than establishing entitlement. He likened mothers to those who had historically been considered intrinsically dependent in law and were without private caretakers: children without parents, the ill with no resources. Justice was a claim of right; charity, a claim of need.

The AALL allowed William Hard, one of the leading journalists advocating mothers' pensions, to respond. He argued that mothers were not dependent; in the work of raising children they earned any money the state might pay them.[21] Advocates and opponents of mothers' pensions agreed on the importance of public service. What they could not agree on was whether mothering qualified.

Despite the position taken by William Hard, Florence Kelley, and to a lesser extent the Federation of Women's Clubs, mothers' pensions *were* based on indigence.[22] Devine argued that the pensions did not break dramatically from poor relief; legally and even constitutionally, he was right. Common law supported the conservatives' position that mothers were legally dependents. If they had no male protectors, they were properly governed by the state; those who were in need would be supported by the state.

Judges treated law as continuous across fields, relying on right principles that made it difficult to change traditional relations of dependency, including those between men and women. Women were naturally and properly dependent on men, just as workers were naturally dependent on employers, servants on masters, and officials on sovereigns.[23] The regulation of women's labor was relevant to mothers' pensions, since both stated women's dependence at law. That dependence, in turn, expressed women's publicly useful role in raising children. As dependents, historically, women had not been free to contract as they chose. Before nineteenth-century legislative reforms, married women were not permitted to hold property. They could not keep their own wages because their labor belonged to their husbands. Since they had no freedom of contract to lose, therefore, the state could step in and set bargains for them, regulating their conditions of work. Women's work in raising children exemplified their dependence, but it was also labor in which the public had an interest, so that regulation to allow women to raise children better was to the benefit of the public and therefore constitutional.[24] Dependence marked regulation for women, as it had marked women's status in the common law, and it is not surprising that it also marked the constitutional framing of pensions for mothers.[25]

Even social insurance advocates such as Devine believed that some widows had earned pensions through their marriages: the families of men killed in industrial accidents should gain pensions in the same way as Civil War veterans' families.[26] Women's access to social insurance payments should remain wholly contingent on their familial status, not on their participation in the labor force or the polity. As Linda Gordon has argued, welfare policy framed a division of labor rooted in gendered expectations.[27] Women raised children; even if they also worked for wages, their employment did not define them, as men's did. Men often worked in dangerous jobs, risking their ability to earn, and they supported dependent wives and children. (Few white activists, however, argued that black women should not work, and though black women activists also idealized home life, they accepted that mothers worked for wages.)[28] Advocates for mothers' pensions did, as Devine contemptuously noted, acknowledge single mothers' need for support.[29] If mothers were dependent and had not earned payments through service, the only way to make mothers' pensions constitutional was to limit them to indigent mothers.

Those who believed that pensions should be paid only to the poor had all the forces of organized charity, financially strapped counties, and established poor relief on their side. Even before any case appeared in state court, the constitutional arguments were there, should anyone choose to remind the women who wanted to reward motherhood how wrong they were. In the California battle in 1913, Emma Wolfe, a socialist activist who was on the losing side of pensions, lamented that constitutionality was the "stone wall against which we are thrown when we attempt to do anything for the mothers. I suppose some day they will say the mothers are unconstitutional, at least they may well say many of them have no constitution."[30] She slyly used "constitution" in both its meanings, denoting health and strength as well as the document that structures governance. Without the support of universal mothers' pensions, women were frail: they had no constitution. They had no strength in governance and no strength to protect themselves in governance. Constitutionality limited mothers' pensions to dependence and indigence; it did not allow states to recognize mothering as publicly valuable.

Western states were among the first to institute mothers' pensions; many enacted them between 1911 and 1913, when other states were considering them.[31] Legal cases contesting their constitutionality naturally arose first in the West as well. Cases regarding conscription payments had come first out of the Northeast, in the states that had had obligations, and the doctrine that state-funded pensions must serve a public purpose had been established in those cases affirming their constitutionality. As soon as mothers' pensions were enacted, taxpayers who were opposed to the new system and county supervisors who resented losing authority over poor relief sued. A few critics contended that the new pensions were less generous than the old combination of almshouses and outdoor relief—a particularly acute problem in the western states, which had little beyond basic provisions for indenture and general almshouses that housed children as well as adults.[32] Judges who believed that states had an obligation to care for the poor might well wonder whether abolishing the old system and replacing it with the new would care for all the children whose parents were poor.

That issue came to the fore in Arizona, which not only abolished almshouses when enacting mothers' and old age pensions but, alone among the states, enacted (by refendum) universal pensions that were not closely means-tested. In all other states the courts ratified the constitutionality of mothers' pensions. What is important here is *why* they were deemed constitutional: the courts' assumption that the most relevant analogies were between mothers' pensions and poor relief, not the military pensions that had proved so useful in justifying pensions for police and firemen.

Challenges to mothers' pensions were sometimes explicit constitutional challenges to the whole program, and at other times challenges to what seemed to be an overgenerous interpretation of the statute.[33] Constitutional challenges included both concerns about public purpose and concerns that the new programs required a blurring of powers that ought to be separate. The tangle as counties and states struggled for control illustrated Frank Goodnow's belief that what he saw as unnecessary rigidity emphasizing constitutionality rather than accountability could characterize American disputes over new programs.

Three types of challenges to mothers' pensions appeared in court. First, taxpayers who objected to paying for the programs sued as soon as they were enacted. Second, the new programs, though similar to existing state systems of poor relief, were not identical: they often gave administrative powers to state officials or juvenile court and probate judges, thus limiting the discretion of county commissioners. Consequently, state and county officials struggled over control and sometimes took their struggles to court. Third, in the years immediately after states enacted pensions, some women appealed to the courts when they were denied them; these appeals were based on the remarkable practice of treating the program as creating legal rights for claimants, not just potentially violating the rights of taxpayers. These three kinds of cases demonstrate the move from the blunt question of whether or not programs were constitutional to Goodnow's more subtle argument that the way to protect constitutional rights was through administration. Courts did not usually strike programs down; rather, they policed both spending and allocation of powers among officials by policing interpretations of the statutes.

Taxpayers' Complaints

The taxpayers who brought many of the challenges to mothers' pensions were not only individuals but businesses that had the status to sue in court and the wherewithal to pursue lawsuits. Railroads, corporations, and plaintiffs identified only as "taxpayers" filed bloodless complaints about mill levies and the purposes of taxation in many of the states that first enacted mothers' pensions.[34] The fact that taxpayers could sue shaped the stories subsequently told in court. The first person to address a court can shape the court's perception of the problem. Taxpayers used complaints about payments to real people only as a way to challenge a program as a whole. No one spoke for a poor woman who was rescued by the payment of a pension, or even described an undeserving woman trying to gain a government pension. The complaint was never that one individual did not deserve a payment but that no one did. Therefore, the cases did not include compelling stories; rather their abstract quality invited judges to engage in disquisitions on public and private responsibility. The first and most stunning came out of Arizona.

Arizona had become a state in 1912, recognizing in its constitution the state's obligation to support its poor, to be met through institutions. Arizona, like other western states, had adopted many of the measures of Progressive reform (including the initiative, which provided a rich and complicated source for new laws). These reforms partly resulted from western states' dependence on eastern money: public utilities and water management required funding from bankers, many of whom supported Progressive reform measures. Unending problems with floods and droughts also led elites to lobby the national government for federal water projects, which would free the localities from the impossible task of funding such efforts from local money. Elites in Arizona were therefore accustomed to working with national ideas and national leadership. Arizona cities also had a much smaller foreign-born population than cities such as Chicago and New York did; whatever whites' concerns about Mexican Americans, they did not have to worry about an unlimited foreign-born population of naturally dependent people to whom state and local money might flow—an issue that did concern easterners.[35]

Arizona enacted mothers' pensions through a ballot initiative in 1914, which stipulated that the program would take effect in January 1915. In the same ballot measure, Arizona became the first state to enact old age pensions, to be granted to any elderly who were "without visible means of support." The two programs were linked because they replaced the previous system of indoor poor relief, which had provided almshouses for all of the indigent poor rather than providing separate care for children, as midwestern and eastern poorhouses had commonly done. Anyone who was unconvinced that almshouses were worse than any other form of care might well worry that abolishing those institutions would mean that some children would get nothing.

The statute did not impose any income restriction on mothers but provided pensions only for those mothers whose husbands had died or who were inmates of state institutions, including prisons and mental institutions.[36] Families that had been deserted by fathers were not eligible; at common law, these men were still liable for the support their children. Finally, only those who had resided in the state for more than five years were eligible. The state would pay $15 per month to eligible adults and $6 per month for each dependent child under the age of sixteen.

L. H. Buckstegge, a plaintiff identified only as a "taxpayer" who lived in Maricopa County (which included Phoenix), filed a complaint on February 20, 1915, the day after the state Board of Control first granted an old age pension and a mother's pension. Buckstegge's lawyers were Harry M. Fennemore and Will Ryan, who had opened a practice together in 1913. A Republican who participated in civic organizations such as the Elks and the Chamber of Commerce, Fennemore had moved to Arizona in 1911 as the lawyer for Mountain States Telephone and Telegraph. In 1916 he joined a law firm in Phoenix, eventually lending his name to the firm. There he continued to represent leading corporations, including the Atchison, Topeka & Santa Fe Railroad, the Pullman Sleeping Car Company, and Kennecott Copper. I can find no evidence that he took the pension case at the behest of any of his corporate clients or any political organization; at least, no corporations were named as plaintiffs. L. H. Buckstegge could have been a local railroad magnate, since Fennemore's clients were the railroads and mining corporations, but he does not appear in local guides to the prominent men in Arizona history. Fennemore possibly took the case simply as a general practice lawyer in a small firm that was building its business.[37]

Railroads, however, *were* plaintiffs in similar cases elsewhere in the West. In fact, railroads dominated the western states and would have noticed the mill levies. They had also long required the lavish attention of lawyers. From the late nineteenth century, attorneys had helped reorganize the railroads to save them from their extensive debt, assisted them in breaking strikes, and, once the Interstate Commerce Commission came into being in 1887, found a lucrative source of business in contesting the ICC's decisions. In addition, they defended railroads against suits brought for compensation by the families of dead and injured employees. In short, railroads were accustomed to retaining attorneys.[38] Perhaps, then, Fennemore did bring the case for his clients, just as railroad attorneys did in other western states. Or perhaps the case represented an effort on the part of state officials to stop a program the voters had approved. The brief for Buckstegge invited the state supreme court to notice that the Board of Control might not really object to the case: it was "one which was not entirely unwelcome."[39]

Buckstegge and his lawyers challenged the new pensions by claiming that they did not provide for the poor as the state constitution required. The state's attorney general, Wiley E. Jones, defended the program, pointing out that Arizona's pensions were so unusually generous that even he could argue for a narrower version of them. The trial court held that the statute left out too many of the poor by abolishing the almshouses and supporting only women (and their children) who were widows or whose husbands were in state institutions. It was not the state's generosity in making mothers' pensions generally available that made the program unconstitutional; the problem lay in the limits of the program—an ironic finding, since advocates had seen these new programs as a way of eliminating the stigma of poor relief. The trial judge explained that the statute "has left out all the men and women who are objects of charity under sixty years of age; it has left out all the children of deserted wives, all the wives of invalid or crippled husbands."[40] The new pensions were thus a shabby substitute for almshouses, which the trial judge assumed had provided for all the poor.

When states used pensions to replace indoor relief rather than add to it, the programs did cover a narrower range of people than almshouses had—but of course, advocates had intended to leave out those whom they thought should be working, including men under sixty. As E. T. Devine had argued, only women without husbands were proper objects of charity. Many critics feared that granting all mothers pensions would give men an incentive to leave their families.[41] Mothers whose husbands were crippled were supposed to be covered by workmen's compensation, which many states had recently taken under consideration.

When the state appealed the trial court's ruling to the Arizona Supreme Court, briefs filed by both sides in September 1915 addressed the analogy between pensions for mothers and those for soldiers. In addition, Fennemore and Ryan compared mothers' pensions to those for civil servants, emphasizing the two cases that had held civil service pensions to be unconstitutional.

Jones, the state attorney general, took a program that had been crafted for the voters' approval and reshaped it for scrutiny by judges. Advocates could not present programs in court in whatever terms they preferred; legal reasoning required them to represent new programs as continuous with previous ones. Lawyers had to emphasize indigence as a criterion for payment and minimize the distinction between paying people directly and paying for an institution. Jones attempted to erase the differences between new programs and old: "We submit that it is immaterial whether the support of the indigent and needy be called a pension, outdoor relief, food, medicine support or whatever designations might be used. . . . The term by which this relief is called cannot affect its constitutionality."[42] The voters had approved a program that eliminated the legal category "pauper," which was just what both social insurance and mothers' pensions advocates wanted. In lawyers' hands, that shift became minor and semantic.

Attorney General Jones never attempted to argue that the pensions should go to all mothers; he treated them as though the state was granting them only to poor women with dependent children. They were intended for the indigent, which was entirely proper, and in providing for needy mothers the program was continuous with provision for poor veterans and for firemen. Jones asserted that payments to the elderly and to mothers were not an unconstitutional gift but a "fulfillment of a public moral obligation which the State owes to its unfortunate members." Only the Minnesota Supreme Court had previously ruled on mothers' pensions, and that court had held the program to be constitutional, he noted. Moreover, mothers' pensions were preferable to indoor relief because they supported the indigent "without breaking of the home ties." Since governments could pay money for reasons of charity or public obligation, pensions were "not a donation or grant to private individuals, when those private individuals are indigent and needy."[43] Jones cited state grants to Confederate soldiers to demonstrate that even those who "had fought against the flag of the nation" could get pensions if they were indigent. Further, recipients of military pensions sometimes only "deserved" charity; they had not earned it. Service could require indigence, collapsing the distinction between soldiers and mothers not because mothers had served but because veterans were indigent.

Fennemore and Ryan argued that only military service qualified as public service; at law, nothing else counted, and even military service did not always merit reward. Buckstegge's lawyers cited cases in which northeastern courts had "refused to concede any public purpose beyond that involved in state recognition, and granting pensions as a reward for meritorious service. In other words, [those courts had] refused to extend the power of the legislature beyond the generally recognized patriotic policy prevalent to the nation and to some states."[44] No state had extended service beyond veterans, they maintained, and only some states had provided payments to veterans. (This argument ignored the police and firemen's cases, many of which had upheld pensions provided by cities.)

Later, Fennemore and Ryan highlighted for the court the two cases that had held against civil service pensions as constituting extra compensation for a job already completed.[45] If the legislature "has no power to pension firemen, teachers, policemen, and other employees in public service, *as reward for past service rendered*," then surely it could not pension the elderly and mothers. Even payments to public employees for past service were only a gift. Mothers and the elderly were not on the state payroll, so payments to them were simply gratuities.[46]

The second question raised by Buckstegge's lawyers concerned not the generosity of pensions but their gaps. The state was obligated to care for "persons whose fight with the world has been a failure; who . . . for reason of infirmities of age, are 'incapable of earning a livelihood.'" The new pensions did not cover all those who had "failed," and the support they did provide was inadequate. Mothers would not receive enough money; for the state to take the place of the father, it had to meet the father's obligations fully, which monthly payments of $15 plus $6 per child did not do:

> We would expect to find upon our public streets babes in baskets, with six dollars tied to their necks, and from those circumstances find fathers pleading "not guilty" to a charge of non-support, as plausibly as we would expect public conscience to be satisfied with doling out fifteen dollars per month and call it "SUPPORT."[47]

The state could no more discharge its obligations by paying $6 per month per child than a father could.

Finally, because old age and mothers' pensions did not cover everyone who might have resorted to an almshouse, they left out too many poor people. Fennemore and Ryan thus emphasized that pensions would further impoverish the poor; almshouses provided better support. Reformers such as Judge Ben Lindsey could argue that women should gain payment for service as soldiers did, but that did not answer the charge that soldiers were never paid enough. Pensions did not furnish

> the support, care and maintenance, which a gracious people intended to those who served their country in the hour of its dire need. State homes were later provided, to the end of full discharge of the duty which the public felt it owed

to those veterans who are no longer able to conserve and apply to their own benefit . . . the pension money formerly paid.[48]

Almshouses, then, were a more generous solution to poverty—a curious position for those objecting *as taxpayers* to pensions.

The state constitution required that the state provide for institutions "as the public good may require."[49] By abolishing almshouses, Fennemore and Ryan argued, the state was abdicating its responsibility to maintain institutions. They insisted that institutions were buildings. Jones, after consulting a dictionary, declared that pensions qualified as an institution, which signified only an "established rule or order"; not all institutions had walls.[50] Fennemore and Ryan countered that it was not legitimate for the state to "pass the funds over to private control and use."[51] Funds maintaining almshouses were under public control, whereas payments made directly to the indigent were in private hands.

Of course, those who had designed the new pensions believed there would and should be a substantial difference between indoor and outdoor relief, but given the constitutional amendment requiring the state to support institutions, Jones could not argue the virtues of the differences between the programs. Instead, he had to argue that for legal purposes the programs were similar, and that ratifying the new program required only thoughtful reflection on the meaning of the word "institution."

The Arizona Supreme Court struck down the new mothers' pensions, focusing on the program's failure to protect the poor: it abolished almshouses and neglected to support some of the poor, while providing for some widows who did not need the money. Because the program was not means-tested, it gave payments to too many women; even women "rich as Croesus" were eligible, which could not possibly have been what the electorate intended in voting for the initiative:

> The theory upon which a pension system of this kind must be sustained is that the state owes a duty to take care of the unfortunate members of society who, by reason of age or mental or physical infirmity, are unable to care for themselves, and are not the owners and possessors of property sufficient to sustain them from want and beggary. Certainly a citizen and taxpayer ought not to be made or required to help pay pensions to those who have enough and to spare of the world's goods. I can think of no principle of law or justice that could be invoked to sustain a law that required him to do so.[52]

As for the military analogy, only dependency justified social spending on those who had not fought in a war. Mothers who were not the widows of soldiers were analogous to the ill and disabled, not to able-bodied soldiers. Nor did this court accept the idea that women served the state by raising children. In sharp contrast with the courts that decided some of the soldiers' pension cases, the court did not agree that mothering was a burden of the citizenship shared by all which happened to fall on women, as military service was a universal burden for young men.

The court did not hand down an absolute "no," however: the state of Arizona could redraft the statute to limit pensions to the indigent and to maintain almshouses. Of course, though, a new program that could pass constitutional muster would no longer resemble the policy that supporters of mothers' pensions had advocated.

The *Arizona Republican,* the state's leading newspaper, published an article on the case the day after the court issued its decision, emphasizing that the primary problem was the many for whom the act did not provide.[53] By abolishing almshouses, the state would fail to ensure that any public institution would support *all* the poor. An accompanying editorial noted that the new program "left orphans and a certain class of indigents without aid and provided aid for a certain class of widows, wives and children who might be in no need of assistance."[54] The denial of benefits to some deserving poor people, as well as their extension to some mothers who were not destitute, generated critical attention.

Constitutional arguments had been anticipated in the arguments leading up to the pensions: "It was patent long before the election of two years ago that the bill was defective. The defects which were pointed out in the lower court and which are emphasized in the supreme court decision were discerned early in the campaign but nothing could be done about them." Unconstitutionality was only a hurdle, though, not an absolute bar. As the editorial wearily noted, most of the problems could be taken care of by redrafting; indeed, the newspaper suggested as the primary problem that those who draft initiatives were "persons unskilled in work of that kind."[55]

Legal problems with statutes always look like someone's unskilled drafting *after* a court has decided against them. People opposed to new programs pay lawyers to find flaws in statutes. Alternatively, lawyers make a perfectly respectable effort to change the law by reinterpreting it as they strategically define and contest such terms as "institution."

Legal problems also stem from the way courts treat established laws. The state constitution only enshrined the responsibility to care for the poor; it did not specify how that responsibility was to be be carried out. Judges did not treat common-law obligations or the ways states and counties met them as a matter of changeable statute, however. Long-standing practices could become part of *the law,* the proper legal order of things. Thus, courts could elevate an existing system of relief to constitutional status, as the Arizona court did. It did not oppose either spending or poor women or the elderly, as an argument that courts were hostile to social spending would suggest. Envisioning a working alternative to existing relief was difficult. Who would know that the poor fed themselves properly if no one spent the money for them? Impassioned reformers who believed the new payments would protect families better than the old system did not control what changes might mean to others. Advocates of pensions believed that payments to individuals would be less expensive than payments to institutions. The courts were trying to limit spending by ensuring that payments went only to the truly needy, but they also resisted abolishing conventional forms of poor relief. If they had intended only to limit public spending, it would not have mattered whether payments went to individuals or to almshouses.

The Arizona Supreme Court acted on the basis of a distinction between public and private purpose that other courts had also found significant. Ironically, they regarded payments to institutions—"whether public or private," as advocates in a later Pennsylvania case would put it—as *protecting* public purpose. Social insurance advocates contended that corruption rested in payments to privately run institutions, not in payments to individuals, but the justices were not persuaded.

Only the Arizona courts held their program to be unconstitutional. Only the Arizona program, though, had made payments mandatory and paid money to women regardless of need. Illinois instituted a generous program in 1911 but limited the plan even before it could get to court.[56] Chicago, second only to New York as a home to immigrants and to the social workers and charity workers who ministered to them, could not be so generous without having the charity world notice. The Russell Sage Foundation, a research and policy organization that opposed mothers' pensions, decided in 1912 to "attack" the Illinois program because it distributed money too readily. The foundation believed the law to be "so badly drawn and of so sentimental rather than practical nature that it has been abused in its application."[57]

This attack was not difficult to mount, because many people opposed universal distribution. The Chicago courts administering mothers' pensions almost immediately changed the program from one designed to distribute benefits universally to one that distributed benefits only after ensuring the applicant's indigence and investigating her moral worth. Some states, including New York, resolved the tension between charity and reward for service in the administration of programs by agreeing that they had been established for worthy objects of charity. In 1913 the Illinois legislature redesigned its program to require indigence.[58] By the time railroads' lawsuits made it to court, the plaintiffs could complain only about the mill levies. They lost.[59]

Lawyers for the Denver & Rio Grande Railroad challenged Utah's statute, though with little success. That state had not made mothers' pensions mandatory, nor did it grant pensions to all women regardless of income. The state supreme court listed the reasons that the statute served a public purpose, most important among them that the state intended to raise good children. In pursuit of that purpose the legislature allowed investigation of the fitness of the mothers receiving pensions. Such requirements showed the state cautiously ensuring that its money would be used to raise good citizens.[60] Should a mother do a bad job, the state could ensure that the children would become good citizens by taking them away from her.[61] The Utah court concluded:

> It will be conceded, we take it, that the proper rearing and bringing up of children, their education, their moral welfare, can all be subserved better by giving to such children the companionship, control, and management of their mothers than by any other system devised by human ingenuity. The object of the act is to provide means whereby mothers who are otherwise unable may be enabled to give such attention and care to their children of tender years as their health, education and comfort require.[62]

Utah would pay mothers' pensions, then, for the sake of the children, not for the sake of the mothers.

The pervasiveness of this reasoning in social policy arguments in the United States has led Virginia Sapiro to argue that women have historically been instruments of state policy, delivering services valued by the state.[63] Moreover, mothers' pensions would ensure that the state would no longer foster criminality through concentrating poor and troubled children in orphanages.[64]

States and localities were left to administer the programs sustained by the courts. County commissioners sometimes lost discretion when states mandated how they were to spend local money. Frustrated, disapproving, and financially burdened, they provided the next round of cases, claiming that the directives blurred powers between executives, judges, and legislatures. That claim was common to new administrative programs that states and the federal government designed in everything from railroad regulation to immigration control to pensions. Progressive lawyers believed accountability in administration would answer the problem of blurred powers. Frank Goodnow's pathbreaking 1893 treatise in administrative law (discussed in chapter five) shows how any one county's complaint resonated with broader disputes over administrative law.

Changing the Structure of Power

Disgruntled county commissioners brought suits that raised new problems in administrative law, particularly regarding the separation of powers. In so doing, though they may have been concerned only with their local budgets and the undeserving poor, they were taking part in the grand debates about whether constitutions could accommodate new programs. If the programs seemed to take away discretion unconstitutionally, it was only under state constitutions, not federal; state constitutions and state courts seemed more changeable and less trustworthy concerning fundamental rights.[65] Nevertheless, like federal judges, state court judges could concern themselves with whether executives were taking on jobs that judges should have.

According to Frank Goodnow, administrative law required a proper understanding of "the relations between executive and administrative authorities." All programs needed to ensure that government officials did not abolish either constitutional rights or rights in statutory and common law. Striking down programs as unconstitutional was a crude instrument that did not allow governments to accomplish new social purposes. Yet government officials administering programs necessarily blurred the traditional separation of powers among legislative, executive, and judicial functions. Administrative law, which analyzed "the rules of law concerning the function of administration," would help new programs to be administered constitutionally. The interpretation of procedures in cases and judicial supervision to ensure the careful application of statutes in individual cases would be much more finely tuned instruments for preventing new administrative powers from encroaching on individuals' rights. Interpreting statutes with regard to their constitutionality was a necessary part of administration; as Goodnow put it, "Constitutional law does, it is true, aim also at the protection of private rights, in so far as it formulates a scheme of inviolable rights, but the remedies offered for their violation, and without which they are valueless, are to be found in the control over administrative action provided by the administrative law."[66] Administrators, judges, commissioners, and state attorneys general built the new law of administration into the details of interpreting programs.

Questions in administrative law appeared with regard to mothers' pensions only because the programs had survived the cruder test of constitutionality. They provided an early site for struggle for control between state and localities. Poor mothers, unlike teachers, were systematically separated from poor relief only in the limited sense that county commissioners in some states lost discretion. They *had* to fund charitable relief for poor mothers, and many did not like it.

New cases resulted from the new structures set up to administer mothers' pension programs in some states. Aid to dependent women and children was no longer a matter solely for the county commissioners, or for the boards of overseers of the poor that had exercised almost total discretion over poor relief. The arbitrary power of local administrators infuriated a wide range of social policy reformers during the late nineteenth and early twentieth centuries. According to Frank Goodnow, local commissioners were not professionals, and they worked without central administrative control: "Seldom do we find any authority which has administrative supervision of any extent over the actions of the other authorities in the locality. . . . Having no opportunity to develop professional habits they thus do not form a special class in the community."[67] The administration of new pensions took a variety of forms in different localities. Some states still left administration to county commissioners, but in many states they lost some control when mothers' pensions replaced poor relief.

Some states set aside money for mothers' pensions within the poor relief fund, which outraged county officials. Other states had special supervisors to check the discretion county officials exercised. In still others, probate courts and juvenile courts distributed money to individual women, replacing county commissioners entirely. Each situation could result in the county's challenging the pension given to a particular woman, if not the structure of the whole program.[68] State officials sometimes espoused the causes of individual women in order to bring county officials into line with the design of new programs. That approach was relevant only where a state was trying to wrest control from the counties; those few states could use all the help they could get.

Pennsylvania was one of the states in which a state agency supervised local administration, and the state attorney general advised counties concerning how they must interpret the law.[69] For example, Carrie Dougherty had lived in Philadelphia between 1891 and 1915, when she applied for a mother's pension. The county would not pay her, and she left Philadelphia to live with her husband's mother in Newark, New Jersey. She claimed that she had left only because she could no longer earn enough to support her children; she intended to move back as soon as Philadelphia agreed to pay her pension. Trustees in Philadelphia, however, believed that she was no longer eligible, since only those who lived in the county could receive payments. The state supervisor took Mrs. Dougherty's case, along with a similar one for a Mrs. Beckman, to the attorney general for clarification. The deputy attorney general confirmed that if Mrs. Dougherty meant to live in Philadelphia, she was still a resident there and eligible for a pension; he concluded, "The act should be construed liberally in favor of the applicant, having in view the humane purposes of its enactment."[70]

The deputy attorney general's opinion tells nothing more about Mrs. Dougherty: whether her husband had died, was in prison, or had deserted her; how she had supported herself before the mothers' pensions came into effect; or how old her children were. Most likely she was a widow, since states seldom awarded pensions to women who were divorced or separated, and she was on good terms with her mother-in-law. Her story is included in the published opinion only because she provided an occasion for a state supervisor to try to force a county to distribute money more freely than the local officials wanted to do. Many cases in appellate courts or an attorney general's office resembled Mrs.

Dougherty's, involving disputes between state and local officials, or between local officials and the courts charged with administering pensions.

States and counties were fighting not only over budgets but also over new state powers. Designating judges as administrators of pension funds was especially controversial, since distributing public funds did not resemble judges' ordinary duties and seemed to violate the principle of separation of powers, a central constitutional doctrine. Separation of powers was formally a question in the United States only at the national level, however, where each branch of government had constitutional status. Counties had no formal constitutional status—they were creatures of the states—but the national-level debates resonated locally as well.

New regulatory programs administered nationally by bureaucracies violated the separation of powers as a matter of course. For example, in setting the rates that railroads could charge, bureaucrats were not simply executing the law Congress had enacted but adjudicating the private property rights of the railroad and, therefore, acting judicially. The answer at the national level, at least according to the courts that were called upon to adjudicate these disputes, was to impose judicial standards of administrative procedure on the bureaucrats.[71]

Goodnow responded to this problem in 1893 by arguing that the separation of powers had never really existed and could not fully exist in practice. The branches of government shared the task of governing, and the powers they exercised to carry out that task were not intrinsically different.[72] He argued that it was mistaken to erect a general theory from historical observation—for example, that because the English Parliament legislated, all legislatures must legislate and only they could legislate. Even in England, lower courts, at that time a collection of local notables who did a variety of tasks, had administered the poor law before 1834.[73] English courts did draw lines around the jurisdiction of branches of the state, particularly the executive. Executives had to proceed within the bounds of the statute and according to principles of natural justice, which approximated what in the United States was called due process. By supervising jurisdiction, the courts in England brought something akin to constitutional principles to bear on a common-law system.[74]

Histories of the separation of powers are told so as to make particular points regarding how the state should work; this is only a special case of the practice of many, especially lawyers, to tell histories in ways that support a certain point of view. Doing so has a purpose only if one believes that history provides a lesson concerning how people should live now, and legal reasoning relies on that commitment.[75] Goodnow tried to counter histories that said recent transformations in governance were unprecedented. He was trying to discredit the separation of powers as a description of public administration in order to correct what he saw as an error in governing that many judges nevertheless acted upon. That mistaken assumption made it difficult to grant new tasks to officials, such as allowing judges to administer pensions.

Questioning the new responsibilities of officials was evident in the debate over pension laws. Concern over the separation of powers provided one more way for frustrated county officials to try to rid themselves of new programs. Justice Richard H. Grace, who sat on the North Dakota Supreme Court, mused:

> The exact line of demarcation where judicial functions end and administrative functions begin is not easily discernible, and is fraught with many difficulties, just as perplexing as it is to accurately determine the exact line of demarcation which segregates the animal from the vegetable kingdom, and as we draw near the extremity of one the shadows of the other, figuratively speaking, are falling across our pathway.[76]

The concurring justice was much more blunt: judges should not try to demarcate shadowy boundaries but, rather, collapse categories. Distributing pensions was neither wholly judicial nor wholly executive, and therefore the legislature could choose the administrative body it preferred, judges or executives.[77]

Throughout the country, once new programs were deemed constitutional, judges would try to apply to bureaucracies forms of control that did not fit neatly into the traditional separation of powers into legislative, executive, and judicial branches. Legal control included supervising through statutory interpretation what administrative organizations did. For example, Pennsylvania's deputy attorney general exercised this role when he informed the mothers' pension supervisor that Mrs. Dougherty should receive her pension. In turn, statutory interpretation evoked the public purposes that made new programs legitimate: Mrs. Dougherty could receive her pension because it was within the act's "humane" purpose. At the state and county level, these pension programs were making new forms of governance. In state appellate courts, judges were trying to determine what this new form of governance would be and how it would be controlled. The lower-court judges, county officials, and corporations that appear in the appellate court cases were struggling over state control of poor relief, which had long been a county function.

Suits Brought by Women

The few women who pursued their own cases through a lawyer appear less vulnerable than those few we can see only faintly through the brief stories told by a pension commissioner who was trying to control a recalcitrant county. In Marion County, Oregon, just outside the state capital of Salem, lawyers brought a flurry of

cases on behalf of women soon after the state enacted pensions in 1913. Only a handful of cases came before the Oregon Supreme Court, but that handful was more
than appeared in any other state. Oregon was unusual in providing for appeals for
those who had been denied pensions. Whether lawyers took these women's cases as
a charitable act, or the local Women's Club helped to sponsor them as a way of fur-
thering mothers' pensions, or there was enough at stake for lawyers to make money
from women who were not financially desperate is anyone's guess.

When Grace Buster's husband died in January 1914, he left her both land and
debt but enough life insurance to pay off the debt and buy a half-acre just east of
Salem. She had a home there, and she cultivated a vegetable garden and kept
chickens to feed her two children. The children also had inherited eighty acres of
uncultivated land from their late father, subject to Mrs. Buster's dower claim.
Thus, though she had little cash and no clear income, she had land. In 1916 she
applied for a mother's pension, and the juvenile court granted her a pension of
$10 a month—less than the statutory maximum on grounds that the children
were not wholly dependent on her. Mrs. Buster argued that they were, and she appealed. The circuit court granted her $17.50 a month. Then the county appealed,
and its lawyer persuaded the supreme court that since Mrs. Buster was not desperately poor, the county owed her nothing more than the juvenile court had first
awarded.[78] Whether or not the pensions had been designed for indigent women,
the local juvenile court judges administering the money had practical discretion
to determine what pensions meant locally. In Oregon they were neither granted
routinely to everyone nor limited to the most desperate of mothers.

Counties in Oregon denied other women pensions when they were divorced or
had been deserted by their husbands, when they had some property, or when for
whatever reason they were not deemed worthy.[79] These women could bring cases
before the state appellate courts but were unlikely to win.[80] If a state legislature
had clearly limited payment to indigent women, the courts could safeguard public purpose through supervising lower-level decisions. The new powers of the state
were worked out not only through the broad-brush decisions made in the legislatures but also through the slow accretion of decisions made by the administrators,
juvenile court judges, and appellate court judges who participated in overseeing
the system.

Whether the restriction was first stated in the statute or in the supervising decisions made by the courts, throughout the country payments were to go to *indigent*
mothers. Even when mothers pensions' had been enacted after reformers advocated transforming those payments from poor relief to desert, the courts con-
curred with many local officials in their refusal to recognize the *work* of mothering. That mothers provided good care was not a sufficient reason to pay them;
only destitute and desperate mothers appeared to them as deserving of public sup-

port. The glimpses of administration available in the appellate cases, however, illustrate its variability. Few women were in any position to appeal, allowing courts and other administrators substantial practical discretion. Consequently, although at law, payments could go only to indigent mothers, the social workers in any particular county might choose to grant them more generously.[81]

American Law Reports, the primary synthesis of state law, summarized the law on mothers' pensions in 1917. Citing *Buckstegge,* the decision from Arizona that had struck down pensions, the journal remarked, "Of course, such statutes should be confined to indigent persons."[82] By disseminating *Buckstegge,* that report settled commentators' uncertainty about whether "public purpose" was a live doctrine. Indeed, as the taken-for-granted character of this comment in *American Law Reports* suggests, the statutes authorizing mothers' pensions *were* based in indigence; Arizona quickly reenacted its program on that basis. Furthermore, virtually all the states limited pensions to widows rather than including women who had children but were unmarried, abandoned, or simply poor.

Conclusion: Women's Dependence

Before 1920, most women's obligations in law were to their husbands and their households; they could not serve the state, because they had no political obligations.[83] The relationship between mother and child was natural, not a matter of political obligation or choice; fatherless children were best off with "their natural protector," their mother.[84] Children's first natural *financial* protector was their father, rather than than the state. The natural relationship between men and their dependents meant that the state could pay pensions to firemen's dependents because the men had earned them, and the natural relationship allowed the state just as easily to grant such funds to dependents. In mothers' pensions cases, the natural relationship allowed the state to pay some women the money they needed to support children. Men's primary responsibility for children brings the legal denial of pensions to divorced or deserted women into sharp focus: whether or not their parents were divorced, children remained the responsibility of their fathers; a child who had a living father, however far away, was thought to have no need of a pension.[85] Mothers' pensions recognized a natural relationship among family members, not a political tie between the state and the mother.

The gendered assumptions that prevailed in the courts were expressed in their language and shaped their decisions. The judges did not cite either civil service pension cases or military pensions to support rulings on the worthiness of mothers' pensions, because those cases did not raise the same issues. Instead, in the judges' way of thinking, mothers' pensions remained similar to poor relief and emerged from the state's obligation to support the poor. For most courts, performance by the intrinsically dependent woman of her quintessential role of mother was not work. Instead, it demonstrated dependence.

Women remained dependent in law even after legal changes increased their independence. In 1918, women still did not have the national franchise, although they could vote in some states.[86] Since the 1840s most states had allowed married women to hold property; they could keep their earnings, thanks to post–Civil War state statutes, but judges often interpreted that power restrictively.[87] Until 1923, protective labor legislation was deemed constitutional for women workers, as it was not for men, because women were not able to make legal contracts freely. Labor legislation could not impinge on a freedom of contract that women did not have.[88]

All the work that women did was seen as marking their dependence and their natural subordination to men. Much of the work that married women performed for wages resembled their unpaid work in the home: they sewed, sold meals to workers, and took in boarders. That similarity made it easy for courts to call a woman's work part of her obligation to her husband.[89] In the struggles waged during the early twentieth century over how far courts could govern labor, judges held fast to the belief that they were governing the natural relationship of master and servant, which legislatures could not change; no more they could change the natural dependence of women.[90] No wonder courts recognized children, rather than women, in ratifying mothers' pensions and approvingly noted that women who received pensions were subject to courts' or caseworkers' tutelage for the quality of their mothering.

Republican citizenship requires contribution more than contract, and those who drew analogies between mothers' pensions and soldiers' pensions tried to explain that child rearing was women's contribution to the polity. The courts could not see that women had a stake in the state based in contract or mutual obligation. Women's contribution to the state was welfare rather than warfare, mothering rather than soldiering or civil service, and it was natural rather than political. Advocates for mothers' pensions could and did consider mothering a contribution.[91] As Carole Pateman has argued, that contribution "is not seen as part of, or as relevant to, their citizenship, but as a necessary part of the private tasks proper to their sex." Sexual reproduction is a precontractual requirement for the reproduction of the political world.[92] In a political world in which contract expresses the political equality of all citizens, to have no contractual stake in the state is to risk exclusion. Yet because rearing children was always exclusive to women rather than something appropriate to citizenship, the courts erased it as a public contribution. Basing women's contribution on biology is troubling, for it does not reflect politically considered action. It can implicitly require motherhood of women. In the early twentieth century in the United States, however, when advocates for women posited child rearing as women's contribution to the polity, at law, they lost.

Courts, ruling in continuity with the common law, regarded motherhood as a disability, analogous to conditions such as blindness or insanity that might make a man eligible for poor relief. In the famous United States Supreme Court case *Muller v. Oregon* (1908), the Court did note the benefit to the public of child rearing. To most of the state courts, though, child rearing was more worthy of pity than of gratitude. No mutual contract for service on the basis of biology and child rearing existed between mothers and the state. Legally, indigent motherhood might entitle a woman to charity, but nothing more. The courts' insistence on service in other pension cases reinforced the advocates' analogy between motherhood and military service, but it was not persuasive legally. The presumption about the lack of contribution also applied to disabled men, who were considered necessarily dependent; it was dependency, of which mothering was only one part, that made payments charity.

In placing mothers' pensions in the category of social welfare benefits for the indigent rather than among those defined as as a reward for service, courts continued to treat women as intrinsically dependent. Women most readily received public support through the underfunded mothers' pensions programs or as dependents of men who had served the state. In insisting on service as a requirement of state payments for people who were not indigent, the courts participated in the uneasy efforts of the elite to stave off the expansion of a dependent class, a category composed of people who lacked the independence that citizenship required.[93] Because work was so central to granting pensions in American life, however, some women who were also teachers also gained pensions; the extremely low pay they received guaranteed desperate dependence after retirement if they had no pensions.[94]

Mothers' pensions did not concern only the place of women in the polity. Instead, the control some states were willing to exert over county commissioners—as when the state board asked for help from the attorney general in Mrs. Dougherty's case in Pennsylvania—represented some of the significant changes in governance during the Progressive Era. In many states, mothers' pensions were a county option and remained without state supervision. Still, Frank Goodnow's belief that the new world of governance lay in the development of accountable administrative powers was evident in judges' puzzled evaluation of the mixing of powers which the new programs brought.

Mothers' pensions, though underfunded and administered with substantial discretion, were nevertheless enacted in most of the states between 1910 and 1920. Workmen's compensation, one of the social insurance advocates' favored programs, also fared well during the same period.

CHAPTER SEVEN

Pensions for the Blind and Workmen's Compensation, 1906–1917

The social workers, economists, and lawyers who took European social policy as their model saw a set of programs the United States ought to borrow, from mothers' pensions to compensation for unemployment, industrial accidents, and old age (the last of these paid for through the fiction of public insurance). The tracks that these energetic and prolific writers left lead to the coherent set of programs that social insurance advocates worked for and their conception of these programs as distinct from poor relief and connected to industrial labor. The language of pensions was an attractive way to frame new spending programs that provided payments for individuals and abandoned almshouses and orphanages as ways of providing for the poor, whoever they were; pensions did not have to be specific to soldiers, mothers, or the elderly.

Pensions were both a reward for service and payment to those who had become disabled. Since disability implied intrinsic dependence, which merited only poor relief whereas service implied capability, instituting payments to those who had become disabled could put to the test questions of what service meant. But one program that does not fit within the framework of service succeeded across the states: payments to the blind. In considering both benefits for the blind and workmen's compensation, state court justices decisively held labor to be service, allowing payments outside of poor relief for those who had been injured. Without labor, no one earned such payments.

Pensions for the Blind

If blindness itself led to a pension rather than poor relief, anything could. The social logic of pensions would have required that the blind receive pensions only if they had been injured at work or in war, yet if they had become blind in either of those settings, workmen's compensation or military pensions should have satisfied claims. Pensions did not come about through an unfolding social logic, however, but through political struggle, and organizations of the blind proved particularly good at those politics, though their skill did not necessarily persuade courts when programs were tested.

In 1904, Ohio became the first state to enact pensions for the blind: the legislature provided individual payments for "dependent people" and eliminated almshouses. The state constitution, however, mandated almshouses for the poor, and nothing in the statute said the pensions could *replace* public relief. This contradiction enabled a county unwilling to pay the new relief to bring a case to court. If the new pensions did not replace public relief, then raising the funds for them would unconstitutionally take taxpayers' property, and eliminating almshouses would violate the constitutional requirement that the states provide institutions for the poor. In 1906 the state supreme court held:

> If a bounty may be conferred upon individuals of one class, then it may be
> upon individuals of another class, and if upon two, then upon all. And if upon
> those who have physical infirmities, then why not upon other classes who for
> various reason may be unable to support themselves? And if these things may be
> done, why may not all property be distributed by the state?[1]

Payments to individuals, rather than to institutions, threatened property rights, the court ruled.

The Ohio legislature responded to the court by revising pensions for the blind, making pensions replace public relief, thereby preempting another court challenge. Only after pensions were revised again in 1913 did the courts once more address their constitutionality. In redrafting the legislation in 1913 the state not only reaffirmed the substitution of pensions for poor relief but also decided that the constitutional requirement of an institution for the blind could be fulfilled by making payments—just as the state of Arizona would argue in eliminating its almshouses and establishing a state-administered program of pensions for mothers with dependent children and the elderly. In a significant departure from previous policy and practice, the state of Ohio made the payment mandatory if blind people did not have the means to support themselves; they no longer had to turn to relatives for support. The Ohio Supreme Court struck down that part of the law; the poor law had made family responsible for the poor first, before the state, and state courts read that requirement into the meaning of indigence. Relief payments for the blind were to be reserved for the indigent, not given to those who might have families who could help.[2]

The Ohio decision became an important precedent in other states and was discussed by legal commentators, who wrote as though legal decisions were statements of general principles. Pensions for the blind seemed generally acceptable when framed as a substitute for poor relief. Other states followed Ohio, enacting pensions for the blind and making clear that they substituted for poor relief.[3] A leading advocate for the blind, Harry Best, acknowledged in his 1919 survey of the history and conditions of blindness in the United States that "pension" usually implied previous service and thus was often inappropriate for the blind, but he relied on the term because "it has such a wide acceptance in popular usage."[4]

Advocates for the blind ensured that Ohio's decision in *Lucas County v. State* would not become lost in the obscurities of state constitutional law. Best's 1919 report, written for the American Red Cross, noted the importance of the Ohio dispute as a general difficulty for states.[5] The next major report on pensions for the blind, which came out in 1929, was commissioned by the American Foundation for the Blind.[6] The authors, Robert Irwin and Evelyn McKay, explained that constitutionality limited state pension laws. They dismissed the common analogy with soldiers' pensions, remarking that service was not a justification for payments to the disabled. They did not highlight men who had been blinded during military or industrial employment, which would have pitched the debate toward service; instead, they presented pensions for the blind as an improved form of poor relief.[7] When "pensions" had become a way of describing any state payments that were not poor relief, even those who advocated such payments could believe the language was overextended.

The language of pensions and charity pervaded public discussion because commentators such as Irwin and McKay ensured that it did. Courts play such a significant role in American political life that lawyers have long had a say in the design of public policy; those who write about the law for public consumption give law an even wider play. The principles that the Ohio court enunciated concerning pensions reached beyond pensions for the blind to the whole range of social insurance programs under discussion, especially workmen's compensation. Because states could comply with the warning signals that *Lucas County* provided by simply enacting pensions in the right form—as the state of Ohio had finally done—any analysis of the place constitutional requirements took in shaping programs was more likely to underestimate than to overestimate their significance. Difficult to miss in the contested politics of the age were the constitutional disputes concerning workmen's compensation. Those injured at work merited payment only when they were completely disabled, as objects of charity, or when they had served in hazardous industries.

Service and Hazard in Workmen's Compensation

The physical risks entailed in industrial employment were a serious problem in the early twentieth century. Accidents left many families without an adult male breadwinner; a man's death or disability could leave an already poor family desperate. Social surveys made the social as well as financial costs of industrial accidents visible to reformers, whose own white-collar jobs posed little risk to life and limb. Surveys documented not only that many suffered injury but also that few received anything from employers thereafter. Most famously, Crystal Eastman analyzed the incidence of industrial accidents in Allegheny County, Pennsylvania, during 1907 and 1908; few people gained any compensation at all from employers, she found.[8] State commissions also collected information on occupational injuries and deaths. Those injured at work were left to poor relief if the legal system did not compensate them.

As scholars have explained so well, both injured people's and employers' use of the legal system led to the creation of workmen's compensation.[9] In the nineteenth century, people who had been injured at work had no other recourse than to sue their employers for compensation. Given the legal doctrines regarding liability, they were unlikely to recover. In the eyes of the liability system's defenders, the ineffectiveness of litigation and the skimpiness of employers' payments were the (correct) result of employers' not being forced to compensate an employee for his own carelessness, which would have been unjust.[10]

Juries, however, sympathized with injured people and found ways to compensate them despite legal obstacles. State appellate courts would sometimes carve out exceptions to the doctrines to allow injured workers to recover from employers. As a result, those employers who faced a large number of suits, particularly railroads, were dissatisfied with the haphazard and unpredictable system of liability that became the standard practice in law. During the late nineteenth century, railroads tried to force people to contract out of their rights by requiring employees to sign an agreement that they would not sue if they were injured at work. State legislatures attempted to prohibit employers from writing such conditions.[11] Advocates for labor deplored the courts' reluctance to hold employers accountable systematically and reliably. By 1910, reformers interested in labor issues were well aware that many European countries had enacted social insurance to compensate people for injuries incurred at work.[12] Some form of regular payment for injuries, administered through the states, could address the difficulties that litigation raised for all sides.

Across the political spectrum, from business federations to labor advocates, those concerned with labor issues were searching to transform the system of liability for injuries at work. States began to settle on workmen's compensation— which was not poor relief because it was paid regardless of a worker's income and assets. It did not put the disabled in almshouses but paid them individually. The employers themselves paid the insurance through taxation, reminiscent of the targeted taxation that had been challenged in the earliest firemen's cases. Since the taxes were not paid out of general funds, however, they would not seem to raise the same problems as general taxation for the benefit of retiring civil servants.

Perhaps labor for an employer did not then have to be identical to public service. Just as with the early cases for firemen's charities, however, because the state raised the money through taxation rather than through a wholly voluntary contribution from employers, the statute was subject to constitutional requirements. The state had to be taxing for a public purpose, which raised all the familiar questions concerning what service was and whether labor was service. Not until this period and the cases it brought did the social insurance advocates' arguments that the soldiers of industry had earned payments, just as military soldiers had, begin to hold any sway in the courts.

Like mothers' pensions, workmen's compensation programs spread rapidly. New York enacted the first in 1910, and the plan had expanded to twenty more states by 1913. These programs were challenged in court: since they were not poor relief, they had to involve payments for service, but the money was going to employees in private industry rather than to public servants. If workmen's compensation were to be deemed constitutional, it would contribute to defining all forms of labor as public service: That is, workers served simply by working. If danger was the key to serving, though, workmen's compensation would have to be limited by law to hazardous occupations. Accepting that risk was part of working, those who drafted the statutes specified coverage for those in hazardous occupations. That might prevent the courts from striking down legislation as transferring money from one private group to another. In workmen's compensation the two strands of public purpose came together: people could be paid because they served, and people could be paid because they were disabled.

Central here is the transformation of employment from something in which one engages as a matter of private gain and private concern to employment as a matter of public concern. American social welfare benefits have often been tied to employment, as public pensions for firemen, soldiers, and civil servants and private pensions for employees of large corporations demonstrate. Not all public employment entailed such benefits, but one had to be either in public employment or pitiable to gain public payments. With workmen's compensation, the logic of employment and pity both expanded. (That expansion opened the way to thinking of old age pensions as constitutional as well, though the existing doctrines still imposed limits.) All of employment could be seen as hazardous and worthy of public payment, at least when public payment was funded through a tax on employers.

The cases challenging workmen's compensation raised questions about how much legislatures could change the common law, since workmen's compensation abolished the requirement that employers be found negligent in order to be held liable for an employee's injury. For purposes of this discussion, however, what matters is the public purpose that made workmen's compensation constitutional. Businesses sued to stop the programs; in particular, not all railroad companies saw them as an improvement over the old system of determining liability based on negligence.

New York established a commission to study employers' liability. The Wainwright Commission, named after the senator who chaired it, recommended in its 1910 report that the legislature adopt a bill for workmen's compensation that would protect employees in a few industries: the construction trades, any work that required explosives, and work on railroads. The commission expected to expand the list of covered trades, but the crucial point was that they had to be inherently dangerous. New York's program did not last long; in 1911, in the very first case to be brought before it, the state's highest court struck down workmen's compensation.[13]

Constitutional debates invite debates concerning all manner of public concerns, and New York's workmen's compensation case led to debate about the courts, disability, and social welfare legislation. Taxation provided the entry point: no one would deny that states or counties had to support the disabled. If they supported those who *could* work, though, they reached beyond the traditional definition of poor relief, and then taxation was nothing more than illegitimately transferring tax money. Therefore, some of the controversy in the New York case, *Ives v. South Buffalo Railway*, centered on the meaning of disability. People were disabled when they became unable to work for the rest of their lives; "disabled" was a status.

Earl Ives, whose injuries occasioned New York's courtroom battle, claimed workmen's compensation after he was injured on the railroad. Theodore Roosevelt criticized the decisions of the New York Court of Appeals by playing up pity for Ives, noting that he could no longer support his family. In response, William Guthrie, the New York corporate lawyer who had been so involved in litigating Progressive Era legislation, noted that Ives had been out of work for only four weeks and that losing wages for four weeks was not a serious hardship.[14] The loss of four weeks' wages is no small matter for people who live paycheck to paycheck; but hardship or not, poor law commissioners would never have paid a man who could return to work. Therefore, neither should any new program, according to Guthrie. If Ives was not truly disabled, then paying him would violate the requirement that the state not pay private groups.

States enacted a variety of programs to try to work around constitutional difficulties.[15] Many states made employers' participation in workmen's compensation programs optional, (although they gave businesses incentives to participate), and voluntary programs meant that the state was not taking property and therefore did not invoke the public purpose requirements. What remained was to have the United States Supreme Court rule concerning whether these new programs violated the U.S. Constitution's Fourteenth Amendment by taking property without due process of law.

The U.S. Supreme Court decided cases involving the constitutionality of various state workmen's compensation plans in 1917.[16] In a pattern familiar from civil service pension cases, the Court approved of states' preventing dependence, or the need for poor relief, by paying money to individuals who had somehow merited or earned the money. The Court also noted the significance of dangerousness, which the states had defined in statutes, and drew on soldiers' pensions to argue that those who risked their lives at work were just as worthy of pensions as those who risked their lives in war. Working for wages at dangerous labor thus became service. Just as civil service pensions had validated all forms of public labor as service, so laboring for a private employer became the equivalent of state service. Dangerousness made it so: like soldiers, men on the railroads risked their lives.

New York Central Railroad Company v. White (1917) tested New York's workmen's compensation against the federal Fourteenth Amendment. Justice Mahlon Pitney, writing for the U.S. Supreme Court, held that pensions would prevent pauperism and thus served a state purpose. The program represented an expansion of the poor law, and providing for the poor had always been a state purpose. He pronounced the newly revised New York workmen's compensation law superior to poor relief: "One of the grounds of its concern with the continued life and earning power of the individual is its interest in the prevention of pauperism, with its concomitants of vice and crime."[17] Workmen's compensation, like civil service pensions, did not represent dependence but prevented it by keeping people who had been disabled in industrial accidents out of almshouses and the demoralization thought to result from institutionalization.

The U.S. Supreme Court decided *Mountain Timber v. Washington* on the same day as *New York Central Railroad Company v. White*. The state of Washington had tried to ensure the general public benefit of its workmen's compensation program by decreeing that virtually all industrial work was hazardous. The lawyers challenging the law argued before the Supreme Court that "life is hazardous. Demonstrably many of the industries named in the law are not extra hazardous as compared with agricultural or domestic occupations. Statistically, agriculture, for example, proves one of the most hazardous of all occupations, more hazardous than railroading. Yet farming is omitted from the act." Citing *Lochner v. New York* (1905), which had struck down regulation of hours for bakers, the attorneys continued: "Legislative fiat cannot make hazard if none exists."[18]

In this case, the Court did not compare occupations but accepted the characterization of work itself as hazardous and of workers as therefore eligible for workmen's compensation. As Justice Pitney explained, workmen's compensation simply prevented the need for poorhouses:

> It hardly would be questioned that the State might expend public moneys to provide hospital treatment, artificial limbs or other like aid to persons injured in industry, and homes or support for the widows and orphans of those killed. Does direct compensation stand on less secure ground?[19]

Of course, expanding public purpose to allow not just poor relief but programs for the *prevention* of pauperism could erase the boundaries of the category, as expansions of categories within legal reasoning often do: *any* state payment to someone who could not work, for whatever reason, could prevent pauperism. Louis Brandeis, the eminent corporate lawyer who was also committed to social welfare legislation, cheered the decision for just that reason.[20] Preventing the necessity of paying for poor relief had appeared on occasion in other state employers' liability cases.[20] But this ruling seems a sudden and expansive departure from precedent unless one understands that judges still believed that general principles governed across fields of law.

Analogies with military pensions were central to the U.S. Supreme Court in a way that had been unthinkable during the nineteenth century, when wage labor was not seen as identical with public service and when a war had been fought on American soil within memory. The Court reinforced its support for workmen's compensation by quoting the Washington state decision: "Under our statute the workman is the soldier of organized industry accepting a kind of pension in exchange for absolute insurance on his master's premises."[21] In *Mountain Timber*, Justice Pitney wrote for the Court:

> A familiar exercise of state power is the grant of pensions to disabled soldiers and to the widows and dependents of those killed in war. Such legislation usually is justified as fulfilling a moral obligation or as tending to encourage the performance of the public duty of defense. But is the State powerless to compensate, with pensions or otherwise, those who are disabled, or the dependents of those whose lives are lost, in the industrial occupations that are so necessary to develop the resources and add to the wealth and prosperity of the State? A machine as well as a bullet may produce a wound, and the disabling effect may be the same.[22]

Perhaps the effect was the same, but in earlier reasoning it was not the effect that was significant but rather the service rendered. In considering workmen's compensation, courts still cited service, but its boundaries had come close to dissolving. By 1917 all hazardous work was service if a legislature said so, allowing workmen's compensation even at a time when the U.S. Supreme Court had a reputation of being hostile to labor legislation. Working for a railroad had become like serving in the military, with no distinction necessary between the railroad and the state. All industrial work had become like soldiering because it was dangerous and also because it was useful, not just to the individual employee who earned wages but to the state as a whole.

Both Supreme Court decisions supported the position of social insurance advocates, who urged that industrial life was of public benefit, so its costs ought to be shared. The Court did not hold that such a program would make people dependent or falsely treat them as dependent when they were poor and working, as the nineteenth-century cases on state aid to business had done. The Court did not address injury as an individual problem at all but saw it rather as a social cost attached to a social benefit. That way, courts could treat all who worked in industry as contributing to the social welfare, whereas only those employed in the public service had been so regarded during the late nineteenth century. The new interpretation also represented a shift from the early cases on the regulation of labor, in which men were treated as working only for their individual benefit. In those cases both the state legislatures and the Supreme Court still took the public purpose doctrine into account by going to the trouble of explaining why new programs fit within it; they suggested that the doctrine was alive even while allowing a dramatic rethinking of what counted as a general social cost and benefit.

Conclusion

In sum, workmen's compensation cases extended the framework of what constituted a public purpose in spending programs, allowing that wage labor could count as service from which the entire society benefited. Workmen's compensation was not charity, so states did not have to pay only those injured or disabled workers who were also indigent. State statutes quickly proliferated and varied in their terms, encouraging litigants to forum-shop.[23] The basic principle established, though, was that the schemes were indeed constitutional.

With thousands of industrial injuries yearly, judges could readily imagine the virtue of service as dangerous and masculine: analogies between industrial labor and military service enabled the program to satisfy the public purpose doctrine. Workmen's compensation was not charity. Although the program was designed in part to prevent dependence on poor relief among the wives and children of men who had been disabled by industrial accidents, no judge or commentator compared it with mothers' pensions. Women figured in these programs only as dependents of men or employees who worked in hazardous trades. The military analogy reinforced the assumption that men earned payments through work, and only hazardousness legitimated public intervention in the conditions of labor for men (no such justification was cited for women workers). In *New York Central Railroad Co. v. White,* the U.S. Supreme Court was clear: the state could limit men's much heralded liberty of contract because it was doing so for hazardous employment, "and the public has a direct interest in this as affecting the common welfare."[24]

Constitutional law allows the rethinking of legal categories; interested parties strategize around constitutional limits all the time, as is evident in the changing definitions of service articulated in the workmen's compensation cases. Yet the legal ethic that a judge must at least engage precedent by citing, following, or differentiating his or her decision from decisions in earlier cases meant that cases such as *State v. Osawkee Township* (1875), which had prohibited aid to farmers as class legislation, provided a basis for continued challenges to new programs as long as even one irate taxpayer could hire a lawyer and raise the old doctrine in court. Legal knowledge shaped the creation of state welfare programs because the courts were so prominent as administrators and arbitrators of how states might take on their new tasks.

In its 1917 decisions the United States Supreme Court endorsed the argument that all hazardous work could be public service, or at least something in which the public had an interest, and state-run payments outside of poor relief could serve legitimate public purposes. The Court also agreed that if paying for hospitals and other institutions for the injured and disabled was legitimate, so was paying them directly. These holdings would suggest that old age pensions, which many states were by then seriously considering, might also be constitutional.[25] The transformation to a system in which constitutionally the states could take on new social welfare functions was slow, however, and old age pensions without a means test simply never happened until the United States undertook them in 1935. Although the decisions upholding civil service pensions and workmen's compensation blurred the distinctions between service and labor, disability and ability, and public- and private-sector employment, justices and lawyers still articulated their thinking in those terms.

CHAPTER EIGHT

Old Age Pensions, 1911–1937

Before pensions were available, many worked until they were incapable of working anymore, whether because of recession or injury or encroaching age. During the nineteenth century, old people who were no longer able to work and had no relatives to care for them were generally relegated to almshouses, although some received outdoor poor relief instead. State and local governments who feared state institutions for their low-wage employees would sometimes retain them despite their inability to work.[1] Counties chose myriad forms of relief, sometimes separating and sometimes mixing the aged, the disabled, and children.[2]

Social insurance advocates made pensions for the elderly a central part of their program, but between 1914 and 1935 their efforts encountered court challenges. Given the expansion of pensions to civil servants and the payments under workmen's compensation, it seemed possible that any labor could merit payments under public purpose requirements in state jurisprudence. Despite stern language, courts did provide a stamp of approval for civil service pensions, continually reshaping public purpose requirements. Rewarding *all* labor as service, however, went further than any court was willing to go. Old age pensions for all who had labored for wages had to await the New Deal.

Old people whose physical infirmities made them unable to work, who had exhausted whatever savings they had been able to accumulate, and who lacked relatives to support them could only rely upon public charity. Such indigent persons were very different from those who had been granted pensions during the decades after the Civil War. Military veterans, firemen and policemen, and other civil servants had framed government payments as a return for the service they had rendered the state. Each group that followed could argue only in the language at hand, claiming that its members, too, had earned payments because they had served and should be spared the ignominy of dependence. Public pensions for all elderly people who had worked for wages, which by 1910 had champions in the states, depended constitutionally on the argument that *all* work—not just dangerous work or work in public employment—constituted service. The legal struggle undertaken by advocates of public pension programs tried to change such pensions from poor relief into payments that recipients were regarded as having earned through honorable service. The easiest way to do that was to build on the cultural practices that had made all waged work significant for citizenship: those who labored, served.

Constitutional requirements, however, mattered beyond the few court cases that disgruntled taxpayers and county commissioners brought. How far they mattered is, once again, impossible to know. Threats of lawsuits could shape decisions *not* to pursue legislation or funding, as it had after World War I concerning bonds raised to pay bounties in New York. Most of the decisions not to pursue a new program no doubt occurred in discussions never recorded, perhaps in a threat made on the floor of a state legislature or among state officials. It is therefore unknown quite how far or how often the expectation of constitutional problems discouraged advocates even before a court had an opportunity to vindicate constitutions as unchanging principles by striking down a state program.

The expectations of problems did leave some traces, however. Reformers kept their ideas circulating in their writings, and by the early twentieth century, commentators were worrying in print about the limits new programs might face. State study commissions also mentioned potential problems in their reports. Remnants of the *state* basis of American citizenship still colored state-paid pensions, giving reformers even greater reason to support federal pensions. Not until the federal government had enacted the 1935 Social Security Act did states answer the courts with constitutional amendments to enable pensions.

Commentary: Keeping the Law Alive

Law professors who were active in the politics of reform and the corporate litigators who were still eager to sue guaranteed the ongoing relevance of constitutional categories to social policy debates. Scholars kept the cases alive by discussing them as serious elements shaping reform possibilities, even while the courts stretched requirements at the behest of lawyers. Frank Goodnow, the scholar of administrative law at Columbia University who wanted to turn conversations away from constitutionality and toward *how* power was exercised, found constitutional limits on social spending programs unavoidable. His 1911 book, *Social Reform and the Constitution,* was part of the series "American Social Progress" which Macmillan published for the "student and general reader" (according to the description inside the book). Many economists, lawyers, and sociologists who were spreading the gospel of social reform in the United States wrote for the series, including Edward T. Devine and Henry Rogers Seager. Americans could not avoid considering constitutional questions if they wanted to talk about social welfare. Courts made the doctrine relevant, and commentators ensured that people knew it.

Although the title of his book referred to *the* Constitution, implying that there was only one, Goodnow addressed the constitutionality of social reform programs at the state as well as the federal level. State courts handled state issues under state constitutions, and Goodnow was right to turn his attention to those. His book, however, chiefly addressed the regulatory powers of the federal government, government ownership, and the constitutionality of government aid to businesses and individuals, including the constitutionality of the new social insurance. In 1912, the *American Political Science Review* published part of the book as an article titled "The Constitutionality of Old Age Pensions," thus spreading the word across the academic reform community. Goodnow observed that state courts had been much more aggressive in limiting what the states could do than the federal courts had been under the U.S. Constitution.[3] Although he noted that state constitutional law was not uniform, the habits of mind that treated law as a uniform and coherent whole persisted, and his discussion of government aid generalized from particular state court cases.

Goodnow made the rapidly emerging but still heretical point that the Constitution was not sacred either in its current interpretation or in its design. The attitude of members of the U.S. Supreme Court blocked some social reform legislation unnecessarily, he contended; state constitutions and the federal Constitution could be reinterpreted in response to social change. Furthermore, if reinterpretation did not go far enough to legitimate new policies, the United States could look to the constitutions of Germany and Canada and revise its own, securing "to the national government greater powers than are believed by many to be accorded to the government of the United States under the present Constitution."[4] Ironically, however, in treating the law as a serious limit on constitutional reform, Goodnow participated in the continuing resurrection of old cases that provided a more serious limit than the constitutional provisions themselves did. *Stare decisis,* the obligation of courts to follow past decisions, made constitutions much less flexible than they might otherwise have been. Goodnow criticized the principle of *stare decisis* because it made new programs so difficult to enact.[5]

Goodnow treated old age, sickness, and unemployment compensation as raising similar constitutional problems. (He never mentioned mothers' pensions, though they were also under consideration in the states; they were simply revised charity and did not raise the same problems that social insurance would.) Although he had denounced the courts for their inflexible commitment to precedent, since courts took it seriously he necessarily engaged in the imaginative work of analogy building and law building when he searched through the cases and envisioned their possible consequences for new programs. After all, in 1911 no state had yet enacted and no state court had ruled upon old age pensions or workmen's compensation. His was a normative and predictive enterprise. In the imagined analogies, one can see how the idea of service continued to shape practice in law.

Civil service pensions provided the only parallel Goodnow could find for old age pensions. But the constitutionality of the one promised little for the other, Goodnow emphasized, for civil servants engaged in government service, and the elderly in general did not.[6] In his 1893 *Comparative Administrative Law,* he had pointed out the significance of service and office, both of which were distinct from mere employment by the state. Civil servants were not generally eligible for pensions in 1893; Goodnow had noted that European countries provided them, whereas the United States did not.[7] Still less would employment in the private sector entitle one to a public pension, or even suggest that such a pension program could be constitutional.

In his 1911 text, Goodnow argued that the United States had long provided for the poor through taxes, and ought to continue to do so. As he saw it, new social spending programs that were distinct from poor relief had to contend with *Loan Association v. Topeka,* the 1874 United States Supreme Court decision holding that under the Fourteenth Amendment states could spend only for a public purpose. Goodnow considered whether "public purpose" was a live doctrine in constitutional law; that the United States Supreme Court had been reluctant in recent years to use it to overturn state regulation made the doctrine less visible and more contested. He concluded that the states could determine what was a public purpose and that the federal courts did not need to govern this matter any longer. State courts still used the doctrine, however, and, as he had already observed, were generally more conservative than federal courts. Turning to the state courts did not promise innovation in approving public spending. His analysis tried to determine what they *had* held to be a public purpose.

Long-established public works programs such as roads and schools, he said, clearly fell within public purpose requirements.

> It is only when we come to the new functions the discharge of which changed economic and social conditions make it seem necessary for the state in either its central or local organizations to assume, that we meet with difficulty. What criterion are we to adopt when we come to consider such subjects as old age, accident and sickness pensions, which in some form appear to be essential parts of the program of social reform in Germany, England and Australasia?[8]

He could find no rulings that were directly relevant to his question. He reluctantly admitted, though, that any

> study of the cases which have held purposes to be private and therefore to be improper purposes of taxation can hardly fail to force the conclusion that any

purpose is an improper purpose for taxation which consists in the grant of public monies to individuals who are not in the service of the government or who cannot be regarded because of their poverty as fit subjects of public charity. An old age, accident or sickness pension which is not conditioned upon poverty would probably be regarded by the courts as unconstitutional where the funds from which it was paid were derived from taxation.[9]

Goodnow carefully explained the state court cases, revealing to the readers of the Macmillan series that current constitutional doctrine would not allow the states to give money to individual citizens for their own benefit; courts would view that as illegitimately transferring money from one private group to another, or a version of class legislation. He reluctantly concluded that "there is no great likelihood that a system of state pensions in the case of old age, sickness or accident which is based even on the indigence of the recipients of such pensions would be regarded as constitutional."[10]

Both his book and the article based on it reached back to *State v. Osawkee Township* (1875) regarding aid to farmers.[11] Although subsequent farm policy cases had directly confronted and respectfully dismissed the reasoning of Justice Brewer, *Osawkee Township* was still the leading case: a Supreme Court justice had decided it, and it took on a life well beyond that of the other state cases supporting farm aid. Ohio's case striking down benefits for the blind, *Lucas County v. Ohio,* also gave Goodnow reason to believe that pensions could not pass constitutional muster. His conclusion that only spending programs restricted to the indigent had a chance of gaining courts' approval was a serious blow to social insurance; conceding indigence as a requirement was just what the social insurance advocates wished to escape.[12]

Goodnow's student Howard McBain also kept the public-purpose doctrine alive while deploring it. McBain gained his Ph.D. in political science at Columbia in 1907. In 1913 he returned to Columbia as a professor of municipal administration and, in 1917, a professor of constitutional law. Like his mentor, McBain concerned himself with the difficulties of enacting pensions. When he wrote about pensions in 1914, he saw the boundaries that judges drew between public and private as real. That is, they were not just an expression of judges' beliefs, as reformers frustrated with federal court decisions limiting social spending had begun to contend. The constitutional limits were not just a curse; they could also ensure that the municipalities did not waste taxpayers' money by giving it away to those who did not merit public payments.

In a 1914 article, "Taxation for a Private Purpose," McBain argued:

while the principle is in one aspect a protection to municipal corporations it is in another aspect a restriction—a restriction which would doubtless present a formidable obstacle in the way of the adoption by American cities of some of the more paternalistic functions and some of the speculative business practices of their European contemporaries.[13]

States could spend, he noted, but only for service, and service was distinct from employment or citizenship. Unemployment or retirement programs funded by taxation and contributions from workers and paid out to *all* workers, not just state workers, could not satisfy constitutional requirements until all wage labor came to be regarded as public service. Even then, unemployment insurance would not be pronounced constitutional until judges viewed unemployment as a collective disaster rather than an individual failure, which would make insuring it of general rather than particular benefit. That decision would await the Great Depression.[14]

Exasperated with the U.S. Supreme Court, Goodnow and later McBain argued that the problem was not only the attitude of justices, which Goodnow deplored.[15] The very principles of the Constitution needed to become much more flexible to accommodate changing social needs, a perspective that expanded into public debate during the 1920s.[16] Goodnow's *Social Reform and the Constitution* articulated that concern: the eighteenth century had bequeathed to Americans a limited federal government that could not take on the tasks that modern society required of the polity.[17] McBain espoused the same position in 1927, arguing for a "living constitution," one that would change in response to social needs. He argued for principles so flexible that to conservative critics they seemed to be no principles at all; Goodnow and McBain seemed to abandon the idea of a constitution as a touchstone text.[18]

Although constitutional principles may have been exasperating, they were not as unbending as Goodnow and McBain feared.[19] Their readings of constitutional provisions were based on legal precedent; they did not capture the continuing expansion that many courts were willing to accept when confronted with new definitions of what made work into service. If workmen's compensation could find favor with the United States Supreme Court (chapter seven), perhaps the public purpose doctrine could stretch again to accommodate the work the elderly had done. State commissions tried that idea out, but when it came to a test in court, the argument failed.

Old Age Pensions in the States

After 1910, as proposals for new social welfare benefits circulated throughout the country, states began to consider pensions for the elderly. They conducted surveys investigating how counties supported their elderly poor, who the elderly poor were, and finally, albeit briefly, how constitutional provisions might limit what the states could do. As a practical matter, state commissions kept the constitutional categories alive in their reports.

Unlike mothers' pensions, pensions for the elderly were not widely adopted. Most states allowed counties to choose whether to implement them, making them an insignificant change from poor relief. Arizona enacted old age pensions in 1914, in the same initiative that created mothers' pensions. Montana, Nevada, and Pennsylvania enacted old age pensions in 1923. Only Arizona's and Pennsylvania's programs would have made pensions mandatory, however. Pension programs remained inoperative in Nevada; in Montana, counties chose whether to pay them or not, and no county administrator or taxpayer challenged them, because they hardly differed from poor relief. Colorado, Kentucky, Wisconsin, Maryland, Minnesota, Utah, Wyoming, and California all enacted old age pension programs between 1925 and 1929, each a matter of county option or dependent on county rather than state funding.[20] As soon as Colorado made old age pensions mandatory in 1931, however, county commissioners, who had no idea how they would pay for them, challenged the program in court. A lawsuit was the last effort when all other opposition to pensions had failed.

The constitutional politics of old age pensions mattered in every state that considered pensions. Some states considered constitutional amendments to allow pensions; in New Hampshire the state supreme court issued advisory opinions. Legal challenges were not brought in every state but all three states that before 1932 enacted mandatory programs not designed as poor relief—Arizona, Pennsylvania, and Colorado—faced constitutional challenges. Not the politics of the individual states or their particular constitutional provisions but the character of the programs they enacted explains whether anyone challenged their programs in court. If they were mandatory *and* were not restricted to the indigent, they landed in court, and judges immediately struck them down.

State commissions guaranteed the ongoing importance of legal knowledge, for their comprehensive reports included discussion of the legal implications of the pension programs they considered. Commission members were often social workers who would be responsible for administering new welfare programs, but invariably they included or consulted with attorneys and legal scholars within the reform community.

A Massachusetts report in 1910 expressed serious reservations about the constitutionality of old age pensions; every subsequent state commission cited it.[21] The commissioners in Massachusetts seriously doubted whether general old age pensions could be constitutional; they accurately distinguished between pensions for firemen and policemen, who had served the public, and those for the elderly as a whole, who had not. (Until 1912, the Massachusetts Supreme Court was even unwilling to allow aid to soldiers; see chapter four.) Later state reports ranged over the gamut of ways that constitutions could be interpreted; Ohio commissioners briefly and contemptuously commented on the obvious unconstitutionality of Arizona's pensions, which could easily be remedied with better drafting.[22]

Other reports took a more reflective approach that treated principles as open to continual reinterpretation. Wisconsin's commission tried to answer the objections voiced in the Massachusetts report:

> A doubt may be raised whether the state has power, under the existing constitu-
> tion, to provide support for the aged poor who are not totally indigent. But to
> argue that such old age relief is not a public purpose is to argue that the state
> has no interest in the material well being of needy citizens who are not paupers.
> To assure a reasonable degree of comfort and security to aged workmen, to so
> distribute the burden of supporting the superannuated that it will not bear too
> heavily upon particular families of the working generation and thereby to secure
> fuller nurture and better education for the young—surely these are legitimate
> objects of public taxation. Old age support is deemed a public purpose in nearly
> all industrial countries outside the United States and will doubtless be so con-
> sidered in this country whenever public opinion is ripe for such a step.[23]

According to the Wisconsin commission, the state constitution did not necessarily require amendment, nor did its current interpretation represent only the arbitrary will of some judges. The people needed not a new constitution or new
judges but a collective willingness to rethink the meaning of constitutional provisions. In short, the constitutional problems mattered but were not insurmount-
able. The Wisconsin commission issued this report in 1915, well before the extended American debate so noticeable during the 1920s concerning the need for a
flexible constitution that would recognize changing social circumstances.[24] Rethinking particularities did not capture the flexibility that this commission
deemed necessary. Close thinking about constitutionality would have been futile
anyway, since the precedent was so thoroughly, if implicitly, hostile to payments
that were neither for charity nor for state service. It seemed better simply to accept
the problem and urge wider reflection on where the United States might fit with
the European industrialized nations that were so eagerly pursuing social welfare
programs.

Commissioners in Pennsylvania tried to strategize around the state constitution. They began with a comprehensive survey of the provision of old age pensions in other countries, discussion of such provision in other states, and the administration of almshouses in Pennsylvania. Much of the commission's effort
went into showing that those who lived in the almshouses were not dissolute or
lazy, as those who opposed pensions believed. Instead, the commission argued,
the difference between those who needed public assistance and those who did not

was their ability to rely on family: those in the almshouses had no family to support them; those who lived in the community did. A summary of the 1919 report stated the case succinctly: "The aged worker is thrown upon his own resources. This condition of impotence is augmented still further by the break-up of the family in modern society which often thrusts the aged worker into a strange country or community without friends or relatives."[25] Moreover, the difference between those who could and could not care for themselves was not attributable to differences in thrift or moral worth. To refute those who denigrated the poor, the commissioners asked former employers of the elderly to testify to their hardworking character. Surely those who had worked all their lives *deserved* state pensions.

Documenting that the elderly in poorhouses had spent their lives working demonstrated that they deserved payments, unlike those who had not worked. By 1919, men's labor was seen as part of citizenship. Paying people for something other than working would create dependence not suitable for the rigors of republican citizenship. The Pennsylvania commission answered the complaint on its own grounds: almshouses did not simply recognize a dependency that already existed; instead, keeping people in almshouses created dependency. Those who had labored had earned any payments they might receive. The commission's reference to the "impotence" of former workers who were living in almshouses also highlighted the connection between manliness and self-support. If fears about creating a dependent population shaped the reluctance to enact social welfare programs, ameliorating impotence was the Pennsylvania commission's concern in recommending old age pensions.[26] An insurance program that provided money only to those who had worked would restore independence, and therefore masculinity, rather than erode it.

The commissions were well aware of the constitutional problems that old age pensions could face. Each state made its own policy within a national conversation. Pennsylvania's constitution included the standard limits on spending, dating from 1873, which had proved decisive in other states. The leading national advocate for old age pensions, however, Abraham Epstein, served as the executive secretary of the Pennsylvania commission, and its report dismissed the concerns about constitutionality that had so worried the Massachusetts commissioners:

> The constitutionality of such a scheme is also questioned by the Massachusetts Commission. Strangely enough, however, it admits that firemen, policemen and teachers who "are not only rendering peculiarly hazardous meritorious services to society, but also have deprived themselves of the full opportunity of earning the largest returns for their services in a competitive way . . . have some claim upon the State for special consideration in the matter of public support in old age. This claim, however, cannot exist in the case of persons employed in the or-

dinary competitive callings." The fallacious method of the Commission's reasoning at this point is self-evident.[27]

Of course the reasoning in Massachusetts was not fallacious; firemen, policemen, and teachers had all served the state. The easiest way to argue that work was service was to dismiss the belief that it was not.

The civil service cases and workmen's compensation cases made it possible to assert that work was service. The Massachusetts commission still distinguished between the two. It observed that public pensions for civil servants whose occupations were not hazardous were constitutional because they had deliberately chosen not to get the "largest returns for their services." Ordinary laborers, however, had not made that sort of sacrifice for the public good. In a competitive labor market, workers ended up with their just deserts; those who were poor had simply not worked hard enough, or scrimped and saved enough, to provide for their old age.[28]

Far from being anomalies, the civil service pension cases shared a doctrinal thread with one of the most well-known cases of the early twentieth century, *Lochner v. New York* (1905), which struck down the regulation of hours for bakers in New York. Bakers made no sacrifices that justified limiting their hours, and baking bread was not especially hazardous, so there was no reason to protect bakers more than other workers from long hours.[29] Perhaps not all the elderly had been in hazardous employment, but the commissions continued to try to explain that workers had become disabled over time, meriting pensions as much as anyone else who had been worn down with service. Although they argued that pensions were earned, the reports also explained the helplessness of the elderly.

The Stories Commissions Told: Debility and Mobility

States could consider public policies as a series of discrete programs—first workmen's compensation, then old age pensions—but troubles often do not afflict people singly or sequentially. One affliction makes another harder to bear: aging makes dismissal from a job more likely, and family illness makes it more difficult to keep a job. Old age policy had implications for workmen's compensation and for the unemployment and sickness insurance that public policy advocates dreamed of. Although these policies were packaged separately, the stories that commissioners collected in their reports did not separate the difficulties workers encountered. Rather, they told of the complex difficulties of marginal employment, a lack of family, and injuries.

Commissions collected statistics on who lived in almshouses, how long they had worked, and how long elderly inmates had resided in the state. Old age pensions that recognized service to the state implied the significance of *state* citizenship and responsibility, even after the nationalization of citizenship that came with the Civil War and its constitutional amendments.[30] Although elderly Americans might have served in some other state, far from where they wished to claim an old age pension, they had to have become poor through no fault of their own and while working in the state in which they would claim a pension.

Even if the elderly were helpless as a result of a long life of service, the stories placed them in a category of helplessness shared by those with other disabilities. People who worked in industry for low wages, the trusting souls who had been cheated by swindlers common in "our present civilization," the widow, the farm laborer: these were the characters peopling the report of the Pennsylvania commission, bringing human interest to the abstract discussion of county boards and European systems of social insurance that otherwise dominated the report. For example, the Pennsylvania report described a woman worker who had been displaced by technological change:

> When the tobacco stripping machine was introduced, [Mrs. R. S.] was found too feeble to be adjusted to the machine and was, therefore, discharged although she was conceded one of the best workers. The company could not provide anything for her. She is now living with the factory foreman who took her in because he could not see her go to the poorhouse and she does her best in helping out with the family work.[31]

As the commission represented her, Mrs. R. S. had worked in the state and was poor through no fault of her own. Like many women, though, she did not end up living in the poorhouse. Men outnumbered women in almshouses; women who still could offer services in exchange for support more often lived with relatives, other families, or on their own.[32]

Housing the elderly in almshouses alongside the insane and the disabled blurred the distinctions that the commissioners wished to make between congenital dependency, degradation resulting from vice, and the debility that followed a lifetime of labor.[33] Old age pensions could not possibly undermine masculinity when men's likely alternative was the poorhouse, where they shared living space with those who were intrinsically dependent, ill, or insane. To commissioners, pensions represented dignity rather than dependency.

The stories the old age commissions told made old age look quite a bit like disability, however much they tried to make the lives of the elderly look like service; pity is difficult to escape. For example, the 1928 California report told the story of Mr. and Mrs. "Sandy Bar Jim," who were California Indians in their seventies. They farmed; he cut wood and sold Indian relics when he could find them, and that sufficed until "sickness brought them to want." Mr. and Mrs. B, who had resided in California for only nine years, had come there seeking health; he was asthmatic. But he could not find work, and she had "worried over their financial condition until she had become sick."[34] Each story the commissions told includes a mixture of working at odd jobs, illness or physical disability, unemployment, distant or nonexistent family, and aging, which made all of those situations more difficult.[35] Although the commissioners conceded that one couple had not lived in the state for all of their work lives, they tried to reassure California taxpayers that pensions would go to residents: the 1928 report noted that of all local residents who might be eligible for pensions, "sixty four percent had resided in the state for more than twenty years."[36]

Skepticism about whether the elderly had served in the state in which they lived could lead to support for national pensions rather than state-paid ones. Donald Sowers wrote a pamphlet for the state of Colorado in 1938 in which he criticized state pensions but strongly supported the federal Social Security Act. Sowers noted that, of all those eligible for pensions under the proposed act, "only 4 percent were born in Colorado," and "two-thirds of the pensioners had located in Colorado since 1900," a point he described as "interesting because of the often repeated statement that the pensioners have devoted their lives to the upbuilding of Colorado and that the pension is a reward for long and faithful service to the State."[37] By today's standards, residing in a state for thirty-five years sounds substantial. To Sowers, however, people not born in Colorado were unlikely to have truly served.

The conventions that would justify pensions color the vignettes and statistics that commissions provided. One such convention stipulated that poverty in old age had to result from low wages and misfortune if the elderly were to deserve pensions. Another specified that recipients should have served a particular state. The concept of service to a state intersected with the practice of the poor law, which made the poor the responsibility of the county in which they were legally settled. But Americans' high rates of geographical mobility made it doubtful whether a program organized around state and county payments would work.

Suspicions regarding whether pensioners would actually have served the state contributed to the general skepticism about whether state courts would uphold new social welfare functions. State responsibility would be replacing local responsibility; government responsibility might be replacing that of the family. Courts sometimes hesitated to allow states to replace common-law obligations with newly imposed statutory obligations. This hesitation explains why both courts and legislatures were often reluctant to grant mothers' pensions to women whose husbands had left: those men still owed child support. Similarly, children were often obligated in law to support their aging parents.

Amending Constitutions

If common-law requirements were part of the constitutional requirements, then amending the state constitutions was one possible response to the problem, as Goodnow pointed out:

> Inasmuch as the constitutions of the states are, comparatively speaking, rather easy of amendment, it has frequently happened that subsequent to a decision of a state court that an act of the state legislature is unconstitutional, the state constitution has been so changed as to remove all objections to the passage of the statute from the point of view of the state constitution. The natural result is that the limitations of the state constitutions as interpreted by the state courts are not serious permanent obstacles to social reform, either in the matter of labor legislation, or, indeed, in any other matter in which change is desired.[38]

Goodnow's passionate commitment to social reform led him to note the obvious solution to the obstacles that state constitutions imposed: amend them. Many states did amend their constitutions during the Progressive Era, not only to authorize new social welfare programs but in the West to institute new forms of municipal governance and to create the initiative and referendum.[39] As Goodnow noted, state constitutions were relatively easy to amend, and nothing in them permanently prevented any program from being enacted and upheld by the courts. Changing a state constitution was more difficult than passing legislation, however, and usually took more time, requiring statewide political mobilization. For some reformers, constitutional amendments conceded too much: to conclude that the state constitution required amending was to admit that the courts were correct in their decisions, rather than to maintain that they had imposed principles from without.[40] For those debating constitutional interpretation, it was enough to say that constitutions could accommodate new meanings, as the state of Wisconsin had urged. Furthermore, state constitutional amendments could not solve the whole problem if interpretations of the federal Fourteenth Amendment by the federal courts would also block new programs.

The blurring of state and federal constitutional requirements, as well as the problems that state constitutions posed, gave reformers good reason to consider amendments. In particular, the 1911 New York Court of Appeals decision that declared workmen's compensation unconstitutional provided a shocking reminder that the bundle of social welfare programs under discussion would require change in American governance.[41] Ohio, for example, responded by amending its constitution in 1912 to make "such decisions as that of the New York Court of Appeals . . . impossible."[42]

New York held a constitutional convention in 1915. The American Association of Labor Legislation proposed an amendment to allow spending for benefit of individuals, overriding the prohibition against gifts, but the proposed revisions failed.[43] Louisiana revised its constitution in 1921 to allow public retirement benefits and mothers' pensions.

Between 1919 and 1921, Pennsylvania sponsored a commission on constitutional revision, just when the commission on old age pensions was meeting. The secretary of the commission was William Draper Lewis, who had been the dean of the University of Pennsylvania Law School and the Progressive Party's candidate for governor in 1912 and 1916; he would later be the first director of the American Law Institute.[44] The commission on constitutional revision adopted a provision specifically designed to allow widows' pensions but framed in more general terms to include military pensions, civil service pensions, and public assistance. Observers expected the amendment to pass.[45] It did not, but probably because of a lack of interest rather than organized opposition.[46]

Constitutional politics left traces that reveal more widespread interest in social welfare programs—and the problems that constitutions posed for them—than the positive enactment of social insurance in a few states suggests. In states that did not enact new social welfare programs, political elites and electorates nevertheless demonstrated their interest, as well as their expectation of constitutional trouble, by enacting constitutional amendments that would authorize social welfare laws. Sometimes the effort to clear the way for pensions did just what it was supposed to: after Louisiana amended its constitution, it became one of the first southern states to enact mothers' pensions.[47]

Testing Old Age Pensions against Elizabethan Poor Laws

Legal challenges inevitably followed programs that constituted a substantial departure from existing poor law. Did the program require the counties to spend more money? Did it limit the discretion of county commissioners? Did it impose state control where spending had previously been a matter of country discretion? Each such provision in the statute increased the likelihood of a lawsuit. County commissioners, with money and power at stake, had access to lawyers and a budget with which to pay them. Suits brought by county officials or people and corporations who did not want to pay the taxes resulted in decisions that captured newspaper headlines and made constitutional limitations a matter of public discussion. If no challenge was brought to court, the reason was not that state constitutions clearly allowed the new program but rather that it represented too small a change to annoy anyone with the ability to sue.

Pennsylvania enacted an ambitious pension program in 1923, even though the proposed constitutional amendment authorizing pensions had failed in 1921. The statute established a state social welfare board, made old age pensions mandatory, and funded the program through the state. Like Arizona, Pennsylvania did not restrict pensions to the indigent; instead, it allowed those who made up to $365 each year and who had up to $3,000 in property to collect them. Nor did it require that family members be the first recourse for anyone who wished to claim a pension; the inability to support oneself, rather than the absence of family, was sufficient qualification. The decisions made by the county board were to be accepted as final. The *American Bar Association Journal,* a widely available legal periodical, immediately noted that the constitutional status of the programs would be worth watching, since so many states were interested in old age pensions.[48] Constitutionality shaped not just decisions from Pennsylvania's trial and appellate courts but also the arguments that advocates offered before the state supreme court. Despite policymakers' intention to pay the pensions to all the elderly, proponents' arguments limited the payments to try to save them, framing them as payments to the poor rather than payments to those who had served.

Pennsylvania's program, like Arizona's, immediately faced a test case. Forty businesses and individuals identified only as "taxpayers" challenged the old age pensions in court as a violation of the state constitutional prohibition on lending the state's money or credit for a private purpose. Mrs. Clara Busser led the list of plaintiffs, individualizing a challenge that actually was part of a concerted political effort. The lawyers for the state were Phillip Moyer, Robert Sterrett and Attorney General George Woodruff. They knew that defending the new program required that they accept the framework of the poor laws, since the existing laws would include the constitutionally acceptable meaning of "poor." They argued that the program was constitutional because it merely extended the old poor laws and was entirely consistent with them. The state almost certainly adopted this argument only to anticipate the limits that the court might find, for it was important to social insurance advocates that the new program had departed from the punitive poor laws.

Judge William Hargest, in the court of Dauphin County (which includes the state capital, Harrisburg), struck down the law on August 4, 1924, not even a year after it was supposed to take effect. He relied on the 1875 case from Kansas, *State v. Osawkee Township,* quoting Judge Brewer: "Cold and harsh as the statement may seem, it is nevertheless true that the obligation of the State to help is limited to those who are unable to help themselves."[49] As Frank Goodnow had feared in 1911, *Osawkee Township* haunted social welfare law, prohibiting the new social welfare programs if a taxpayer decided to sue. Judge Hargest noted that relief for the poor in almshouses had been in place when the state constitution was drafted;

had its writers meant to change the policy establishing almshouses, they would have said so.

The social welfare journal the *Survey* protested Judge Hargest's decision by arguing that pensions for "soldiers of industry" should not be unconstitutional if military pensions were not.[50] The logic that courts had found persuasive for workmen's compensation did not prevail at the state level, however. Although the United States Supreme Court had held that "soldiers of industry" earned payments as military soldiers had, the state court considering general old age pensions decided otherwise: service to *private employers* did not justify state payments, even if they were funded by contributions from employers and employees. Wage labor was important to citizens' participation in the United States, but it still was not service.

In response to Judge Hargest's decision, the state not only appealed but also mobilized public support. The Pennsylvania Commission on Old Age Pensions collected statements from the administrators of all the county poor boards in support of the old age assistance program and published them in 1925. Leon Baynes of the Tioga County board posed a pointed question:

> To my mind these poor old people who have given the best they had in labor and good citizenship, and many of them raised large families of children, who are now contributing their bit to industry and to their State and Nation, should be as much entitled to a pension as our ex-judges who received enough during their term of office so they should be able to take care of themselves. How do they get around the Constitution to pay such pensions?[51]

His frustrated question made clear how little sense a legal distinction between service and work could make to nonlawyers by 1925. The lawyers for the state disagreed with those representing Clara Busser and the corporations that had brought the suit about whether the state could pay the elderly for service or only for their helplessness, and whether the new form of administration fit with American forms of accountability or, instead, constituted yet another "irresponsible bureaucracy." Because each side knew the law, the attorneys argued positions that were the reverse of those they might have advocated outside of court: Moyer, Sterrett, and Woodruff argued that the new pensions were no more than a new poor law; Clara Busser's lawyers argued that they paid people who were not indigent. These arguments represented an inversion of those made by, respectively, the proponents and opponents of old age pensions, demonstrating the power that constitutional logic wielded over the ways social welfare programs were defined and defended.

Despite all the work that the commission had done to demonstrate that all elderly people deserved pensions because they had worked long and hard, Moyer, Sterrett, and Woodruff argued before the state's supreme court:

> There is no express prohibition in said Section 18 against an appropriation to a general class of *aged indigent* citizens any more than there is an express prohibition against an appropriation to a general class of *aged infirm* citizens, or to *institutions for aged infirm or mentally afflicted citizens* whether the same be publicly or privately owned.[52]

Like the lawyers who redefined the term "institution" in Arizona, those arguing in support of pensions in Pennsylvania knew that almshouses were constitutional; the trick was to make pensions appear to be like almshouses. Social insurance advocates had sought to dignify pension programs by differentiating them from the ignominy of the almshouse, with its debilitating mixture of the elderly, the insane, and the ill, as well as to insulate them from the problems of political patronage. Legal reasoning required making the two look just alike, since judges elevated long-standing practices to constitutional status. To them, paying those incapable of working had a charitable purpose, whatever form it took.

Not only did Moyer, Sterrett, and Woodruff downplay the distinction between almshouses and payments to individuals; they downplayed the idea that pensions rewarded service. Instead, they argued, pensions were a charitable response to the helplessness that almost invariably accompanied old age: "When a person has reached the age of seventy it is true with rather rare exception, that it is reasonable to presume that so far as his own labors are concerned he has reached a state of 'helplessness.' "[53] If old age pensions were intended for the helpless, the indigent, and the infirm, then they resembled mothers' pension programs, according to the state. Abraham Epstein and the other experts who had served on the old age pension commission, like social insurance advocates across the country, had instead argued that the elderly had *earned* the pensions by working throughout their lives.[54] In the legal arena, however, caution advised and stressing continuity with previous policies.

Drawing on every possible case and conceivable argument, the state moved on to contend that the new pensions also resembled those for civil servants.[55] Busser's lawyers responded with disdain that civil service pensions were akin to military pensions, mothers' pensions were just like charity, and old age assistance was like neither. The new program provided old age assistance to those who were not indigent and to those who had not served, placing it beyond constitutional bounds on both counts.

On February 2, 1925, the Pennsylvania Supreme Court struck down old age pensions. In both Arizona and Pennsylvania, the only states in which both generous and mandatory pensions had been enacted, the courts had immediately found them unconstitutional, giving reformers good reason to fear that the elderly would not fare as well in court as taxpayers and county commissioners.

The richness of the arguments before the court was not entirely apparent in the final opinion. In explaining its decision, the state supreme court took the austere position of insisting that it was making a pronouncement on the law rather than taking a stance in political debates. It insisted that it could neither rule against the pension program on the grounds that it was "socialistic," as the plaintiff argued, nor rule for it because it benefited the state, as the defendant argued. Rather, held Judge John W. Kephart, writing for the court, no matter what the initial purpose of the 1873 constitutional provision prohibiting grants for private purposes might have been, the judges had to follow the literal meaning—and that meaning made old age pensions unconstitutional.[56]

The court separated the provision from its historical connection to the hostility toward the railroads and the support some states granted them, as well as to the corruption of charitable politics in the cities. Historical practices mattered, though: the only people for whom the state could provide were those who had always been included in the poor law. The court explained the poor law as the proper kind of charity to answer the claim made by the state that the law was only a slightly reconceived poor law:

> It is earnestly contended that the Old Age Assistance Act should be sustained as a poor law. . . . The poor laws of Pennsylvania were taken from the Elizabethan Law of 1601 (43d Eliz. chap. 11), and our Act of March 9, 1771 (1 Smith's Laws, pp. 332, 338, 8 Stat. at L. p. 75), continued in effect until the Act of June 13, 1836, P.L. 541. No material change has been made in these laws except, as contended for by appellant, by the act now under consideration. It is urged that the state may define and classify poor persons; if this be true, it is only so to a limited extent; in either attempt it cannot encroach on the manifest prohibition expressed in the Constitution by section 18 of article 3, now under consideration.[57]

The court understood the state constitutional provision as embodying the common law, which extended to old statutes that had gained constitutional status; the state could not change them by enacting new statutes.

The English Elizabethan poor law was not part of Pennsylvanian, or even American, law. Under current theories of legal interpretation and legislative choice, a legislature should readily be able to change a statute if leaders can find the votes. Constitutions, not statutes, limit the choices legislatures can make, yet that distinction makes no sense if, in trying to discern the meaning of a constitutional provision, a court turns to old statutes. This Pennsylvania court held to an older and different understanding of the law: common-law decisions were evidence of the right way to govern, illustrative of correct principles; statutes could embody those general right principles, and for that reason judges would defer to them. No question about the legitimacy of political choice tainted the court's discussion of the Elizabethan poor law and of the eighteenth-century Pennsylvania statute. That these laws had long been on the books made them legitimate.

The court could not uphold the act as a poor law, which would have been constitutional, because poor people were defined as helpless dependents in need of assistance, entirely unable to support themselves, whereas the act in question granted pensions to people with some property. According to the judge, "poor" people were not the same as "not rich" people: "In appropriating money, the minute the historical definition of poor persons is broken through, the act enters the field of forbidden legislation through sec. 18 of article 3 and falls as a poor law."[58]

The state supreme court also rejected efforts to recognize the elderly as independent and deserving a reward for service, distinguishing between civil servants and the elderly. According to the court, old age pensions were charitable, whereas retirement acts were "neither charitable nor benevolent" but "founded on faithful, valuable services actually rendered to the Commonwealth over a long period of years."[59] If the elderly were dependent, as understood in ordinary poor relief, then payments to them were exempt from the prohibition against gifts. But state payments would invite dependency; the commission's insistence that payments would end dependency by being a reward for work had failed to persuade the court.

The form as well as the substance of the program gave grounds for complaint. Like other administrative programs, it raised constitutional questions concerning governance in an emergent administrative state. Were new welfare boards with substantial discretion legal? How were their decisions to be supervised? Although the lawyers for Clara Busser and the corporations raised this point, the court did not resolve it. The state contended that no more discretion was vested in the new state welfare board than had always been vested in the county boards that the poor law established. But Busser's lawyers urged that the new commission was completely unaccountable and thus unconstitutional; moreover, the commission had not provided clear enough guidelines for its decisions. To put the problem in the common language of the separation of powers, the new board was an executive authority but would exercise legislative authority, which made it unconstitutional. In addition, a dissatisfied applicant would have no appeal, for no procedures ensuring that private rights would be respected within the structure of the new program were in place—Frank Goodnow had suggested safeguards for new programs, and the courts had insisted on them for federal regulation at the behest of the railroads.

The state tried to appeal to commonalities with existing practices, which was certainly a sensible strategy given legal reasoning. The plaintiffs, however, emphasized the novelty of the state pension system, maintaining that it contained nothing akin to a legal duty to support anyone, which the poor law had provided. In a supplemental brief, the lawyers for Busser and the other taxpayers and corporations concluded, "The Old Age Assistance Commission is, in effect, nothing more nor less than part of a new appointive and irresponsible bureaucracy."[60] That fact, they said, made it a violation of a state constitutional provision vesting the legislative power in the state Senate and House of Representatives. The state could not delegate its legislative powers to an executive body.[61]

Elizabethan poor laws, doubts about eliminating almshouses, insistence that new spending programs must explicitly replace public relief: all these factors provided grounds for courts to declare new policies unconstitutional. In judicial ordering, to say that things were done in a certain way in the past is often enough to justify doing them the same way today, however exasperating commentators such as Frank Goodnow found such a view. The courts did not lose the power to maintain old meanings until the New Deal. They could and did assist those who wanted to maintain payments as public charity.

The political system was not working toward one clear and unified meaning of public spending, nor did it enact an integrated social welfare system. Instead, separate institutions—state legislatures, courts, bureaucracies, and counties—allowed multiple meanings to coexist. American public policy with regard to pensions had a "patterned disorder."[62]

Pennsylvania's governor, Gifford Pinchot, a progressive Republican who had made his national reputation as a forest conservationist, immediately reconstituted the state commission on old age pensions, which in 1927 recommended a constitutional amendment to authorize pensions. Under Governor John Fisher, who took office in January 1927, a proposal for old age pensions failed in the legislature, and Pennsylvania did not enact anything further before the New Deal.[63] Advocates in Pennsylvania had tried to enact old age pensions for eight years, from the first commission report in 1919 until 1927. Constitutional politics had proven a significant stumbling block, one of many ways to block policies in a complex political system.

Elsewhere, the push for old age pensions picked up momentum. Four states enacted them in 1929; the American Federation of Labor endorsed pensions that same year. In 1930–1931, legislators introduced bills across the country. By the time the Roosevelt administration took office in 1932, the push for pensions had became a mass movement, led most visibly by Francis Townsend, a populist and policy entrepreneur from California.[64] Nevertheless, the constitutional problems persisted until the New Deal.

The Separation of Powers and the Delegation of Authority

The "irresponsible bureaucracy" that Clara Busser and the other plaintiffs had condemned in Pennsylvania was the source of concern to legal elites carving out a new administrative law across the United States. Addressing the question of how to enable bureaucracy to take on new tasks while ensuring that it remain accountable became a veritable industry for corporate lawyers whose clients were trying to shape government regulation. By the 1930s, it had become a fertile field for legal commentators as well. Unlike European states, American governments were trying to develop reliable programmatic bureaucracies at the same time as they were developing new programs; American governance had no history of a civil service insulated from electoral politics and accountable only through a clear hierarchy.[65] Lawsuits compounded the difficulty. In the other two states whose courts considered old age pensions during the 1930s, New Hampshire and Colorado, justices heard challenges to bureaucracy. Once again, federalism allowed different state courts to answer questions of accountability differently.

Questions concerning who could decide and what kind of power the deciders were exercising threatened to blur the line that scholars were drawing between constitutional and administrative law. Frank Goodnow had argued that administrative law ought to be the law of what administrators did; it included issues of the separation of powers, but such a limited constitutional matter hardly exhausted the topic. Ernst Freund, first of New York and later of Chicago, largely agreed.[66] These commentators, however, eventually lost the argument in a way that had long-standing implications for the field.

In 1931 the supreme court justices in New Hampshire revisited old age pensions at the request of the state legislature. (Both the legislature and the governor could request advisory opinions from the state supreme court; as Governor John G. Winant noted in a radio address after the decision was issued, the state constitution was unusual in allowing them.)[67] The court had previously addressed the subject in 1917, before the state enacted any program. In 1931 the justices focused on the separation of powers rather than on indigence, which had been central in 1917. That the proposed new statute assigned administration of the pensions to the probate courts would, in the opinion of the justices, unconstitutionally give executive powers to judges. The justices acknowledged that divisions were not always clear: "Many things to be done call for the exercise and passing of judgment, and the law ordinarily regards such things as judicial acts. But the judicial charac-

ter of acts does not test the department of government to which they are assigna-
ble."[68] Therefore, the tasks of administering pensions could share in a judicial
character but still belong properly to the executive—exactly contrary to what the
North Dakota court had held in its mothers' pensions case. In so holding, the
New Hampshire justices struck down the law as unconstitutional on grounds easily remedied by a legislature, for it was not the substance of the pension that was
wrong. Reasoning in administrative cases addressed whether the right institution
was deciding according to the right procedure, a question that focused not on
what governments might do but on the subtler matter of *how* they might do it.

The Depression had spread across the country when the New Hampshire court
advised in 1931 that old age pensions would be unconstitutional. The justices'
opinion shared top billing in the *Manchester Union,* the state's very conservative
leading newspaper, with an opinion rejecting an income tax: "Income Tax, Old
Age Pensions Law Held Invalid; Two Important Decisions Made by the High
Court."[69] The *Union* editorialized: "The Court also emphasized that only a law
giving assistance to the aged because of poverty comes within the limits of the
Constitution. This ruling eliminates the pension proposal and bring [*sic*] such
legislation as may be undertaken in this regard under the head of relief measures."[70] In fact, the justices had ruled on the matter of administration rather than
on the qualifications of recipients, but indigence always reappeared in public discussion. The state senator who read the opinion aloud, Clark Greer, stated that
the problems in the bill could be remedied and vowed to reintroduce a revised
bill.[71] The New Hampshire Supreme Court could and did block the pension proposal, but its judgment was neither sacred nor final.

Separation of powers appeared alongside arguments about service in Colorado
as well, after that state made its pensions mandatory in 1931.[72] When the state had
first enacted old age pensions in 1927, they were optional. Counties could avoid
them, and they all did; no one, then, had any reason to sue. Once pensions became mandatory, however, county commissioners filed suit to overturn them,
since countries often lacked the funds. Even before the new law took effect, Abraham Epstein said that "county attorneys all over Colorado are waging a battle to
destroy the law."[73] By March 1932 the Denver county commissioners had brought
the compulsory system to court in what the *Rocky Mountain News,* one of Denver's two main papers, called a test case.[74] Other county officials joined the Denver board as friends of the court in contesting the pensions. The county commissioners did not argue against the pension system on financial grounds, however.
Instead, they raised questions of service to the state and the appropriate division
of responsibilities between judges and administrators.

In what did become the test case, Anna Lynch had applied for a pension, but
the Denver board denied her. She and her sister had spent their lives doing

"women's work": they had cooked professionally and taken boarders into their home in central Denver. By 1931 they were tired and no longer able to support themselves. The Lynch sisters satisfied the age requirements, but old age alone seldom captured people's problems, as the commission reports from California and Pennsylvania had noted earlier. Old age, debility, and economic downturns compounded one another. During the Great Depression the Lynch sisters could no longer find boarders, making an old age pension more urgent.[75]

The firm of Quiat and Cummings took the case. Ira L. Quiat was the state senator who had sponsored the 1931 legislation making the pensions mandatory.[76] George Blickhahn was also an attorney for Lynch; long an attorney for the city of Walsenburg in southern Colorado, he later became a judge there.[77] As a city attorney, Blickhahn is likely to have known the budget complaints that the county commissioners had. The case included attorneys as amici curiae, probably for other counties in Colorado. The courts provided another place to continue the political argument that had engaged the legislature for years.

Service and indigence once again appeared in the arguments before the court but disappeared in the opinion; the court considered the statute's constitutionality on the basis of separation of powers. This shift was the reverse of what had taken place in the Pennsylvania case; there, the lawyers questioned the delegation of authority to a bureaucracy, but the court sidestepped the issue. Still, just as the Pennsylvania lawyers had done, the Colorado lawyers quickly abandoned what the champions of old age pensions saw as most attractive about them: their distance from poor relief. The brief supporting the Lynch sisters' claim argued that pensions for the elderly were poor law provisions, just as mothers' pension laws were; they were not "a true pension law akin to the soldiers pension acts."[78] For that reason, the lawyers asserted, service to the state was unnecessary to make the payments constitutional; like poor relief, they did not require service.

Nevertheless, just in case the court noticed that the new pensions were in fact distinct from poor relief, Quiat and Cummings and Blickhahn tried to explain how all the elderly did satisfy the requirement of having served the state. They first reminded the court of Colorado's pioneer legacy (which was a romantic image in Denver in 1932): pioneers who had built the state had earned anything the state could pay them. "And the man who builds a house," they continued, "who digs in the street or who farms and raises the food to feed the rest of the state, all in a measure are serving the public and serving the state of Colorado. It is not necessary to bear a gun and kill or maim an enemy to serve one's state."[79] By 1931, many localities were paying pensions not only to firemen and police but also to teachers, other civil servants, and even judges. Yet the military imagery of independence and service was so prevalent that lawyers had to remind the courts that one did not have to kill to serve. Building houses would not have been considered service to the state in most of the nineteenth-century cases; it would have been the sort of ordinary work that Judge Brewer had long ago held did not deserve payment. Furthermore, the kinds of work cited to exemplify service were distinctly masculine. Farm women worked alongside men to raise the food that fed the state, but the lawyers' imagery portrayed men, not women, building the economy. Ironically, that image persisted even though the occupations of the Lynch sisters, the plaintiffs in this case, were typical of urban women's work.

Finally, in drawing analogies with mothers' pensions, Quiat, Cummings, and Blickhahn wavered between portraying mothers' pensions as an extension of the poor laws and justifying them as a reward for service. They asked, "Shall we say that it is constitutional to hear the cry of a child because it is helpless, but it is unconstitutional to hear the moan of the old folk?"[80] Constitutionally, mothers' pensions were for the children, not the mothers; children's helplessness, not mothers' service, was crucial. According to the *Denver Post*, which advocated pensions with an eye to the problem of constitutionality, old people moaned for help as babies did; they did not earn payments through service.

The local newspapers published the arguments in this case. During the New Deal years the confrontation between President Roosevelt and Congress and the United States Supreme Court was so prominent, some commentators quipped, that Americans could discuss the Constitution over their morning coffee. In the early 1930s, however, that honor was not reserved for the Federal Court and Constitution. As state courts engaged issues that concerned many Americans, their ways of thinking about constitutional matters also became popularly available. Frank Goodnow had warned as early as 1911 that these questions were not something to be left to the specialist, given the attitudes of Supreme Court justices and the need for amendments in the states. By 1931, anyone who saw a newspaper could talk about the arguments.

The Colorado Supreme Court split in *Denver v. Lynch:* one of the three judges recused himself, and the other two disagreed.[81] One judge, then, was able to strike down the law. He did so on the grounds that it conferred judicial powers on the county commissioners, whereas determining the proper amount of a pension payment was, in his opinion, a judicial matter.[82] The statute had largely assumed that point: judges were to fix the pension, but the county commissioners had the statutory power to approve what the judges did. Nevertheless, the state supreme court held that although there were other constitutional issues, striking the statute down on the one ground of violating separation of powers was enough. Perhaps when the legislature met next, it would address the constitutional problems without requiring a judicial decision.

Sorting the threads of governance—who deserved payment and who did not, how boards could be organized—by constitutionality allowed legally trained officials to maintain power; they did not need to appeal to a broader constituency in order to remain politically significant. Conversely, though, since these narrow legal arguments addressed politically popular programs, they contributed to an atmosphere in which Americans could talk about constitutions and what they meant. In addition, the legal principle that law is not timebound but forms an integrated and perpetual governing system meant that the constitutional grounds on which pensions were fought might have very little popular currency yet still matter.[83] Local political concerns, though influential, were not the primary force in determining the constitutionality of pensions. County officials' primary concern in opposing them may have been financial, but they had to express those concerns through constitutional arguments: that it was wrong to spend tax money on pensions and that judicial, executive, and legislative powers should be kept separate. In Colorado, as in Pennsylvania, legal doctrine coupled with a willingness to mobilize it contributed to the difficulty of enacting old age pensions. Difficulties rested in long-standing judicial supervision of the economy—much of which, however, had emerged as judges ratified pension legislation, not overturned it.

The passage of the federal Social Security Act in 1935, requiring that states establish programs for old age social security, did not end the controversy. In Colorado, where the Townsend movement remained strong, eleven groups supporting old age pensions drafted a constitutional amendment and got it on the ballot by petition.[84] In November 1936, Colorado voters approved a constitutional amendment that raised existing old age pensions from $30 to $45 per month.[85] The amendment also excluded applicants' homes and personal property from consideration in assessing their eligibility. Since the payments from the new federal program would remain the same, the new amendment could cost the state of Colorado substantial sums of money. Officials thus had the same reason to oppose the pensions as in 1932.

In December 1936, only a month after voters approved the amendment, "Colorado's old-age pension problem was dragged out into the open . . . and dumped into the lap of Attorney General Byron G. Rogers."[86] The state auditor asked for an opinion regarding whether the new system needed legislation to make it effective. The attorney general stated that the new amendment did require action by the legislature before it could take effect; the *Denver Post* announced his decision in banner headlines.[87] In turn, the governor requested an opinion from the state supreme court, and the federal government withheld the money that was to go to Colorado until the court clarified the question.[88]

The state supreme court held that the new amendment was constitutional; it did not violate the due process clause of the Fourteenth Amendment. Furthermore, it was self-executing, an issue that had been at the center of controversy in

Denver.[89] Even this decisive ruling did not quiet all objections, however; in March 1938 the *Rocky Mountain News* called the new pensions amendment "cruel, because it robs those on relief, the blind, and crippled and will end by discrediting all social welfare including old age pensions."[90]

Conclusion

During the 1930s, states joined in the remaking of state constitutions in order to allow social welfare spending. Some state courts followed the example set by Colorado, ratifying their new spending programs after the federal Social Security Act was enacted, and some passed constitutional amendments.[91] A third possibility was to treat constitutions as flexible, open to multiple interpretations, as the commissioners in Wisconsin had argued.

Without attending to constitutional struggles over pensions, one misunderstands the timing of pension programs—particularly because states revised and enacted programs whose previous forms had been struck down as unconstitutional. Without attending to the ongoing doctrines of public purpose and separation of powers, one is likely to conclude that in three states—Arizona, Pennsylvania, and Colorado—pensions were held to be unconstitutional, as though the cases and doctrines represented idiosyncratic preferences of particular judges, unconnected to the ongoing disputes over responsibility and poverty that constitutional doctrines represented.[92] Instead, the constitutional problems that old age pensions had in every state that made them mandatory before the New Deal were entirely predictable from the political contests over local responsibility and the long history concerning public purpose that preceded them. State constitutional transformation was long and slow. Legal frameworks had shaped political struggles for a long time before the federal constitutional crisis of 1937. States relied on one another's rulings and on interpretations of the Fourteenth Amendment to the U.S. Constitution throughout the early twentieth century.

Scholars often conclude that the New Deal finally won in the United States Supreme Court because the Court "opened its eyes," or because the Court followed the election returns, or because the New Deal represented a "constitutional moment" during which the nation revised its constitutional understandings.[93] The United States Supreme Court is only one part of the story, however. Many state courts evaluated the constitutionality of social welfare programs, both before and after their enactment on the federal level; because all spending programs were at least nominally state spending programs, just as old age social security was, the states would have to go along with the programs. They did go along, but not until officials had argued about the law. Well before 1937, when the United States

Supreme Court began to ratify the New Deal measures, the states had begun to amend constitutions, and state courts had revised constitutional interpretation so as to hold that the Fourteenth Amendment and state constitutional provisions did not stop the payment of pensions.

This interpretation, where it occurred, was not the result of a single constitutional moment or revision. The conception of what counted as service to the state had broadened during the previous years in evaluations of civil service pensions, although it remained narrow in what are now considered welfare programs, such as mothers' pensions. Legally speaking, civil service pensions and workers' compensation made it possible for the attorneys in the Colorado old age pension case to argue in 1932—however unsuccessfully—that farming and building houses counted as service to the state just as soldiering did.

Mothers' pensions had also been enacted in most of these states, though they did not raise the same constitutional issues that social insurance did. In Colorado, Ira Quiat and George Blickhahn drew an analogy between old age pensions and mothers' pensions in order to persuade the state supreme court that pensions for the elderly were constitutional because they were a form of poor relief. But when old age pensions and unemployment insurance were established without means tests and placed under the control of administrative agencies, they broke with past legal interpretations of poor relief. Courts then struck them down, just as they did mothers' pensions that were mandatory for counties and not means-tested.

Some state officials tried to make all debilitating wage labor qualify as service, including women's work. That expansive understanding of service was not accepted by courts that were considering state-paid pensions for the elderly, despite commissions' enthusiastic reports. Defining wage labor as service could justify employment-based social insurance programs but could never provide a publicly acceptable rationale for mothers' pensions. Even at its most expansive, when ordinary wage labor that was not especially dangerous qualified as service, the amorphous and shifting legal understanding of service required that the work be compensated with wages, which made the household and child-rearing work of mothers no work at all. Furthermore, if pensions were acceptable only as a return for service already completed, a woman who had not yet been able to perform, say, twenty years of service would have a difficult time making a legitimate claim on the state for funds. Child rearing is work in progress and work to come, not work past.

State court judgments made it difficult to enact the particular forms of state pensions that some legislatures supported. The state courts did not always have the final word, however. States reenacted pension programs; state commissioners, public commentators, and newspapers all contributed to laying the groundwork for changing interpretations of public purpose. Eventually, as the courts came to uphold any program that state legislatures could say was of general benefit, the question of public purpose largely disappeared.[94] This long, slow change in the states had important implications for an understanding of American constitutional transformation.

Conclusion
State Constitutions and Public Spending

extbooks still tell undergraduates studying American constitutional law that the United States Supreme Court, staffed with justices who held conservative political views, was hostile to legislation protecting labor or otherwise giving government new tasks from the late nineteenth century until 1937. Then a switch by one justice and a subsequent rash of new appointments by President Franklin D. Roosevelt allowed the Supreme Court to follow the popular will. That popular will supported Roosevelt's New Deal, in which the government took on everything from managing national agriculture to creating old age pensions.[1] G. Edward White calls this narrative the "conventional account" of constitutional change.[2]

For a long time the primary task for scholars was to explain how this shift might have come about. Some have argued that the Supreme Court follows the election returns. Bruce Ackerman has taken that point further and argued that the Constitution itself was transformed through the support that Roosevelt found in the election of 1936, that in constitutional politics the New Deal led to a new governing system as much as the Civil War led to new constitutional governance, and that Supreme Court justices obligingly reread doctrine to accord with Roosevelt's popular support even before he appointed the seven justices who joined the Court between 1937 and 1941.[3]

In contrast to this view of abrupt change, recent scholarship has demonstrated long, slow change in constitutional governance, with no one clear point marking a new constitutional regime—a less dramatic but perhaps more accurate story. During the New Deal the United States Supreme Court joined debates concerning what made legislation illegitimately class-based, how to regulate interstate commerce, and how to structure emergent administrative government. Barry Cushman, Howard Gillman, Julie Novkov, Melissa Saunders, and G. Edward White have all argued that internal doctrinal reasons, along with new legislation that raised problems for the courts, account for challenges better than external political reasons do.[4] Since the Supreme Court cites internal doctrinal reasons for what it does, and since the ethic of legal reasoning requires that the Supreme

Court act on the reasons it states, starting there to explain cases has the virtue of parsimony.

Like the issues about class legislation that Gillman analyzes or about the delegation of administrative authority that concerns White, the Social Security Act and questions as to its constitutionality had a rich history, as the foregoing chapters demonstrate. The proliferation of programs governed by the public purpose doctrine made it extremely difficult to continue to apply the doctrine in any kind of coherent fashion, Howard Gillman has argued.[5] It collapsed as its internal structure required ever more ornate buttresses. As programs proliferated, the category of service expanded, so much so that no court could any longer sustain service as separate from work, particularly in conjunction with the transformations represented by governing through state boards rather than local commissioners. It did not expand so far as to include retirement payment from the government for all those who had labored, or for poor women with children, even after the New Deal. State legislation had laid the groundwork, however, including a basis for holding such spending constitutional. Early New Deal legislation was badly enough drafted and the litigation defending it badly enough done that the Court had good standard legal reasons to strike down certain acts. The legislation it began to uphold in 1937 (by the same narrow 5–4 margin) was better drafted and defended, and the Court no longer had to respond to popular support for Roosevelt.[6]

Another part of the story of the transformation in governance that occurred in the early part of the century was the creation of administrative accountability. When state courts did not strike down programs regulating railroads or the purity of food and drugs or immigration, they nevertheless imposed new structures of accountability through judicial supervision. Judges ensured that bureaucratic officials provided hearings for those whose businesses they were regulating, that they made decisions according to evidence, that the railroads and other businesses always had an opportunity to appeal to courts. Judges structured their version of fairness via internal administrative procedures.[7] New social welfare law in the states experimented with the new bureaucratic forms of accountability. The least rights-based program, mothers' pensions, was sometimes as much an innovation in giving some authority to the state over the counties as it was in distributing money to poor women. Social welfare law was part of the bureaucratic shift in administrative law.

In pensions, transformation came via state, not federal, legislation and constitutions. State constitutions receive little attention in their relationship to federal constitutional interpretation; they often seem to be too legislative, with too many provisions and too many details, to be truly constitutive documents. Nevertheless, many of the most basic struggles concerning what made a welfare state arose from *state* constitutional interpretation.[8] State constitutions allowed courts to approve or strike down programs; the programs they did approve hinted at all the programs they would not. Granting pensions to firemen *because* they had served implied that the elderly, who had not necessarily served, should not get pensions. Whenever they had the chance, state courts affirmed those hints that so worried state commissions studying pensions programs not tied to some version of service and not means-tested lost in court. The state constitutional governance of social welfare programs shaped what was possible.

Dependence and Independence

Starting with state constitutional governance leads in a different direction from beginning with social welfare. Concern about poor women has motivated many of the efforts to understand gender in the welfare state; that concern invites a focus on programs that addressed women. Mothers' pensions have often provided a focus but offer only a slender basis for explaining how the welfare state has been gendered. Mothers' pensions were always needs-based and highly stigmatized. They never represented a substantial change from poor relief, despite what many advocates wanted.[9] Expanding analysis to programs that address women beyond mothers' pensions provides a salutary introduction to the variety of programs that have addressed women but do not allow comparative thinking across programs addressing men *and* women. For example, Gwendolyn Mink states her central problem as that of "inequality in the welfare state." She therefore discusses not only mothers' pensions but education, infant health, and labor policy, all within programs focusing on women.[10] Molly Ladd-Taylor also provides a rich understanding of what she calls mother-work, addressing the politics and policies for women in the early twentieth century.[11] Joanne Goodwin details disputes concerning the administration of public assistance in Chicago in the early twentieth century, opening the question of just how much mothers' pensions changed poor women's lives.[12]

Gender is a relational construct, however, as studies that compare mothers' pensions with social insurance demonstrate.[13] Public policy imagines what it means to be properly masculine or feminine, without mapping those meanings neatly onto real women and men.[14] That insight leads to a comparison of mothers' pensions with public spending that we no longer even think of as different from private, such as police pensions. Studying these civil pensions illuminates just how administrators and judges could divide programs into those for dependent and independent people. The lines of cases sometimes did *not* speak to each other, despite their similarity as social welfare programs, because they relied upon a dichotomy between independent and dependent, which in turn implied gender.[15] The marker of independence changed in constitutional law from danger-ousness to work so as to allow spending while preserving the independence that had once precluded spending.

Using the mutually defining categories of dependence and independence has il-luminated connections between payments to volunteer firemen in antebellum New York, aid to farmers in drought-stricken Kansas, and old age pensions in Pennsylvania in the 1920s. The degrading category of dependency was not re-served solely for women. Anyone making claims on state payments they had not earned in public service—indeed, through the nineteenth century, service that could somehow be understood as dangerous—was the object of pity and received payment only via charity. Male workers *ought* to be independent; it was not that they naturally and always were. To understand the associations carried by depen-dence and independence one must map the whole of the constitutional doctrine and the context in which it emerged, rather than just examining the sporadic cases that specifically addressed old age pensions or mothers' pensions.

State Constitutions through the New Deal

What is the evidence that state constitutions mattered in social welfare before the New Deal? For payments to soldiers before Reconstruction, there were chal-lenges to local efforts to raise taxes in most states in the Union. Those challenges were unsuccessful, but the way the courts decided the cases made it possible to doubt the constitutionality of state aid to veterans even as late as post–World War I and it shaped the market for bonds throughout the country. Pensions for each group of civil servants that municipalities employed, from firemen to policemen to teachers, were subject to suits from skeptical taxpayers or disappointed claimants. In 1916 the one state, Arizona, that made mothers' pensions and old age pensions mandatory for counties and not closely means-tested found itself in court under state constitutional doctrine. Mothers' pensions were deemed consti-tutional in other states largely because they continued to meet state obligations to aid the desperate poor. The primary change that mothers' pensions represented was the loss of control for some county commissioners, leading to questions—which also occupied federal courts—of how to define new administrative powers not neatly slotted as legislative, executive, and judicial. Given the pervasiveness of constitutional challenges to social welfare programs and the courts' ongoing belief in the value of traditional poor relief, the fact that mothers' pensions programs met only limited trouble could be ascribed only to the courts' perception that mothers' pensions were continuous with poor relief.

In Arizona, Pennsylvania, and Colorado, the states that made old age pensions mandatory and not means-tested before the New Deal, taxpayers and county commissioners challenged the programs in court and won. The further pensions moved from a basis in state service and from means-testing, the less likely they were to be held constitutional. The consistency of such rulings shows that cross-state constitutional principles mattered much more in handing these losses to the states than did the political culture of individual states or the constitutional provisions within them.

Court cases leave clear traces, but all the activity before someone sues need not. If a court battle loomed, programs could be dropped before they were enacted. More likely, programs could become means-tested after commissions interpreted prior court pronouncements. Traces of attention to constitutionality outside the court remain. Once the practice of commissioning studies to justify and explain programs began about 1910, those studies sometimes specified constitutionality as a problem. Reactions ranged from Wisconsin's statement that when people want old age pensions to become a public purpose they would become one to Pennsylvania's effort to enact a constitutional amendment that would allow old age pensions. Debates in the early twentieth century concerning flexibility in constitutions became practical realities when they moved from the scholar's book to the policy advocate's report. The Wisconsin report would have it that constitutions were living, flexible documents that could reflect the point of view of the culture taken as a whole: not until that whole believed pensions were constitutional would they become so. The attempt in Pennsylvania to get a constitutional amendment may have reflected nothing more than the fact that pensions were a real possibility in Pennsylvania, as they perhaps were not in Wisconsin. Rather than waiting until some unknown time when the state supreme court might agree that pensions were constitutional, Pennsylvanians who wanted to get pensions enacted had to get their constitution amended soon. Even if doing so conceded that pensions did represent a fundamental change in constitutional governance, practicalities demanded that concession.

Not only did commission reports show the indirect influence of constitutionalism in shaping programs, but so also did some of the leading commentary on social welfare, especially Frank Goodnow's *Social Reform and the Constitution*. His work made the concerns of a legal elite available to an educated public. Many popular magazines discussed the proposed pensions without focusing on whether they were constitutional, but when courts decided cases, magazines prominent in policy and law circles covered their reasoning. Furthermore, the possibility that courts *would* determine the fate of new programs made legal knowledge relevant to the circles of social workers and economists who were discussing how to institute reform. Abraham Epstein, not a lawyer but an economist prominent in social welfare circles, immediately warned the Colorado public that county commissioners would be eager to sue concerning its proposed old age pension program.

County commissioners did not think they could afford the new payments, and questioning their constitutionality provided one way of trying to stop them.

The federal government, also recognizing the significance of constitutionalism, reinforced its importance by recirculating it. The Roosevelt administration's Works Progress Administration (WPA) commissioned studies of state constitutions with an eye toward new social welfare law and issued the resulting reports between May 15 and June 1, 1937. The United States Supreme Court had upheld the most controversial provisions of the Social Security Act on May 24, 1937, so the studies were certainly commissioned before anyone could be certain the Social Security Act would be deemed constitutional. A. Ross Eckler, the statistician who headed the Division of Social Research within the WPA, hired researchers for a Legal Research Section to investigate "constitutional provisions affecting public welfare." Complementing its digests of public welfare laws, the section issued reports on ten states in total.[16] Nothing in them explains why those ten states and not others; perhaps the Supreme Court's ratification of the national Social Security Act provided reason enough to stop producing the reports. Those that the WPA did produce briefly addressed public-purpose limits on taxation as well as provisions concerning the use of credit, special sessions of the legislature, and ways of amending the constitution.

In any case, constitutionality in the states rapidly became a non-issue as states enacted constitutional provisions that would allow them to legislate old age pensions and unemployment relief, not least to take advantage of federal government grants once the Social Security Act was in place.

The WPA's Division of Social Research had also expended considerable effort in describing poverty in the United States.[17] The researchers did painstaking empirical work, providing unparalleled and still-useful information on poverty during the Depression. Someone in the division clearly also thought it necessary to study the state laws. In order to understand poor relief in the United States, unlike in any other country in the world, one had to understand state constitutional provisions and their interpretation. That became unimportant only as the federal government enacted social welfare programs, and states complied by enacting amendments which the Supreme Court proved willing to hold constitutional.

Other scholars too found researching constitutional problems for social welfare worthwhile. The long-standing local control of poor law made such research fruitful for Edith Abbott's students at the Chicago School of Social Work. She had learned law from the eminent New York legal scholar Ernst Freund, who, like his friend and colleague Frank Goodnow, believed that the way forward for reformers and legal scholars rested in administrative law. Edith Abbott brought his lessons to the next generation. In the 1930s her doctoral students produced dissertations focusing on the poor law of individual states from Rhode Island to Montana, totaling eight reports. Each one discussed the local law of settlement, the responsibilities of kin for their poor family members, and the special local conditions that shaped poor law, such as the vulnerability of farming to drought. Where Justice Brewer in Kansas had held farm aid unconstitutional, or the justices in Ohio had struck down relief during the Depression as unconstitutional, the student reported it and discussed constitutional requirements in detail.[18]

Abbott herself wrote most of the introductions to these dissertations. Her colleague Sophonisba Breckinridge wrote the others and collected court decisions. Abbott stated her frustration with the local administration of the poor law, a system that led to what she saw as fundamental unfairness and pointless litigation among townships eager to rid themselves of burdens they genuinely could not afford. The constitutional organization of federalism, including local financing, was responsible for this system, Abbott believed. She also explained that the public purpose doctrine seriously limited what states could do.[19]

The reports Abbott sponsored are part of the evidence, then, that shows state constitutions as the subject of debate and disapproval for years before the New Deal brought the 1935 Social Security Act. The debates gradually changed over the years, but concerns about the way constitutions might thwart spending for individuals dated to the 1880s, when states and localities paid individual veterans and began to pay pensions to police and firemen. The transformation from that time forward was one of gradual expansion to include a wider range of state workers, then workers generally, in the category of servants who had earned additional compensation from the state. By the time of the New Deal, the category of service had so broadened that it had become close to useless in drawing the line between legitimate and illegitimate spending. "Service" had expanded because states had increased the kinds of payments they made, bringing new situations before judges and making the line-drawing increasingly difficult. Judges throughout the period continued to rule as though constitutional principles were sacred and as though statutory requirements must embody—though in greater detail—and only gradually conceded that determining what constituted a public purpose was a legislative rather than a judicial question.

Without attending to political struggles over state constitutional doctrine, cases such as *Buckstegge* (1916) in Arizona and *Busser* (1925) in Pennsylvania—the mothers' pensions and old age pensions cases—look like arbitrary twentieth-century interventions from conservative courts rather than the contributions to long-standing constitutional doctrine that they actually were. Indeed, in some scholarship on struggles over the American welfare state these cases seem to be arbitrary interventions, requiring no explanation. For example, Russell Hanson has argued that federalism itself partly explains the uneven development of the American welfare state. Federalism, he claims, allowed the tremendous variability in mothers' pensions and the Social Security Act's Aid to Dependent Children enacted in the 1930s.[20] The variability across states includes amendments enacted in several to authorize the borrowing required to support the New Deal's ADC.[21]

Since mothers' pensions were most often constitutional when enacted, and only the recalcitrant southern states needed amendments to get them enacted, Hanson's oversight is understandable. Ignoring constitutional problems in old age pensions, however, is not. In every state in which they were made mandatory, someone challenged them in court. Yet Ann Shola Orloff, in her comprehensive study of the creation of old age pensions in the United States, only briefly notes that the Arizona and Pennsylvania programs were struck down by the state supreme courts.[22] Constitutionality mattered much more than that: Colorado's program was also struck down, and every state report mentioned the problem. As all the commission reports and WPA findings made clear, it was not only public purpose that limited what states could do. Since judges still believed that it was possible and constitutionally necessary to separate judicial, legislative, and executive powers, new pensions under state control raised the same problems as other bureaucratic programs.

Administrative Law in the States

State welfare programs raised the same problems concerning bureaucratic governance as those prevalent at the federal level. Commentators everywhere worried about how to create accountability with new forms of governance, and whether it was possible to maintain the separation of powers into legislative, executive, and judicial when administrators had so much authority. Two kinds of answers were possible. On the one hand, Frank Goodnow, in his 1893 treatise *Comparative Administrative Law*, argued that new programs such as the regulation of interstate commerce and of immigration would require careful interpretation by state officials to ensure that they were not encroaching on private rights. Understanding administration required attention to the details of the work administrative agencies did. He had an ally in Ernst Freund, a scholar who trained leading social work figures in law and administration. Felix Frankfurter, on the other hand, turned to courts as the instruments for holding bureaucrats accountable in his 1932 treatise on administrative law: administrative law was a specialized branch of constitutional law.[23]

Goodnow and Frankfurter agreed that new forms of governance through administrative agencies required that no one have a rigid understanding of the separation of powers. Goodnow approached his critique of the separation of powers historically, arguing that it was a mistake to elevate contingent settlements concerning the division of responsibility in England into something eternal.[24] Frankfurter, for his part, seemed to have years of federal constitutional law on his side: the courts had not insisted on a strict separation of powers between legislatures and agencies as long as legislatures provided standards for agencies. Half his case-book explicated separation of powers doctrine.[25]

Separation of powers exploded into view in the United States Supreme Court in 1935, when the Court struck down the National Industrial Recovery Act as un-constitutional for delegating too much authority to administrative agencies.[26] What the Court did seemed to go against years of judicial acceptance of adminis-trative agencies, though observers argued that the National Industrial Recovery Act had been particularly free in delegating legislative authority to bureaucra-cies.[27] Even if the issues had faded in the federal courts, though, pensions in the states had raised precisely the problems of delegation for state courts. In the states, taxpayers won gratifying victories against old age pensions, mothers' pensions and teachers' pensions on just those grounds.

Frankfurter's emphasis on administrative law as a subset of constitutional law triumphed because the courts were willing to revisit the constitutional questions. Separation of powers remained a live doctrine, notably in the state courts in pro-grams that presaged the New Deal. Goodnow was aware that when he was writ-ing, new spending programs were within the states' purview, not the federal gov-ernment's.[28] Where the courts mused about the separation of powers and the unconstitutionality of delegating legislative authority to a board, as they did in Pennsylvania, Colorado, and New Hampshire regarding old age pensions (and even Nebraska, when it enacted pensions in anticipation of the federal Social Se-curity Act), Goodnow would have advised them to abandon a time-bound vision of neatly contained governmental powers. The state courts in the programs were much less willing, however, to see state boards gain new legislative authority than Goodnow would have wished.

The 1935 federal decisions striking down the National Industrial Recovery Act are even less surprising than recent scholarship has made them out to be, if we note the concerns the state courts had. In both New Hampshire and Colorado, over-enthusiastic delegation of legislative authority to bureaucracies gave state courts reason to strike down old age pensions, and in other states questions about delegation provided reasons to question mothers' pensions. When the United States Supreme Court revisited the question of how much authority Congress could delegate, it participated in a conversation the states had pursued.

Goodnow's approach would not have eliminated court decisions, but it would have made court cases turn not on constitutionality but on bureaucratic account-ability: Were lower level officials doing what the legislature told them to do? That was the crucial issue for the cases and opinions of the attorney general in Pennsyl-vania regarding mothers' pensions. Mothers' pensions were constitutional because the legislature said they were; supervising lower level officials ensured proper pursuit of the program's purposes (particularly through an attorney general, who should have a commitment to executing the legislature's laws). Goodnow had argued that professionalization of the bureaucracy was crucial to fair administration. To avoid taking property unjustly via taxation, a constitutional requirement, bureaucrats would have to spend money just as legislatures intended them to. (It should not be up to the courts to determine that the legislature was wrong.) Local officials in the United States would have to become professional administrators rather than the underpaid amateurs they had been. Bureaucratic rationality would be the way to reconcile private rights and public purpose.

The social spending programs I have examined provide only a small glimpse of the questions the courts tried to resolve as old forms of judicial accountability were partially transformed into ones of bureaucratic accountability. These transformations happened in the myriad programs the states and federal governments were administering.

New Deal Programs and Public Purpose

By the time Congress enacted the Social Security Act of 1935, much of the legal groundwork concerning why spending for individuals benefited the public had been laid in the states. The Social Security Act expanded federal authority in taking responsibility for the welfare of individuals. By allowing payments to elderly people who were not indigent, it also directly countered Arizona's 1916 decision and decisions from the 1920s in Pennsylvania and Colorado. Popular movements for old age pensions and the national crisis of the Great Depression had transformed visions of public welfare.[29] The gradual expansion in pensions from firemen to police and teachers, however, had already built a framework to permit spending for individuals who were not indigent. The new boards controlling spending had contributed to the ongoing struggles over agency governance, which in the twentieth century ranged from decisions to exclude the Chinese on the West Coast to decisions to raise freight rates on railroads throughout the country.[30]

The conflict between the courts and Congress that has been so prominent in studies of the New Deal had a long history in the states as well as the federal government, one that had been building as governments took on new tasks. Barry Cushman has argued that the prominent cases lost by Roosevelt's New Deal administration were lost because the programs were badly drafted in light of decisions the courts had long been making.[31] G. Edward White has similarly argued that judges had for some time been struggling with what constitutional law was and what it required of them. Judgment could require what he calls "boundary pricking," or defining acceptable and unacceptable actions according to unchanging principles. Judges came to abandon that ideal as impossible for judging, accepting instead that the United States Constitution contained flexible principles and required them to discern what those principles were, not just to apply them to new and changing circumstances. This trouble, White argues, had been brewing for years before the New Deal.[32]

Reading the federal cases and disputes over federal authority, then, shows that the New Deal was a much more ambiguous legal period than the oft-told story of conflict between a politically motivated Supreme Court and an innovative administration indicates. The collapse of categories in law—between public and private, between service and work, categories that an expansion in programs made virtually untenable—applies not just to federal cases and federal courts but to state courts and state court cases as well. State implementation of the Social Security Act was constitutional in the courts because the cases concerning firemen, policemen, and teachers—alongside the workmen's compensation cases and state commission reports from states as different as Wisconsin, California, Pennsylvania, and Massachusetts—had made it possible to think of all wage labor as service. Where it was not, states amended their constitutions.

In response to complexity that threatened to make nonsense of distinctions, commentators and courts began to see defining public purpose as the legislature's job. In 1924 an article in *Corpus Juris,* the major synthesis of state law, gamely tried to describe the law while noting that it was very difficult to tell exactly what constituted a public purpose; by then the authors had dozens of cases to cite.[33] Judges had begun to concede that determining public purpose was a job for legislatures.[34] Legal commentary supported that concession: it was just why scholars such as Howard McBain had spent the 1920s arguing for a "living constitution," one that would allow changing perceptions of needs to change interpretations of principles.[35]

As McBain's argument for a living constitution implied, the concessions to the legislature were not limited to social welfare law. Labor law had historically been within the jurisdiction of the courts in Anglo-American law, and courts had been reluctant to allow legislatures to govern it. Relations between employers and employees were, within legal doctrine, a matter of natural hierarchy, similar to relations between parents and children, or husbands and wives. The common law represented governance via a natural order, suitable to these natural hierarchies; legislation represented disruption of these hierarchies.[36] To cede control of labor to the legislature was to say that this was not an area of law peculiarly within the expertise of the courts rather than the legislature. In a world with a natural order, conceding that legislatures could violate the principles of natural hierarchy seemed akin to saying that they could try to change the law of gravity. Since courts were only loosely coordinated, however, the shift away from that view was uneven.

If determining public purpose was a legislative task, all the popular and intellectual changes in the interpretation of the troubles that befell people mattered in law. By the turn of the century, labor activists had begun to see public works not as a matter of poor relief but as a requirement for coping with expected downturns in the economy.[37] From commentators on state court cases to Keynesian explanations of unemployment and what to do about it, the groundwork had long been laid for the acceptance of legislatures' definitions of unemployment and poverty in old age as problems for the polity, not just for the individual poor. Although Arizona's supreme court in 1916 had taken it for granted, requiring no citations, that states could help only the indigent, and the Pennsylvania court in the 1920s held that old age pensions could provide only for the indigent, other states and the federal courts were at the very same time upholding workmen's compensation. Those cases explained why dangerous work was beneficial to the general public. The conclusion the *Corpus Juris* writers had reached in 1924—that determining public purpose was the responsibility of the legislature—became national constitutional law in 1937 in the New Deal Social Security cases *Steward Machine Co. v. Davis* (1937) and *Helvering v. Davis* (1937), which decided the constitutionality of federal payroll taxes for unemployment and old age pensions, respectively.

The New Deal reconfiguration of public power required a rethinking of the public-purpose doctrine in the state courts as well as in the United States Supreme Court. To avoid problems of federalism and limits on what the federal government could legitimately do, the Social Security Act of 1935 established a complicated scheme requiring states to have their own unemployment compensation, old age pensions, and Aid to Dependent Children. Such a format meant that if someone challenged any of those plans, a state supreme court had to decide whether the program accorded with that state's interpretation of public purpose. As chapter eight explains, after the Pennsylvania and Colorado courts had struck down old age pensions, many states enacted amendments allowing the new pensions, particularly once the New Deal made them a reality. Unemployment compensation, one of the schemes that social insurance advocates believed should protect workers from the devastation that the business cycles of industrial capitalism could bring, raised the same constitutional questions as other social insurance schemes. State supreme courts approved these programs before the United States Supreme Court did: as legislation proliferated, state courts acceded to the position that what constituted public purpose was a matter for the legislature to determine, not the courts.[38] Widespread unemployment was a disaster general enough to make unemployment insurance a matter of general public welfare, not class legislation.

The Supreme Court affirmed state unemployment schemes in *Carmichael v. Southern Coal and Coke Co.,* decided on the same day as *Helvering* and *Steward Machine Co.* The Alabama Supreme Court had already held that the program was constitutional under both state and federal constitutions; the United States Supreme Court took the Alabama court's holding as simply a statement of the law rather than as something the high court could check, and it also held, by the one-vote margin common to decisions in 1937, that the unemployment compensation scheme was constitutional.

In *Carmichael,* the Supreme Court held that determining a public purpose was for legislatures, not justices or judges, just as the writers in *Corpus Juris* had said in 1924: "The existence of local conditions which, because of their nature and extent, are of concern to the public as a whole, the modes of advancing the public interest by correcting them or avoiding their consequences, are peculiarly within the knowledge of the legislature, and to it, and not to the courts, is committed the duty and responsibility of making choice of the possible methods."[39] There was no longer any law to apply, as there had been throughout the nineteenth and, sometimes, the early twentieth century.

That the problems of unemployment in *Carmichael* and *Steward Machine Co.* and old age in *Helvering* were problems of the public as a whole also made the programs satisfy remnants of the public-purpose doctrine:

> It suffices to say that [studies] show that unemployment apparently has become a permanent incident of our industrial system. . . . The evils of the attendant social and economic wastage permeate the entire social structure. Apart from poverty, or a less extreme impairment of the savings which afford the chief protection to the working class against old age and the hazards of illness, a matter of inestimable consequence to society as a whole, and apart from the loss of purchasing power, the legislature could have concluded that unemployment brings in its wake increase in vagrancy and crimes against property, reduction in the number of marriages, deterioration of family life, decline in the birth rate, increase in illegitimate births, impairment of the health of the unemployed and their families and malnutrition of their children.[40]

Unemployment was no longer a sign of hard times that strong men endured, as drought had been in the *Osawkee Township* case in 1875. Then, assistance implied developing dependence in people who should rely on themselves, friends, and Christian charity. Robert Jackson, one of the attorneys for the government litigating New Deal cases, said of *Carmichael,* "The decision allowed the states to put unemployment insurance on the basis of a right instead of charity."[41] In short, unemployment payments need not be limited to the indigent. Similarly, in *Helvering v. Davis* the Supreme Court held that poverty in old age raised national, not just individual problems, and that Congress had its hands on enough studies to demonstrate that old age pensions would serve a public purpose.[42] Public purpose was still live enough that the Court majority thought itself obligated to explain why Congress could determine that insurance programs divorced from public service and indigence could serve a public purpose.

Aid to Dependent Children, enacted in the Social Security Act to replace mothers' pensions, raised no constitutional problems in the states because mothers' pensions had been deemed constitutional, just as poor relief had been. Poor women never had the category of service expanded to include them. Aid to Dependent Children was drafted hurriedly by women in the Children's Bureau, the federal bureau that was responsible for the welfare of children. They did not see it as controversial, or even as the bureau's top priority.[43] Mothers' pensions had had the support of the charity workers and middle-class women activists who always worried about poor women, whereas the elderly in the 1930s had popular spokesmen and mass movements to support making old age pensions into something other than poor relief. Even though old age pensions were struck down as unconstitutional in every state in which they had been made mandatory before the New Deal, the enactment at all by state legislatures had made it imaginable that they could be something other than poor relief.

The elderly also never won a claim to service constitutionally before the New Deal. That awaited the determined work of political executives who believed that by explaining to Americans that the elderly were receiving payment for work they had done, they would be able to eliminate the stigma of that form of public assistance.[44] The constitutional story of transformations in payments parallels the political story: each new pension judged constitutional separated its recipients from the poorhouse and from recipients of poor relief. That never happened for poor women with children.

Good legal reasons for upholding the Social Security Act included the reconsideration in the state courts concerning the meanings of indigence and dependence, the move from service as public work to service as work. Rethinking the Constitution did not occur just through the switch in the Supreme Court, however it is understood, after Roosevelt's second election. The changes went on in the states as well, through constitutional amendments and public discussions of them that made visible the contest over constitutional meanings. When the United States Supreme Court decided *Carmichael*, it cited Alabama's decision that alleviating unemployment was a public purpose, deferring to the state's decision on the meaning of its constitution. To repeat, many of the most basic struggles concerning what made a welfare state arose from state, not only federal, constitutional interpretation. Constitutional change is long and slow with loose and jolting connections between intellectual currents, the frustrations of litigants, and judges' decisions; no particular moment stands out as a guide to interpreting the Constitution properly today. That past offers paths rather than definitive breaks with what has come before. The paths chosen in a loosely coordinated federalism make the world of antebellum firemen and collective obligation very distant from today's disputes over private investment of social security funds.

Stretching the service justification to include all paid work has helped to eliminate from discussion of welfare the payments of pensions to civil servants, veterans, and the elderly. Constitutionally, each was once subject to the same suspicion concerning a dependent population that still plagues discussion of payments to poor women with children and, less visibly, to men eligible only for state public relief. Revisiting nineteenth-century and early-twentieth-century constitutional debates over what kinds of spending would encourage dependency invites a rethinking of welfare and of constitutional revision in American history.

Appendix

Cases Cited

Adkins v. Children's Hospital, 261 U.S. 525 (1923)

Ahl v. Gleim, 52 Pa. 432 (1866)

Aetna Fire Ins. Co. v. Jones, 78 S.C. 455 (1907)

Angle v. Runyon, 38 N.J.L. 403 (1876)

Attorney General v. Connolly, 193 Mich. 499 (1916)

Badura v. Multnomah County, 87 Or. 466 (1918)

Barber v. Camden, 51 Me. 608 (1865)

Bartholomew v. Harwinton, 33 Conn. 408 (1866)

Bartlett v. Ackerman, 21 N.Y.S. 53 (1893)

Beach v. Bradstreet, 85 Conn. 344 (1912)

Beeland Wholesale Co. v. Kaufman, 174 So. 516 (1937)

Board of Education v. Bladen, 113 N.C. 379 (1913)

Board of Education v. City of Louisville, 288 Ky. 656 (1941)

Booth v. Town of North Branford, 32 Conn. 49 (1864)

Booth v. Town of Woodbury, 32 Conn. 118 (1864)

Bosworth v. Harp, 154 Ky. 559 (1913)

Bowler v. Nagel, 228 Mich. 434 (1924)

Bowles v. Landaff, 59 N.H. 164 (1879)

Bradwell v. Illinois, 83 U.S. 130 (1873)

Briscoe v. Allison, 43 Ill. 291 (1867)

Broadhead v. Milwaukee, 19 Wis. 624 (1865)

Brown v. Russell, 166 Mass. 14 (1896)

Buckstegge v. State Board of Control of Arizona, #8308, Superior Court of the State of Arizona in and for Maricopa County

Bush v. County of Orange, 159 N.Y. 212 (1899)

Busser v. Snyder, 5 Pa. D. & C. 842 (1924)

Busser v. Snyder, 282 Pa. 440 (1925)

Busser v. Snyder, 37 A.L.R. 1515 (1925)

Buster v. Marion County, 84 Or. 624 (1917)

Butler v. Town of Putney, 43 Vt. 481 (1871)

Carmichael v. Southern Coal and Coke Co., 301 U.S. 495 (1937)

Carver v. Creque, 48 N.Y. 385 (1872)

Cass County v. Nixon, 35 N.D. 601 (1917)

Cass Township v. Dillon, 16 Ohio St. 38 (1864)

Chamberlin, Inc. v. Andrews, 271 N.Y. 1 (1936)

Chamberlin, Inc. v. Andrews, 299 U.S. 515 (1936)

Champion v. Ames, 188 U.S. 321 (1903)

Chicago, M. and St. P. Railway Co. v. Minnesota, 134 U.S. 418 (1890)

City of Lowell v. Oliver, 8 Allen 247 (1864)

Civil Rights Cases, 109 U.S. 3 (1883)

Cobbs v. Home Ins. Co., 18 Ala. App. 206 (1920)

Coffman v. Keightley, 24 Ind. 509 (1865)

Comer v. Folsom, 13 Minn. 219 (1868)

Commonwealth ex rel. Attorney General v. Schlager, 18 Lackawanna Jurist 16 (1917)

Commonwealth ex rel. Firemen's Relief Assn. v. Barker, 211 Pa. 610 (1905)

Commonwealth ex rel. Mothers' Assistance Fund v. Powell, 256 Pa. 470 (1917)

Commonwealth ex rel. Philadelphia Police Pension Fund Assn. v. Walton, 182 Pa. 373 (1897)

Cooley v. Board of Wardens, 12 How. 299 (1851)

Cox v. Mt. Tabor, 41 Vt. 28 (1868)

Crowell v. Hopkinton, 45 N.H. 9 (1863)

Davis v. Landgrove, 43 Vt. 442 (1871)

DeBrot v. Marion County, 164 Iowa 208 (1914)

Deering and Co. v. Peterson, 75 Minn. 118 (1898)

Delaware County v. Town of Delaware, 93 N.Y.S. 954 (1905)

Denver v. Lynch, 92 Colo. 102 (1932)

Denver and Rio Grande Railroad Co. v. Grand County, 170 Pac. 74 (1917)

Dinehart v. La Fayette, 19 Wisc. 677 (1865)

Dred Scott v. Sandford, 19 How. (60 U.S.) 393 (1857)

Eddy v. Morgan, 216 Ill. 437 (1905)

Elder v. Collier, 100 Ga. 342 (1897)

Feldman and Co. v. City Council of Charleston, 23 S.C. 57 (1885)

Finley v. Marion County, 81 or. 294 (1916)

Fire Department of the City of New York v. Noble, 3 E. D. Smith 440 (1854) 391

Fire Department of the City of New York v. Wright, 3 E. D. Smith 453 (1854)

Fire Department of Milwaukee v. Helfenstein, 16 Wis. 136 (1862)

Firemen's Benevolent Association v. Lounsbury, 21 Ill. 511 (1859)

Franklin v. State Board of Examiners, 23 Cal. 173 (1863)

Freeland v. Hastings, 10 Allen 570 (1865)

Frisbie v. U.S., 157 U.S. 160 (1895)

Gillum v. Johnson, 62 P.2d. 1037 (1936)

Gould v. Raymond, 59 N.H. 260 (1879)

Grim v. Weissenberg School Dist., 57 Pa. 433 (1868)

Gustafson v. Rhinow, 144 Minn. 415 (1920)

Hammitt v. Gaynor, 144 N.Y. Supp. 123 (1913)

Haven v. Ludlow, 41 Vt. 418 (1868)

Helvering v. Davis, 301 U.S. 619 (1937)

Henderson v. Lagow, 42 Ill. 360 (1866)

Hilbish v. Catherman, 14 P. F. Smith 154 (1870)

Howes Bros. Co. v. Unemployment Compensation Commission of Massachusetts, 5 N.E.2d. 720 (1936)

Hughes v. Traeger, 264 Iɪɪ. 612 (1914)

Inhabitants of Poland v. Inhabitants of Wilton, 15 Me. 363 (1839)

In re House Roll, 284 31 Neb. 505 (1891)

In re Hunter, 97 Colo. 279 (1936)

In re Interrogatories of the Governor, 99 Colo. 591 (1937)

In re Koopman, 146 Minn. 36 (1920)

In re Opinion of the Justices, 100 A. 49 (1917)

In re Opinion of the Justices, 154 A. 217 (1931)

In re Roche, 141 N.Y. App. Div. 872 (1910)

In re Rumsey, 102 Neb. 302 (1918)

In re Sharp, 88 Or. 594 (1918)

In re Snyder, 93 Wash. 59 (1916)

In re Walker, 49 N.D. 682 (1923)

In re Wolfe, 81 Or. 297 (1916)

Ives v. South Buffalo Railway, 201 N.Y. 271 (1911)

Kelly v. Marshall, 69 Pa. 319 (1871)

Lander County v. Humboldt County, 21 Nev. 415 (1893)

Laughton v. Town of Putney, 43 Vt. 485 (1871)

Le Duc v. City of Hastings, 39 Minn. 110 (1888)

Leonard v. Wiseman, 31 Md. 201 (1869)

Loan Association v. Topeka, 20 Wall. 655 (1874)

Lochner v. New York, 198 U.S. 45 (1905)

Londoner v. Denver, 210 U.S. 373 (1908)

Lowell v. Boston, 111 Mass. 454 (1873)

Lucas Co. v. State, 75 Ohio State 114 (1906)

Mahon v. Board of Education of the City of New York, 171 N.Y. 263 (1902)

McKay v. Welch, 6 N.Y.S. 358 (1889)

Mead v. Acton, 139 Mass. 341 (1885)

Milheim v. Moffat Tunnel Improvement District, 72 Colo. 268 (1922)

Milheim v. Moffat Tunnel Improvement District, 262 U.S. 710 (1923)

Miller v. Korns, 107 Ohio State 287 (1923)

Misner v. Bullard, 43 I11. 470 (1867)

Mothers' Pensions, 28 Pa. Dist. Rep. 244 (1919)

Mountain Timber Co. v. Washington, 243 U.S. 219 (1917)

Muller v. Oregon, 208 U.S. 412 (1908)

Munn v. Illinois, 94 U.S. 113 (1877)

New York Central Railroad Co. v. White, 243 U.S. 188 (1917)

North Dakota v. Nelson County, 1 N.D. 88 (1890)

O'Dea v. Cook, 176 Cal. 659 (1917)

Opinion of the Justices, 166 Mass. 589 (1896)

Opinion of the Justices, 175 Mass. 599 (1900)

Opinion of the Justices, 186 Mass. 603 (1904)

Opinion of the Justices, 190 Mass. 611 (1906)

Opinion of the Justices, 211 Mass. 608 (1912)

Opinion of the Justices, 45 N.H. 593 (1864)

Panama Refining Co. v. Ryan, 295 U.S. 388 (1935)

Paul v. Virginia, 8 Wall. (75 U.S.) 168 (1869)

Pecoy v. Chicago, 265 I11. 78 (1914)

Pennie v. Reis, U.S. 464 (1889)

People v. Fire Association of Philadelphia, 92 N.Y. 311 (1883)

People v. Home Insurance Co., 92 N.Y. 328 (1883)

People v. Westchester County National Bank, 231 N.Y. 465 (1921)

People ex rel. Detroit and Howell R. R. v. Township Bd. of Salem, 20 Mich. 452 (1870)

People ex rel. Kroner v. Abbott, 274 I11. 380, 385 (1916)

People ex rel. Peake v. Board of Supervisors of Columbia County, 43 N.Y. 130 (1870)

People ex rel. Stuckart v. Chicago, 270 I11. 477 (1915)

People ex rel. Stuckart v. Klee, 282 I11. 440 (1918)

People ex rel. Stuckart v. New Jersey Sandberg Co., 282 I11. 245 (1918)

People ex rel. Waddy v. Partridge, 172 N.Y. 305 (1902)

People ex rel. Westchester Fire Insurance Co. v. Davenport, 91 N.Y. 574 (1883)

Personnel Administrator of Massachusetts v. Feeney, 442 U.S. 256 (1979)

Philadelphia Assn. v. Wood, 39 Pa. St. 73 (1861)

Phoenix Assur. Co. v. Fire Dept., 117 Ala. 631 (1897)

Pierce v. Society of Sisters, 268 U.S. 510 (1925)

Pierce County v. Rugby, Pierce County, 47 N.D. 301 (1921)

Pollock v. Farmer's Loan and Trust Co., 157 U.S. 429 (1895)

Potter v. Canaan, 37 Conn. 222 (1870)

Powers v. Shepard, 48 N.Y. 540 (1872)

Railroad Retirement Board v. Alton Railroad Co., 295 U.S. 330 (1934)

Ryan v. Foreman, 262 Iɪɪ. 175 (1914)

Schechter Poultry Corp. v. United States, 295 U.S. 495 (1935)

Seymour v. Marlboro, 40 Vt. 171 (1868)

Shackford v. Newington, 46 N.H. 415 (1866)

Shapiro v. Thompson, 394 U.S. 618 (1969)

Sharpless v. Mayor of Philadelphia, 21 Penn. St. Rep. 147 (1853)

Smith v. Aplin, 80 Mich. 205 (1890)

Smithberger v. Banning, 129 Neb. 651 (1935)

Spaulding v. Andover, 54 N.H. 38 (1873)

Speer v. Blairsville, 14 Wright 150 (1865)

Startup v. Harmon, 59 Utah 329 (1921)

State v. Baltimore, 52 Md. 398 (1879)

State v. Demarest, 32 N.J.L. 528 (1866)

State v. Edmondson, 89 Ohio 351 (1913)

State Board of Control of Arizona v. Buckstegge, 18 Ariz. 277 (1916)

State ex rel. Anderson v. Harris, 17 Ohio St. 608 (1867)

State ex rel. Atwood v. Johnson, 176 N.W. 224 (1920)

State ex rel. Bates v. Richland Twp., 20 Ohio St. 362 (1870)

State ex rel. Board of Commissioners v. District Court of Second Judicial District, 204
   Pac. 600 (1922)

State ex rel. Cline v. Wilkesville Township, 20 Ohio St. 288 (1870)

State ex rel. Cryderman v. Wienrich, 54 Mont. 390 (1918)

State ex rel. Dudgeon v. Levitan, 181 Wis. 326 (1923)

State ex rel. Griffith v. Osawkee Township, 14 Kan. 418, 421 (1875)

State ex rel. Haig v. Hague, 37 N.D. 583 (1917)

State ex rel. Hart v. Clausen, 113 Wash. 570 (1921)

State ex rel. Heaven v. Ziegenhein, 144 Mo. 283 (1898)

State ex rel. Jackson v. Kurtz, 11 Ohio C.D. 705 (1900)

State ex rel. Jennison v. Rogers, 87 Minn. 130 (1902)

State ex rel. McCurdy v. Tappan, 29 Wis. 664 (1872)

State ex rel. Morris v. Handlin, 38 S.D. 550 (1917)

State ex rel. Snyder v. Abbey, 15 Ohio 261 (1911)

State ex rel. Stearns County v. Klasen, 123 Minn. 382 (1913)

State ex rel. Walker v. Derham, 61 S.C. 259 (1901)

State ex rel. Ward v. Hubbard, 12 Ohio C.D. 87 (1901)

State of Louisiana v. Merchants Ins. Co., 12 La. Ann. 802 (1857)

State of Nebraska ex rel. Haberlan v. Love, 89 Neb. 149 (1911)

State Supervisor, Mothers Assistance Fund, 28 Pa. Dist. Rep. 244 (1918)

Stebbins v. Leaman, 47 Ill. 352 (1868)

Stertz v. Industrial Insurance Commission, 91 Wash. 588 (1916)

Steward Machine Co. v. Davis, 301 U.S. 619 (1937)

Taber v. Erie County, 6 N.Y.S. 91 (1889)

Taylor v. Mott, 123 Cal. 497 (1899)

Taylor v. Thompson, 42 Ill. 9 (1866)

Town of New Hartford v. Town of Canaan, 52 Conn. 158 (1884)

Town of South Hampton v. Town of Hampton Falls, 11 N.H. 134 (1840)

Trustees of Dartmouth College v. Woodward, 4 Wheat. (17 U.S.) 518 (1819)

Trustees of Exempt Firemen's Benevolent Fund v. Roome, 93 N.Y. 313 (1883)

Tyson v. School Directors of Halifax Township, 1 P. F. Smith 9 (1865)

United States v. Cruikshank, 92 U.S. 542 (1875)

United States v. Hall, 98 U.S. 343 (1878)

United States v. Hartwell, 6 Wallace 385 (1867)

United States v. Marks, 2 Abb. (U.S.) 534

United States v. Teller, 107 U.S. 64 (1883)

Verdery v. Walton, 137 Ga. 213 (1911)

Veterans' Welfare Board v. Riley, 206 Pac. Rep. 631 (1922)

Walton v. Cotton, 60 U.S. 355 (1856)

Washington County v. Berwick, 56 Pa. 466 (1867)

Webster v. Town of Harwinton, 32 Conn. 131 (1864)

Weismer v. Village of Douglas, 64 N.Y. 91 (1876)

Weister v. Hade et al., School Directors, 2 P. F. Smith 474 (1866)

Willoughby v. Holderness, 62 N.H. 227 (1882)

Wilson v. Buckman, 13 Minn. 441 (1868)

Winchester v. Corinna, 55 Me. 9 (1866)

Wood v. Simmons, 4 N.Y.S. 368 (1889)

Woodall v. Darst, 71 W.Va. 350 (1912)

Zachary v. Polk County Court, 74 Or. 58 (1914)

Notes

1. Social Welfare in the States

1. Abner Louima was battered, including being sodomized, by New York City police officers in 1997. In 1999, Amidou Diallo, an unarmed West African immigrant, died in a hail of police gunfire. Both incidents provoked public outpourings of grief and protest. See Jim Dwyer, "No Way Out," *New York Times Magazine,* June 23, 2002, 20; Dean E. Murphy and David M. Halbfinger, "9/11 Bridged the Racial Divide, New Yorkers Say, Gingerly," *New York Times,* June 16, 2002, 25.

2. See Linda K. Kerber, *No Constitutional Right to Be Ladies* (New York: Hill & Wang, 1998), chap. 5.

3. Http://www.arlingtoncemetery.com/fireman-01.htm. I am grateful to Sheri Englund for this citation.

4. Steven R. Weisman, *The Great Tax Wars: Lincoln to Wilson: The Fierce Battles over Money and Power That Transformed the Nation* (New York: Simon and Schuster, 2002).

5. Gwendolyn Mink, introduction to *Whose Welfare?* ed. Gwendolyn Mink (Ithaca: Cornell University Press, 1999); Rickie Solinger, "Dependency and Choice: The Two Faces of Eve," 7–35, and Dorothy Roberts, "Welfare's Ban on Poor Motherhood," 152–167, both in Mink, *Whose Welfare?*

6. Gwendolyn Mink, "Aren't Poor Single Mothers Women? Feminists, Welfare Reform, and Welfare Justice," 171–188, in Mink, *Whose Welfare?;* Linda Gordon, *Pitied but Not Entitled* (New York: Free Press, 1994), 1–13.

7. See, e.g., "Small Blessings," *People,* February 25, 2002, 48.

8. Amy Dru Stanley, *From Bondage to Contract: Wage Labor, Marriage, and the Market in the Age of Slave Emancipation* (New York: Cambridge University Press, 1998).

9. See, e.g., Kerber, *No Constitutional Right,* 221–302.

10. Judith Shklar, *American Citizenship* (Cambridge: Harvard University Press, 1991), 63–104; Stanley, *Bondage,* 1–17.

11. Lawrence Glickman, *A Living Wage: American Workers and the Making of Consumer Society* (Ithaca: Cornell University Press, 1997), 1–2, 17–24; Stanley, *Bondage,* 19–23, 98–137.

12. T. H. Marshall, *Citizenship and Social Class* (1950; London: Pluto Press, 1992). Even in the British centralized state, rights of citizenship emerged from local conditions. Margaret R. Somers, "Rights, Relationality, and Membership: Rethinking the Making and Meaning of Citizenship," *Law and Social Inquiry* 19, no. 1 (1994): 63–112.

13. Gordon, *Pitied,* 145–182; Theda Skocpol, *Protecting Soldiers and Mothers: The Political Origins of Social Policy in the United States* (Cambridge: Harvard University Press, 1992), 160–194; Kathryn Kish Sklar, "The Historical Foundations of Women's Power in the Creation of the American Welfare State, 1830–1930," in *Mothers of a New World: Maternalist Politics and the Origins of Welfare States,* ed. Seth Koven and Sonya Michel (New York: Routledge, 1993), 43–93.

14. The literature on these transformations is vast. See Douglas Ashford, *The Emergence of the Welfare States* (New York: Basil Blackwell, 1986); Gordon, *Pitied;* Michael B. Katz, *In the Shadow of the Poorhouse: A Social History of Welfare in America* (New York: Basic Books, 1986); Daniel Levine, *Poverty and Society: The Growth of the American Welfare State in International Comparison* (New Brunswick, N.J.: Rutgers University Press, 1988); Ann Shola Orloff, *The Politics of Pensions: A Comparative Analysis of Britain, Canada, and the United States, 1880–1940* (Madison: University of Wisconsin Press, 1993);

Daniel Rodgers, *Atlantic Crossings: Social Politics in a Progressive Age* (Cambridge: Harvard University Press, 1998); Skocpol, *Protecting*.

15. For the importance of maternalism across Western industrialized states, see Koven and Michel, *Mothers of a New World*.

16. Joanne L. Goodwin, *Gender and the Politics of Welfare Reform: Mothers' Pensions in Chicago, 1911–1929* (Chicago: University of Chicago Press, 1997); Gordon, *Pitied*, 102–104.

17. Gordon, *Pitied*, 22–24, 39–64, 70–88; Kathryn Kish Sklar, *Florence Kelley and the Nation's Work: The Rise of Women's Political Culture, 1830–1900* (New Haven: Yale University Press, 1995); Ellen Fitzpatrick, *Endless Crusade: Women Social Scientists and Progressive Reform* (New York: Oxford University Press, 1990); Skocpol, *Protecting*, 430.

18. Candice Lewis Bredbenner, *A Nationality of Her Own: Women, Marriage, and the Law of Citizenship* (Berkeley: University of California Press, 1998); Hendrik Hartog, "Mrs. Packard on Dependency," *Yale Journal of Law and the Humanities* 1 (1988): 79–103; Nancy Isenberg, *Sex and Citizenship in Antebellum America* (Chapel Hill: University of North Carolina Press, 1998), 155–190.

19. Norma Basch, *In the Eyes of the Law: Women, Marriage, and Property in Nineteenth-Century New York* (Ithaca: Cornell University Press, 1982); Reva B. Siegel, "Home as Work: The First Woman's Right Claims concerning Wives' Household Labor, 1850–1880," *Yale Law Journal* 103 (1994): 1073–1182; Stanley, *Bondage*, 204–17.

20. Rogers M. Smith, *Civic Ideals: Conflicting Visions of Citizenship in U.S. History* (New Haven: Yale University Press, 1997), 230–235, 337–342; Stanley, *Bondage*, 175–218.

21. Hendrik Hartog, *Man and Wife in America: A History* (Cambridge: Harvard University Press, 2000), 32–39, 295–308.

22. Roberts, "Welfare's Ban," 156–163; Skocpol, *Protecting*; Gordon, *Pitied*.

23. Skocpol, *Protecting*, 67–152.

24. Laura S. Jensen, "Entitlements and the Constitution of the American Nation" (manuscript, 2001); Laura S. Jensen, "The Early American Origins of Entitlements," *Studies in American Political Development* 10, no. 2 (1996): 360–404; Megan J. McClintock, "Civil War Pensions and the Reconstruction of Union Families," *Journal of American History* 83, no. 2 (1996): 456–480.

25. Orloff, *Politics of Pensions*.

26. Suzanne Mettler, *Dividing Citizens: Gender and Federalism in New Deal Public Policy* (Ithaca: Cornell University Press, 1998), 5–6, 15–22.

27. Gwendolyn Mink, *The Wages of Motherhood: Inequality in the Welfare State, 1917–1942* (Ithaca: Cornell University Press, 1995), 127, 130, 137.

28. Mettler, *Dividing Citizens*, 72–73.

29. Barbara J. Nelson, "The Origins of the Two-Channel Welfare State: Workmen's Compensation and Mothers' Aid," in *Women, the State, and Welfare,* ed. Linda Gordon (Madison: University of Wisconsin Press, 1990), 124, 133, 145.

30. Ibid.; Theda Skocpol, "The Limits of the New Deal System and the Roots of Contemporary Welfare Dilemmas," in *The Politics of Social Policy in the United States,* ed. Margaret Weir, Ann Orloff, and Theda Skocpol (Princeton: Princeton University Press, 1988); Mettler, *Dividing Citizens*, 211–223; Gwendolyn Mink, *Welfare's End* (Ithaca: Cornell University Press, 1998).

31. Joel F. Handler, "Low-Wage Work 'As We Know It': What's Wrong/What Can be Done," in *Hard Labor: Women and Work in the Post-Welfare Era,* ed. Joel F. Handler and Lucie White (Armonk, N.Y.: M. E. Sharpe, 1999); Kathryn Edin and Christopher Jencks, "Reforming Welfare," in Christopher Jencks, *Rethinking Social Policy: Race, Poverty, and the Underclass* (Cambridge: Harvard University Press, 1992), 229; Solinger, "Dependency and Choice"; Eileen Boris, "When Work Is Slavery," in Mink, *Whose Welfare?*; Roberts, "Welfare's Ban."

32. Frances Fox Piven, "Welfare and Work," in Mink, *Whose Welfare?* 83–99.

33. For discussions of sociological jurisprudence and legal realism, see Laura Kalman, *Legal Realism at Yale, 1927–1960* (Chapel Hill: University of North Carolina Press, 1986); John Henry Schlegel, *American Legal Realism and Empirical Social Science* (Chapel Hill: University of North Carolina Press, 1995), chaps. 2–4; N. E. H. Hull, *Roscoe Pound and Karl Llewellyn: Searching for an American Jurisprudence* (Chicago: University of Chicago Press, 1997).

34. Frank J. Goodnow, *Comparative Administrative Law: A Comparison of the Administrative Systems, National and Local, of the United States, England, France, and Germany,* 2 vols. (New York: Putnam, 1893).

35. Fitzpatrick, *Endless Crusade,* 44–46; Goodwin, *Gender,* 92–94. During the 1930s, Edith Abbott and Sophonisba Breckinridge of the Chicago School of Social Work sponsored a number of dissertations on the poor law in different states. See see Sophonisba P. Breckinridge, *The Illinois Poor Law and Its Administration* (Chicago: University of Chicago Press, 1939); Grace A. Browning, *The Development of Poor Relief Legislation in Kansas* (Chicago: University of Chicago Press, 1935); Isabel Campbell Bruce and Edith Eickhoff, *The Michigan Poor Law* (Chicago: University of Chicago Press, 1936); Margaret Creech, *Three Centuries of Poor Law Administration: A Study of Legislation in Rhode Island* (Chicago: University of Chicago Press, 1936); Alice Shaffer, Mary Wysor Keefer, and Sophonisba P. Breckinridge, *Indiana Poor Law: Its Development and Administration* (Chicago: University of Chicago Press, 1936); Martha Branscombe, *The Courts and the Poor Laws in New York State, 1784–1929* (Chicago: University of Chicago Press, 1943). Edith Abbott also used case law to illustrate questions of who counted as a pauper in her own comprehensive study of poor law in the United States, *Public Assistance* (Chicago: University of Chicago Press, 1940), vol. 1.

36. Roscoe Pound, "Fifty Years of Jurisprudence," *Harvard Law Review* 51, no. 5 (1938): 779. Barry Cushman also relies upon Roscoe Pound to elucidate readings of cases in *Rethinking the New Deal Court* (Oxford: Oxford University Press, 1998), 42.

37. Pound, "Fifty Years," 789.

38. Robert Gordon, "Critical Legal Histories," *Stanford Law Review* 36 (1984): 57.

39. G. Edward White, *The Constitution and the New Deal* (Cambridge: Harvard University Press, 2000), 3–4, 36–37.

40. Since scholars have argued this point in many different areas of law, what is remarkable is the persistence of some clarity. See Stanley Fish, *There's No Such Thing as Free Speech and It's a Good Thing Too* (New York: Oxford University Press, 1994), 141–179.

41. For a discussion of law as an "authoritative social discourse," see Christopher Tomlins, "Subordination, Authority, Law: Subjects in Labor History," *International Labor and Working Class History* 47 (spring 1995): 56–90.

42. White offers a summary of what he calls the conventional account, as well as a critique of it, in *Constitution,* 11–32. Other scholars who have revised the conventional account include Howard Gillman in *The Constitution Besieged* (Durham, N.C.: Duke University Press, 1993); Cushman in *Rethinking;* and Julie Novkov, *Constituting Workers, Protecting Women: Gender, Law, and Labor in the Progressive Era and New Deal Years* (Ann Arbor: University of Michigan Press, 2001).

43. Karen Orren, *Belated Feudalism: Labor, the Law, and Liberal Development in the United States* (New York: Cambridge University Press, 1991), 211–215.

44. Howard Gillman, "The Antinomy of Public Purposes and Private Rights in the American Constitutional Tradition, or Why Communitarianism Is Not Necessarily Exogenous to Liberal Constitutionalism," *Law and Social Inquiry* 21 (1996): 67–77.

45. William Novak, *The People's Welfare: Law and Regulation in Nineteenth-Century America* (Chapel Hill: University of North Carolina Press, 1996), 235–245.

46. Susan M. Sterett, "Constitutional Law and Administrative Law: Public Pensions in the United States, 1860s–1930s," *Oxford Journal of Legal Studies* 17, no. 4 (1997): 587–610.

47. Karen Orren and Stephen Skowronek, "Beyond the Iconography of Order: Notes for a 'New Institutionalism,'" in *The Dynamics of American Politics: Approaches and Interpretations,* ed. Lawrence C. Dodd and Calvin Jillson (Boulder, Colo.: Westview Press, 1994), 323–328.

2. Independence and Dependence

1. For a systematic discussion of the public purpose doctrine regarding police power, see Gillman, *Constitution Besieged.*

2. Ibid.; Michael Les Benedict, "Laissez-Faire and Liberty: A Reevaluation of the Meaning and Origin of Laissez-Faire Constitutionalism," *Law and History Review* 3 (fall 1985): 243–331; Cushman,

Rethinking; Paul Kens, "The Source of a Myth: Police Powers of the States and Laissez Faire Constitutionalism, 1900–1937," *American Journal of Legal History* 35 (1991): 70–98; Charles McCurdy, "Justice Field and the Limits of Laissez-Faire Constitutionalism," in *American Law and the Constitutional Order,* ed. Lawrence Friedman and Harry N. Scheiber (Cambridge: Harvard University Press, 1978); Harry N. Scheiber, "The Road to *Munn:* Eminent Domain and the Concept of Public Purpose in the State Courts," in *Law in American History,* ed. Donald Fleming and Bernard Bailyn (Cambridge: Harvard University Press, 1971).

3. Gillman, *Constitution Besieged,* 7–15, 28–33.

4. Smith, *Civic Ideals,* 165–167; Stanley, *Bondage,* 9–11, 20.

5. Benedict, "Laissez-Faire"; William Forbath, "The Ambiguities of Free Labor: Labor and the Law in the Gilded Age," *Wisconsin Law Review* (1985): 767–817; Gillman, *Constitution Besieged,* 44–45, 114–131; McCurdy, "Justice Field."

6. Orren, *Belated Feudalism,* 73–91; David Roediger, *The Wages of Whiteness* (New York: Verso Press, 1991), chap. 4.

7. Orren, *Belated Feudalism,* 92–102.

8. David Montgomery, *Citizen Worker* (New York: Cambridge University Press, 1993), 28, 30.

9. Stanley, *Bondage,* 1–17.

10. Eric Foner, *Nothing but Freedom* (Baton Rouge: Louisiana State University Press, 1983), chap. 3; Stanley, *Bondage,* 40–44, 123–129.

11. Stanley, *Bondage,* 102.

12. Ibid., 108–109.

13. Ibid., 110–113.

14. *Munn v. Illinois,* 94 U.S. 113 (1877). For discussions, see Benedict, "Laissez-Faire"; Cushman, *Rethinking;* Gillman, *Constitution Besieged,* 271–272; Paul Kens, *Justice Stephen Field: Shaping Liberty from the Gold Rush to the Gilded Age* (Lawrence: University Press of Kansas, 1997); McCurdy, "Justice Field"; Samuel R. Olken, "Justice George Sutherland and Economic Liberty: Constitutional Conservatism and the Problem of Factions," *William and Mary Bill of Rights Journal* 6, no. 1 (1997): 1–88; Scheiber, "Road to *Munn.*"

15. Karen Orren, "The Primacy of Labor in American Constitutional Development," *American Political Science Review* 89, no. 2 (1995): 386.

16. Gillman, *Constitution Besieged,* 47, 52, 55.

17. Melissa L. Saunders, "Equal Protection, Class Legislation, and Colorblindness," *Michigan Law Review* 96 (November 1997): 255–259.

18. Louis Hartz, *Economic Policy and Democratic Thought: Pennsylvania 1776–1860* (Chicago: Quadrangle Books, 1948), 122–125, discussing *Sharpless v. Mayor of Philadelphia* 21 Penn. St. Rep. 147 (1853); Morton Keller, *Affairs of State* (Cambridge: Harvard University Press, 1977), 111–114; William A. Russ, "The Origin of the Ban on Special Legislation in the Constitution of 1873," *Pennsylvania History* 11, no. 4 (1944): 260–275; Matthew Crenson, *Building the Invisible Orphanage: A Prehistory of the American Welfare System* (Cambridge: Harvard University Press, 1998).

19. Morton J. Horwitz, *The Transformation of American Law, 1870–1960: The Crisis of Legal Orthodoxy* (New York: Oxford University Press, 1992), 21.

20. Gillman, *Constitution Besieged,* 53, 55–56.

21. Analyses of how judges saw the law in the nineteenth century have used different terms but have agreed on the importance of their belief in general, definable law. Chief Justice Joseph Story was the first to try to synthesize American common law; see R. Kent Newmyer, *Supreme Court Justice Joseph Story: Statesman of the Old Republic* (Chapel Hill: University of North Carolina Press, 1985), 271–281. See also Edward Purcell, *Brandeis and the Progressive Constitution* (New Haven: Yale University Press, 2000), 51–63; and White, *Constitution,* 174–176.

22. Paul D. Carrington, "Law as 'The Common Thoughts of Men': The Law-Teaching and Judging of Thomas McIntyre Cooley," *Stanford Law Review* 49 (1997): 498–499, 515–516; Robert Stevens, *Law School: Legal Education in America from the 1850s to the 1980s* (Chapel Hill: University of North Carolina Press, 1983), 52–56.

23. Gerald Berk, *Alternative Tracks: The Constitution of American Industrial Order, 1865–1917* (Baltimore: Johns Hopkins University Press, 1997); Horwitz, *Transformation*, 23.

24. Keller, *Affairs of State*, 345–347; Clyde E. Jacobs, *Law Writers and the Courts* (Berkeley: University of California Press, 1954), chaps. 4–5.

25. Carrington, "Law as 'The Common Thoughts,'" 540–542.

26. Arlien Johnson, *Public Policy and Private Charities: A Study of Legislation in the United States and of Administration in Illinois* (Chicago: University of Chicago Press, 1931), 39.

27. Crenson, *Building the Invisible Orphanage*, 48.

28. Johnson, *Public Policy*, 106–111.

29. "Charity Appropriations," *New York Times*, November 26, 1874, 2; Crenson, *Building the Invisible Orphanage*, 47; "The Bearing of the Recent Amendments . . . ," *New York Times*, March 11, 1875, 6.

30. Crenson, *Building the Invisible Orphanage*, 47–48.

31. *Weismer v. Village of Douglas*, 64 N.Y. 91 (1876).

32. California Constitution of 1879, art. 13, sec. 25.

33. Harry N. Scheiber, "Race, Radicalism, and Reform: Historical Perspective on the 1879 California Constitution," *Hastings Constitutional Law Quarterly* 17 (1989): 57–65.

34. California Constitution of 1879, art. 4, sec. 22.

35. *Loan Association v. Topeka*, 20 Wall. 655 (1874), 663–664.

36. Molly Selvin, "The Public Trust Doctrine in American Law and Economic Policy, 1789–1920," *Wisconsin Law Review* (1980): 1403–1442.

37. For consideration of Brewer's thought and background, see Joseph Gordon Hylton, "David Josiah Brewer and the Christian Constitution," *Marquette Law Review* 81 (1998): 417–425; Joseph Gordon Hylton, "David Joseph Brewer: A Conservative Justice Reconsidered," *Journal of Supreme Court History* (1994): 45–64; Joseph Gordon Hylton, "The Judge Who Abstained in *Plessy v. Ferguson:* Justice David Brewer and the Problem of Race," *University of Mississippi Law Journal* 61, no. 2 (1991): 315–364.

38. See Kens, *Justice Stephen Field*.

39. Hylton, "Judge Who Abstained," 316–317.

40. Michael J. Brodhead, *David J. Brewer: The Life of a Supreme Court Justice, 1837–1910* (Carbondale: Southern Illinois University Press, 1994), 22.

41. Brodhead, *David J. Brewer*, chap. 1. For an early consideration of Brewer's career as a conservative U.S. Supreme Court justice, see Benjamin Twiss, *Lawyers and the Constitution: How Laissez-Faire Came to the Supreme Court* (Princeton: Princeton University Press, 1942), 91–92, 199.

42. Purcell, *Brandeis*, 46–63.

43. Brodhead, *David J. Brewer*, 29.

44. Kansas Constitution, art. 7, sec. 4.

45. *State ex rel. Griffith v. Osawkee Township*, 14 Kan. 418, 421 (1875).

46. Brodhead, *David J. Brewer*, 29.

47. In 1873 the Massachusetts court decided on a similar basis that the state could not aid those who had lost buildings in the 1872 Great Boston Fire. See Aviam Soifer, "The Supreme Judicial Court of Massachusetts and the 1780 Constitution," in *The Supreme Judicial Court of Massachusetts, 1692–1992*, ed. Russell K. Osgood (Boston: Judicial History Society, 1993), 223.

48. On what women owed to their husbands, see Siegel, "Home as Work," 1073; Stanley, *Bondage*, 198–217.

49. *State ex rel. Griffith v. Osawkee Township*, 424, 422.

50. Nancy Fraser and Linda Gordon, "A Genealogy of *Dependency:* Tracing a Keyword of the U.S. Welfare State," *Signs* 19, no. 2 (1994): 309–336; Stanley, *Bondage*, 105–108.

51. *State ex rel. Griffith v. Osawkee Township*, 422. On the same grounds, courts in Massachusetts and South Carolina struck down disaster relief after fires in Boston and Charleston: *Lowell v. Boston*, 111 Mass. 454 (1873); *Feldman and Co. v. City Council of Charleston*, 23 S.C. 57 (1885).

52. For an excellent overview of the shifting meanings of dependence, see Fraser and Gordon, "Genealogy of *Dependency*."

53. Quoted in Brodhead, *David J. Brewer,* 176.

54. Skocpol, *Protecting,* 95–96.

55. Frank J. Goodnow, *Social Reform and the Constitution* (New York: Macmillan, 1911), 292, 302–304; Browning, *Development of Poor Relief Legislation,* 21–22, 79, with Edith Abbott's introductory note, ix–xii.

56. *North Dakota v. Nelson County,* 1 N.D. 88 (1890). See also *In re House Roll 284,* 31 Neb. 505 (1891); *State ex rel. Cryderman v. Wienrich,* 54 Mont. 390 (1918).

57. *Deering and Co. v. Peterson,* 75 Minn. 118 (1898).

58. Hylton, "Brewer: A Conservative Justice," 54–57.

59. H. R. Wilgus, "The Constitutionality of Teachers' Pensions (I)," *Michigan Law Review* 11 (May 1913): 451–477.

60. Albert DeForest Tyler and Francis J. Ludes, "Taxation," *Corpus Juris* 61 (1924): secs. 21–23.

61. For a useful overview of the poor law in Kansas, see Browning, *Development of Poor Relief Legislation.* On the importance of English settlement law to legal practice in eighteenth-century Massachusetts, see Hendrik Hartog, "The Public Law of a County Court; Judicial Government in Eighteenth-Century Massachusetts," *American Journal of Legal History* 20 (1976): 292–299.

62. For a discussion of domicile and the problems it led to in divorce, see Hartog, *Man and Wife,* 34–35, 266–270.

63. Gerald Neuman, *Strangers to the Constitution: Immigrants, Borders, and Fundamental Law* (Princeton: Princeton University Press, 1996), 23–31.

64. Each volume of the studies that Edith Abbott's students wrote on the poor law in different states criticized the local administration. See, e.g., Aileen E. Kennedy, *The Ohio Poor Law and Its Administration* (Chicago: University of Chicago Press, 1934), 2, with Abbott's introductory note, ix.

65. *Town of New Hartford v. Town of Canaan,* 52 Conn. 158 (1884); *Inhabitants of Poland v. Inhabitants of Wilton,* 15 Me. 363 (1839); *Lander County v. Humboldt County,* 21 Nev. 415 (1893); *Town of South Hampton v. Town of Hampton Falls,* 11 N.H. 134 (1840). For discussion, see Abbott, *Public Assistance,* volume 1.

66. David Eastwood, *Governing Rural England* (New York: Oxford University Press, 1994), 109–115.

67. Montgomery, *Citizen Worker,* 73–74.

68. Browning, *Development of Poor Relief Legislation,* 19–20.

69. *Wood v. Simmons,* 4 N.Y.S. 368 (1889). See also *McKay v. Welch,* 6 N.Y.S. 358 (1889); and *Delaware County v. Town of Delaware,* 93 N.Y.S. 954 (1905).

70. For reorganization of poorhouses in Ohio, see Kennedy, *Ohio Poor Law,* 42–47. For the criticisms of both indoor and outdoor relief, see Katz, *In the Shadow of the Poorhouse,* 3–58; 85–112.

71. Crenson, *Building the Invisible Orphanage,* 50.

72. Lawrence M. Friedman and Jack Ladinsky, "Social Change and the Law of Industrial Accidents," in Friedman and Scheiber, *American Law.*

73. In his discussion of employers' liability and the poor law in England, A. W. B. Simpson, *Leading Cases in the Common Law* (New York: Oxford University Press, 1995), chap. 5, has argued that the workhouse alternative to outdoor relief in the 1834 reforms spurred judges to hold employers liable for workplace injuries.

74. *Bartlett v. Ackerman,* 21 N.Y.S. 53 (1893), 54.

75. Branscombe, *Courts and the Poor Laws,* 205–207, 309, discusses the New York poor law settlement cases.

76. Novak, *People's Welfare,* 238–243.

77. Scheiber, "Road to *Munn*"; Gillman, *Constitution Besieged,* 7–8, 45–56.

78. For a similar explanation of the collapse of public purpose in police powers jurisprudence, see Gillman, *Constitution Besieged,* 11.

3. Payments to Firemen and Soldiers

1. Smith, *Civic Ideals,* 273–277; Kerber, *No Constitutional Right,* chap. 5; R. Claire Snyder, *Citizen-Soldiers and Manly Warriors* (Lanham, Md.: Rowman and Littlefield, 1999). For a conceptual overview

of classical political theory with regard to military service, see J. G. A. Pocock, "The Ideal of Citizenship since Classical Times," in *The Citizenship Debates,* ed. Gershon Shafir (Minneapolis: University of Minnesota Press, 1998), 31–42.

2. Kerber, *No Constitutional Right,* chap. 1.

3. Smith, *Civic Ideals,* 111.

4. Ibid., chaps. 7–8.

5. Amy S. Greenberg, *Cause for Alarm: The Volunteer Fire Department in the Nineteenth-Century City* (Princeton: Princeton University Press, 1998), 70, 75–76.

6. Smith, *Civic Ideals,* 220–225.

7. John F. Dillon, *Law of Municipal Corporations,* 2d ed. (New York: James Cockcroft, 1873), 2:830; John F. Dillon, *Commentaries on the Law of Municipal Corporations* (Boston: Little, Brown, 1911), 2:1108, sec. 915.

8. Hendrik Hartog, *Public Property and Private Power: The Corporation of the City of New York in American Life, 1730–1870* (Chapel Hill: University of North Carolina Press, 1983), 3.

9. Novak, *People's Welfare,* 51–82; Hartog, *Public Property,* 127–128.

10. Greenberg, *Cause for Alarm,* 24.

11. Sean Wilentz, *Chants Democratic: New York City and the Rise of the American Working Class, 1788–1850* (New York: Oxford University Press, 1984), 259–260, 269–270.

12. Greenberg, *Cause for Alarm,* 60–62.

13. Robyn Cooper, "The Fireman: Immaculate Manhood," *Journal of Popular Culture* 28, no. 4 (1995): 139–170; Greenberg, *Cause for Alarm,* 45, 58–59, 66–70, 84–90.

14. Wilentz, *Chants Democratic,* 259, 263.

15. Roediger, *Wages of Whiteness,* chap. 6.

16. Wilentz, *Chants Democratic,* 264.

17. Even in New York today, firefighting is still largely white, and African American recruiters find it difficult to convince young black adults that it does not have to be. See "Race and the FDNY," *Weekend Edition Saturday,* February 16, 2002 (http://www.npr.org).

18. Novak, *People's Welfare,* 773.

19. Greenberg, *Cause for Alarm,* 128–134.

20. John Bainbridge, *Biography of an Idea: The Story of Mutual Fire and Casualty Insurance* (Garden City, N.Y.: Doubleday, 1952), 85–86.

21. Greenberg, *Cause for Alarm,* 133–141.

22. Robin Einhorn, *Property Rules* (Chicago: University of Chicago Press, 1991), 149–150.

23. Charles McCurdy, "American Law and Marketing Structure of the Large Corporation, 1875–1890," *Journal of Economic History* 38, no. 3 (1978): 631–649.

24. Morton Keller, *The Life Insurance Enterprise, 1885–1910* (Cambridge: Harvard University Press, 1963), 200, has noted the taxation of life insurance companies by the states later in the century. He suggests that in New York, insurance regulation began in 1859 at the instigation of fire insurance companies, which is just after the New York court decisions I discuss.

25. Greenberg, *Cause for Alarm,* 146–148.

26. *Fire Department of the City of New York v. Noble,* 3 E.D. Smith 440 (1854); *Fire Department of the City of New York v. Wright,* 3 E.D. Smith 453 (1854), 457.

27. Augustine E. Costello, *Our Firemen: A History of the New York Fire Departments, Volunteer and Paid* (1887; New York: Knickerbocker Press, 1997).

28. *Fire Department v. Wright,* 463.

29. Ibid., 471.

30. *Fire Department v. Noble,* 451–452.

31. Ibid., 450–451.

32. *Fire Department v. Wright,* 458.

33. *Fire Department v. Wright,* 475.

34. *Trustees of Dartmouth College v. Woodward,* 4 Wheat. (17 U.S.) 518 (1819); see Lawrence M. Friedman, *A History of American Law* (New York: Simon and Schuster, 1973), 273–274.

35. *Fire Department v. Wright,* 458.

36. *Firemen's Benevolent Association v. Lounsbury,* 21 Ill. 511 (1859), 515.

37. Ibid. For other challenges to taxation from fire insurance companies in New York, see, for example, *People ex rel. Westchester Fire Insurance Co. v. Davenport,* 91 N.Y. 574 (1883); *People v. Fire Association of Philadelphia,* 92 N.Y. 311 (1883); *People v. Home Insurance Co.,* 92 N.Y. 328 (1883). The New York Court of Appeals continued to uphold taxes on fire insurance companies. The Aetna Fire Insurance actually won its claim in South Carolina as late as 1907. *Aetna Fire Ins. Co. v. Jones,* 78 S.C. 445 (1907).

38. Further cases brought by insurance companies in which state courts tried to ensure that those who benefited paid for the service included *State of Louisiana v. Merchants Ins. Co.,* 12 La. Ann. 802 (1857); *Philadelphia Assn. v. Wood,* 39 Pa. St. 73 (1861); *Fire Department of Milwaukee v. Helfenstein,* 16 Wis. 136 at 145 (1862); and *Phoenix Assur. Co. v. Fire Dept.,* 117 Ala. 631 (1897).

39. Einhorn, *Property Rules,* 1–9, 17–18; Novak, *People's Welfare,* 19–50, 90–95.

40. Hartog, *Public Property,* 60–65, 202–204; Hartz, *Economic Policy,* 79–102.

41. *Paul v. Virginia,* 8 Wall. (75 U.S.) 168 (1869), 177, 183.

42. Alexis de Tocqueville, *Democracy in America* (1840; New York: Knopf, 1945), 1:236.

43. James M. McPherson, *Battle Cry of Freedom: The Civil War Era* (New York: Oxford University Press, 1988), 603.

44. Ibid., 308–312, 326.

45. McPherson, *Battle Cry,* 602.

46. Iver Bernstein, *The New York City Draft Riots* (New York: Oxford University Press, 1990), 17–42.

47. Ibid., 201–202.

48. McPherson, *Battle Cry,* 604, 601.

49. Thomas R. Kemp, "Community and War: The Civil War Experience of Two New Hampshire Towns," in *Toward a Social History of the American Civil War,* ed. Maris A. Vinovskis (New York: Cambridge University Press, 1990), 53, 55–56.

50. Ibid., 74. Some Vermont towns that had promised bounties tried later to rescind them, claiming they had been unconstitutional anyway. The state supreme court held in several cases that "a soldier's town credit was, during the war, property, and as such had a pecuniary market value" (*Haven v. Ludlow,* 41 Vt. 418 [1868]). The towns had to come through on their promises: *Butler v. Town of Putney,* 43 Vt. 481 (1871); *Cox v. Mt. Tabor,* 41 Vt. 28 (1868); *Davis v. Landgrove,* 43 Vt. 442 (1871); *Seymour v. Marlboro,* 40 Vt. 171 (1868). See also *Smith v. Aplin,* 80 Mich. 205 (1890); *Opinion of Justices,* 45 N.H. 593 (1864); *Willoughby v. Holderness,* 62 N.H. 227 (1882); *Winchester v. Corinna,* 55 Me. 9 (1866).

51. Peter Levine, "Draft Evasion in the North during the Civil War, 1863–1865," *Journal of American History* 67, no. 4 (1981): 820, 822.

52. McPherson, *Battle Cry,* 601–604.

53. *Booth v. Town of Woodbury,* 32 Conn. 118 (1864), 120, 121.

54. Linda Kerber, *No Constitutional Right,* chap. 1, provides an excellent interpretation of women's lack of a political obligation to the state. For the unity between husband and wife before 1922, see also Candice Lewis Bredbenner, *A Nationality of Her Own: Women, Marriage, and the Law of Citizenship* (Berkeley: University of California Press, 1998), 4–7, 15–79.

55. *Booth v. Town of Woodbury,* 123–124.

56. For the argument that women's exclusion from citizenship meant that women owed no obligations to the state, see Linda K. Kerber, "A Constitutional Right to Be Treated like American Ladies: Women and the Obligations of Citizenship," in *U.S. History as Women's History,* ed. Linda K. Kerber, Alice Kessler-Harris, and Kathryn Kish Sklar (Chapel Hill: University of North Carolina Press, 1995). These military cases do not address the same issue, but women were still legally subjects of their husbands.

57. *Booth v. Town of Woodbury,* 126. See also *Carver v. Creque,* 48 N.Y. 385 (1872).

58. *Booth v. Town of Woodbury,* 128.

59. See also *Weister v. Hade et al., School Directors,* 2 P. F. Smith 474 (1866); *Hilbish v. Catherman,* 14 P. F. Smith 154 (1870).

60. *Weister v. Hade,* 482.

61. See also *Butler v. Town of Putney; Cox v. Mt. Tabor; Davis v. Landgrove; Franklin v. State Board of Examiners*, 23 Cal. 173 (1863); *Seymour v. Marlboro; Haven v. Ludlow.*

62. *Weister v. Hade*, 483.

63. *Webster v. Town of Harwinton*, 32 Conn. 131 (1864); *Tyson v. School Directors of Halifax Township*, 1 P. F. Smith 9 (1865). See also *Bowles v. Landaff*, 59 N.H. 164 (1879); *Cass Township v. Dillion*, 16 Ohio St. 38 (1864); *Comer v. Folsom*, 13 Minn. 219 (1868); *Crowell v. Hopkinton*, 45 N.H. 9 (1863); *Dinehart v. La Fayette*, 19 Wisc. 677 (1865); *Freeland v. Hastings*, 10 Allen 570 (1865); *Gould v. Raymond*, 59 N.H. 260 (1879); *Henderson v. Lagow*, 42 Ill. 360 (1866); *Kelly v. Marshall*, 69 Pa. 319 (1871); *Misner v. Bullard*, 43 Ill. 470 (1867); *People ex rel. Peake v. Board of Supervisors of Columbia County*, 43 N.Y. 130 (1870); *Potter v. Canaan*, 37 Conn. 222 (1870); *Powers v. Shepard*, 48 N.Y. 540 (1872); *Shackford v. Newington*, 46 N.H. 415 (1866); *Spaulding v. Andover*, 54 N.H. 38 (1873); *Speer v. Blairsville*, 14 Wright 150 (1865); *State v. Baltimore*, 52 Md. 398 (1879); *State v. Demarest*, 32 N.J.L. 528 (1866); *State ex rel. Anderson v. Harris*, 17 Ohio St. 608 (1867); *State ex rel. Bates v. Richland Twp.*, 20 Ohio St. 362 (1870); *State ex rel. Cline v. Wilkesville Township*, 20 Ohio St. 288 (1870); *Stebbins v. Leaman*, 47 Ill. 352 (1868); *Wilson v. Buckman*, 13 Minn. 441 (1868).

64. *Hilbish v. Catherman*, 160. See also *Barbour v. Camden*, 51 Me. 608 (1865); *Butler v. Town of Putney; City of Lowell v. Oliver*, 8 Allen 247 (1864); *Coffman v. Keightley*, 24 Ind. 509 (1865); *Le Duc v. City of Hastings*, 39 Minn. 110 (1888); *Taylor v. Thompson*, 42 Ill. 9 (1866). Only the Wisconsin court was willing to see payments to individual soldiers as constitutional during and immediately after the Civil War: *Broadhead v. Milwaukee*, 19 Wis. 624 (1865).

65. See, e.g., *Freeland v. Hastings.*

66. Thomas M. Cooley, *A Treatise on the Constitutional Limitations Which Rest upon the Legislative Power of the States of the American Union* (Boston: Little, Brown, 1868), 219.

67. Ibid., 220.

68. Thomas M. Cooley, *A Treatise on the Law of Taxation, including the Law of Local Assessments* (Chicago: Callaghan and Co., 1876), 100.

69. Ibid.

70. For the connection between the celebration of firefighting and a cult of masculinity, see Cooper, "Fireman."

71. Russell S. Hanson, "Federal State Building: The Case of ADC," in *Changes in the State: Causes and Consequences*, ed. Edward S. Greenberg (Newbury Park, Cal.: Sage, 1990), 95.

4. Military Pensions in the Courts

1. McPherson, *Battle Cry*, 308–312.

2. Cecilia O'Leary, *To Die For: The Paradox of American Patriotism* (Princeton: Princeton University Press, 1999), 125–127; 205–208.

3. Montgomery, *Citizen Worker*, 93–104.

4. Pound, "Fifty Years," 789.

5. William H. Harris, *Keeping the Faith: A. Philip Randolph, Milton P. Webster, and the Brotherhood of Sleeping Car Porters, 1925–1937* (Urbana: University of Illinois Press, 1977), 29–30; Richard Polenberg, *Fighting Faiths* (New York: Penguin Books, 1987), 4–42; Theodore Kornweibel Jr., *No Crystal Stair* (Westport, Conn.: Greenwood Press, 1975), 18–23.

6. Kornweibel, *No Crystal Stair*, 89–92; O'Leary, *To Die For*, 208–219; Mario T. Garcia, *Mexican Americans: Leadership, Ideology, and Identity, 1930–1960* (New Haven: Yale University Press, 1989), 28–30.

7. Smith, *Civic Ideals*, 165.

8. Ibid., 346.

9. Novak, *People's Welfare*, 238–241.

10. William E. Nelson, *The Fourteenth Amendment: From Political Principle to Judicial Doctrine* (Cambridge: Harvard University Press, 1988), 24–25, 70, 123, 163; Smith, *Civic Ideals*, 328–342.

11. Purcell, *Brandeis*, 61–63, 200–201; Smith, *Civic Ideals*, 340.

12. Kerber, *No Constitutional Right,* 261–263.

13. Kristie Ross, "Arranging a Doll's House: Refined Women as Union Nurses"; and Lyde Cullen Sizer, "Acting Her Part: Narratives of Union Women Spies," both in *Divided Houses: Gender and the Civil War,* ed. Catherine Clinton and Nina Silber (New York: Oxford University Press, 1992).

14. Sizer, "Acting Her Part," 132.

15. Eric T. Dean Jr., *Shook over Hell: Post-Traumatic Stress, Vietnam, and the Civil War* (Cambridge: Harvard University Press, 1997), 78–79.

16. Kerber, *No Constitutional Right,* 221, 227.

17. Brenda Moore, *To Serve My Country, to Serve My Race: The Story of the Only African American WACS Stationed Overseas during World War II* (New York: New York University Press, 1996).

18. David W. Blight, "No Desperate Hero: Manhood and Freedom in a Union Soldier's Experience"; Jim Cullen, " 'I's a Man Now': Gender and African American Men"; and Reid Mitchell, "Soldiering, Manhood, and Coming of Age: A Northern Volunteer," all three in Clinton and Silber, *Divided Houses.*

19. For a superb fictional treatment of battlefields as sites of helplessness, similar to the helplessness that poor women experienced at home, see Pat Barker, *Regeneration* (New York: Dutton, 1991), esp. 107–108.

20. Dean, *Shook over Hell,* chaps. 3, 5, 7, 8.

21. Edward Shorter, *A History of Women's Bodies* (New York: Basic Books, 1982), 130–135, 101–102.

22. Jensen, "Early American Origins," 368.

23. McClintock, "Civil War Pensions," 463; Skocpol, *Protecting,* 107.

24. On the problems of missing records for pension administration, see McClintock, "Civil War Pensions," 472.

25. Ibid., 474–479.

26. Amy E. Holmes, " 'Such is the Price We Pay': American Widows and the Civil War Pension System," in Vinovskis, *Toward a Social History of the American Civil War,* 191–192.

27. McClintock, "Civil War Pensions," 467–468.

28. Skocpol, *Protecting,* 132.

29. One attorney challenged the limit on fees as an impairment of the liberty of contract. That was a good claim to make in the late nineteenth century, when the federal courts found that many statutes regulating labor—including minimum wage and maximum hours laws—impaired the workers' liberty of contract. The U.S. Supreme Court, however, consistently treated bounties as a matter of the generosity of the national government, not something to which anyone had a claim outside what the statutes provided. The government had created the bounties and could take them away, which would of course have abolished any demand for lawyers' services; therefore, Congress could regulate the fees lawyers charged. See *Frisbie v. U.S.,* 157 U.S. 160 (1895); *United States v. Marks,* 2 Abb. (U.S.) 534.

30. *U.S. v. Teller,* 107 U.S. 64 (1883).

31. The administration of federal pensions has a rich history beyond the scope of this book. My only purpose in addressing federal pensions is to note the specific reason federal pensions were constitutional, and to contrast national with state citizenship. For an extended treatment of the history of federal pensions, see Jensen, "Entitlements."

32. *Walton v. Cotton,* 60 U.S. 355 (1856).

33. *United States v. Hall,* 98 U.S. 343 (1878), 351.

34. See also *Manning v. Spry,* 121 Iowa 191 (1903); Jensen, "Early American Origins," 368.

35. Skocpol, *Protecting,* 102–153; Jensen, "Early American Origins," 361–363; McClintock, "Civil War Pensions," 458.

36. Smith, *Civic Ideals,* 186–190, 203.

37. K. Walter Hickel, "Medicine, Bureaucracy, and Social Welfare: The Politics of Disability Compensation for American Veterans of World War I," in *The New Disability History: American Perspectives,* ed. Paul K. Longmore and Lauri Umansky (New York: New York University Press, 2001); Skocpol, *Protecting,* 120–124, 261–278.

38. In Ohio the state court did uphold payments for those who had not previously received a bounty: *State ex rel. Snyder v. Abbey,* 15 Ohio 261 (1911).

39. *Mead v. Acton,* 139 Mass. 341 (1885); *Brown v. Russell,* 166 Mass. 14 (1896); *Opinion of the Justices,* 166 Mass. 589 (1896); *Opinion of the Justices,* 175 Mass. 599 (1900); *Opinion of the Justices,* 186 Mass. 603 (1905); *Opinion of the Justices,* 190 Mass. 611 (1906); *Opinion of the Justices* 211 Mass. 608 (1912). See also *Bush v. County of Orange,* 159 N.Y. 212 (1899); and *Beach v. Bradstreet,* 85 Conn. 344 (1912).

40. Kerber, *No Constitutional Right,* 225–226; *Brown v. Russell.* Eighty years later, in 1979, the United States Supreme Court held that preferences for veterans in civil service employment were constitutional. By then the distinction between state and federal service had been erased in law. *Personnel Administrator of Massachusetts v. Feeney,* 442 U.S. 256 (1979).

41. *Mead v. Acton,* 343–344.

42. Ann Shola Orloff and Theda Skocpol, "Why Not Equal Protection? Explaining the Politics of Public Social Spending in Britain, 1900–1911, and the United States, 1880s–1920," *American Sociological Review* 49 (1984): 743.

43. *Opinion of the Justices,* 175 Mass. 599 (1900).

44. *Opinion of the Justices,* 186 Mass. 603 (1905), 607.

45. *Opinion of the Justices,* 211 Mass. 608 (1912).

46. *Brown v. Russell.*

47. *Opinion of the Justices,* 166 Mass. 589 (1896), 599–600. Soifer, "Supreme Judicial Court of Massachusetts," 224–226, discusses these cases and advisory opinions.

48. *Opinion of the Justices,* 175 Mass. 599 (1900), 603.

49. Orloff, *Politics of Pensions,* 182.

50. Then the courts had to decide only the rather ornate cases of entitlement that could arise when men who had bought substitutes claimed that the county had promised to pay. *Carver v. Creque,* 48 N.Y. 385 (1872); *Taber v. Erie County,* 6 N.Y.S. 91 (1889).

51. Edward Durand, *The Finances of New York City* (New York: Macmillan, 1898), 104.

52. Twiss, *Lawyers and the Constitution,* 215–217.

53. William D. Guthrie, *Lectures on the Fourteenth Article of Amendment to the Constitution of the United States: Delivered before the Dwight Alumni Association, New York, April–May, 1898* (Boston: Little, Brown, 1898).

54. *Pollock v. Farmer's Loan and Trust Co.,* 157 U.S. 429 (1895); *Champion v. Ames,* 188 U.S. 321 (1903); *Pierce v. Society of Sisters,* 268 U.S. 510 (1925). On Guthrie's conservative work before the Supreme Court, see Barbara Bennett Woodhouse, " 'Who Owns the Child?': *Meyer* and *Pierce* and the Child as Property," *William and Mary Law Review* 33, no. 4 (1992): 1070–1080.

55. William D. Guthrie, "Constitutional Morality," *North American Review* 196 (1912): 154.

56. *Bush v. County of Orange,* 217.

57. Kemp, "Community and War," 73. For skepticism about the value of paying pensions to people who probably had not served within the state, see *Beach v. Bradstreet.*

58. O'Leary, *To Die For,* 121–128.

59. See, e.g., the *Civil Rights Cases,* 109 U.S. 3 (1883); *United States v. Cruikshank,* 92 U.S. 542 (1875).

60. Skocpol, *Protecting,* 139–143; Maris A. Vinovskis, "Have Social Historians Lost the Civil War? Some Preliminary Demographic Speculations," in Vinovskis, *Toward a Social History of the American Civil War,* 22.

61. *Board of Education v. Bladen,* 113 N.C. 379 (1913); *Elder v. Collier,* 100 Ga. 342 (1897); *Verdery v. Walton,* 137 Ga. 213 (1911); *State ex rel. Walker v. Derham,* 61 S.C. 259 (1901); *Woodall v. Darst,* 71 W.Va. 350 (1912).

62. *Bosworth v. Harp,* 154 Ky. 559 (1913), 565, 567.

63. Drew Faust, "Altars of Sacrifice: Confederate Women and the Narratives of War," in Clinton and Silber, *Divided Houses,* 177–178.

64. *Bosworth v. Harp,* 569.

65. Seth Koven, "Remembering and Dismemberment," *American Historical Review* 99, no. 4 (1994): 1167–1202.

66. John Whiteclay Chambers II, *To Raise an Army: The Draft Comes to Modern America* (New York: Free Press, 1987), 167, 175.

67. David M. Kennedy, *Over Here: The First World War and American Society* (New York: Oxford University Press, 1980), 210–215, 218–223.

68. Lucy E. Salyer, "The All-American Soldier: Military Service, Citizenship and Race in World War I" (manuscript in possession of the author, n.d.).

69. Moore, *To Serve My Country;* Gerald Astor, *The Right to Fight: A History of African Americans in the Military* (Novato, Calif.: Presidio Press, 1998), 23–43, 108–110, 145–150.

70. Roger Daniels, *Prisoners without Trial: Japanese Americans in World War II* (New York: Hill & Wang, 1993), 69–70.

71. "Banks Won't Buy State Bonus Bonds; Validity Doubted," *New York Times,* June 4, 1921, 1; Benjamin S. Dean, Letter to the Editor, *New York Times,* June 10, 1921, 12.

72. Chambers, *To Raise an Army,* 179–180, 251–254.

73. "State Files Suit to Test Validity of Bonus Bonds," *New York Times,* June 12, 1921, 1.

74. *People v. Westchester County National Bank,* 231 N.Y. 465 (1921), 480.

75. *Gustafson v. Rhinow,* 144 Minn. 415 (1920); *State ex rel. Hart v. Clausen,* 113 Wash. 570 (1921); *State ex rel. Atwood v. Johnson,* 176 N.W. 224 (1920); *Veterans' Welfare Board v. Riley,* 206 Pac. Rep. 631 (1922); *State ex rel. Morris v. Handlin,* 38 S.D. 550 (1917).

76. *State ex rel. Hart v. Clausen,* 575.

77. *State ex rel. Atwood v. Johnson,* 225.

78. *Veterans' Welfare Board v. Riley,* 632.

79. Ibid., 637–638.

80. Salyer, "All-American Soldier," 8.

81. Ibid.; Ian F. Haney-Lopez, *White by Law: The Legal Construction of Race* (New York: New York University Press, 1996), 60, 88.

82. "Annotation: Constitutionality of Statutes Providing for Bounty or Pension for Soldiers," *American Law Reports* 7 (1920): 1636–1637; "Annotation: Constitutionality of Statutes Providing for Bounty or Pensions for Soldiers," *American Law Reports* 13 (1921): 587–589; "Annotation: Constitutionality of Statues Providing for Bounty or Pensions for Soldiers," *American Law Reports* 15 (1921): 1359–1360.

83. "Annotation" (1921), vol. 15, 1360.

5. Civil Service Pensions

1. Costello, *Our Firemen,* 714–715.

2. Orloff, *Politics of Pensions,* 275.

3. John E. Mollenkopf, *The Contested City* (Princeton: Princeton University Press, 1983), 22.

4. U.S. Bureau of Labor Statistics, *Public Service Retirement Systems,* bulletin 477 (Washington, D.C.: Government Printing Office, 1929), 76–77.

5. Ibid., 1, 25.

6. *Bowler v. Nagel,* 228 Mich. 434 (1924).

7. Stanley, *Bondage,* 1–9; Nancy Fraser and Linda Gordon, "Contract versus Charity: Why Is There No Social Citizenship in the United States?" in *The Citizenship Debates,* ed. Gershon Shafir (Minneapolis: University of Minnesota Press, 1998), 122–123.

8. Fraser and Gordon, "Contract versus Charity," 124–125; Shklar, *American Citizenship,* 63–104.

9. Rodgers, *Atlantic Crossings,* 268.

10. Goodnow, *Comparative Administrative Law,* 1:vi.

11. Rodgers, *Atlantic Crossings,* 85.

12. Ibid., 268.

13. Goodnow, *Comparative Administrative Law,* 1:7–8; Charles G. Haines and Marshall E. Dimock, introduction to *Essays on the Law and Practice of Governmental Administration: A Volume in Honor of Frank Johnson Goodnow,* ed. Charles G. Haines and Marshall E. Dimock (Baltimore: Johns Hopkins Press, 1935).

14. Goodnow, *Comparative Administrative Law,* 1:231–234.

15. See White, *Constitution,* 103–104; Susan M. Sterett, "Legality in Britain and the United States: Toward an Institutional Explanation," *Comparative Political Studies* 25 (July 1992): 195–228.

16. Karen Orren, "The Work of Government: Recovering the Discourse of Office in *Marbury v. Madison,*" *Studies in American Political Development* 8 (1994): 60; Karen Orren, "Officers' Rights: Toward a Unified Field Theory of American Constitutional Development," *Law and Society Review* 34, no. 4 (2000): 885–890; Goodnow, *Comparative Administrative Law,* 2:68.

17. Goodnow, *Comparative Administrative Law,* 2:2, quoting *United States v. Hartwell,* 6 Wallace 385 (1867).

18. Goodnow, *Comparative Administrative Law,* 2:2.

19. Orren, "Work of Government," 63.

20. Goodnow, *Comparative Administrative Law,* 2:62–64, 68–71.

21. Greenberg, *Cause for Alarm,* 24.

22. Ibid., 125–151.

23. Eric Monkkonen, *Police in Urban America, 1860–1920* (New York: Cambridge University Press, 1981), 52–55; 152–156.

24. James Leiby, *A History of Social Welfare and Social Work in the United States, 1815–1972* (New York: Columbia University Press, 1978), 211.

25. Goodnow, *Comparative Administrative Law,* 2:73; *In re Roche,* 141 N.Y. App. Div. 872 (1910).

26. H. R. Wilgus, "The Constitutionality of Teachers' Pensions (II)," *Michigan Law Review* 12 (November 1913): 27–49.

27. *Trustees of Exempt Firemen's Benevolent Fund v. Roome,* 93 N.Y. 313 (1883), 327.

28. Greenberg, *Cause for Alarm,* 153.

29. See especially *Commonwealth ex rel. Philadelphia Police Pension Fund Assn v. Walton,* 182 Pa. 373 (1897); *State of Nebraska ex. rel Haberlan v. Love,* 89 Neb. 149 (1911); and *Cobbs v. Home Ins. Co.,* 18 Ala. App. 206 (1920).

30. Mr. Crawford of Manchester, *Journal of the Constitutional Convention of New Hampshire,* June 20, 1912, 442–443.

31. Mr. Folsom of Dover, ibid., 438.

32. Ibid., 441.

33. For a historical overview of pensions and their constitutionality in Illinois, see Illinois State Legislative Council, *Pensions for Policemen and Firemen,* Publication 67 (Springfield, Ill., 1945), 3.

34. Louise de Koven Bowen, "Women Police," *Survey* 30 (April 12, 1913): 64–65.

35. "Not Entitled to These Pensions," *Chicago Daily Tribune,* May 8, 1911, 8.

36. "Police Pensions Hit Snag," *Chicago Daily Tribune,* May 10, 1911, 4.

37. "Sticks to Amendments," *Illinois State Journal,* May 10, 1911, 1.

38. "Attack Police Pension Law," *Chicago Daily Tribune,* July 1, 1911, 2.

39. U.S. Bureau of Labor Statistics, *Public Service Retirement Systems,* 118.

40. *Eddy v. Morgan,* 216 Ill. 437 (1905), 449; see also *Pecoy v. Chicago,* 265 Ill. 78 (1914) and *Commonwealth ex rel. Firemen's Relief Assn. v. Barker,* 211 Pa. 610 (1905).

41. *People ex rel. Kroner v. Abbott,* 274 Ill. 380, 385 (1916); see also *O'Dea v. Cook,* 176 Cal. 659 (1917). Dillon, *Commentaries on the Law of Municipal Corporations,* vol. 1, sec. 430. For an opposite resolution to the question, see *State ex rel. Heaven v. Ziegenhein,* 144 Mo. (1898).

42. Thomas M. Cooley, *A Treatise on the Constitutional Limitations: Which Rest upon the Legislative Power of the States of the American Union,* 7th ed. (Boston: Little, Brown, 1903), 1:189, as cited in *People ex rel. Kroner v. Abbott,* 388.

43. *People ex rel. Kroner v. Abbott,* 385.

44. *People ex. rel. Waddy v. Partridge,* 172 N.Y. 305 (1902).

45. *Ryan v. Foreman,* 262 Ill. 175 (1914), 175, 181.

46. Karen Orren, "Officers' Rights," 887–888, 897–898.

47. *Pennie v. Reis,* 132 U.S. 464 (1889). See also *Mahon v. Board of Education of the City of New York,* 171 N.Y. 263 (1902).

48. Fraser and Gordon, "Genealogy of *Dependency*"; Smith, *Civic Ideals,* 170–173.

49. Eric Foner, *Free Soil, Free Labor, Free Men: The Ideology of the Republican Party before the Civil War* (New York: Oxford University Press, 1970); Stanley, *Bondage,* 35–42.

50. W. E. B. Du Bois, *The Souls of Black Folk* (1903; New York: Washington Square Press, 1970), chap. 1; Foner, *Nothing but Freedom;* Stanley, *Bondage,* 122–130.

51. Guyora Binder, "The Slavery of Emancipation," *Cardozo Law Review* 17 (1996): 2063–2102; Foner, *Nothing but Freedom;* Du Bois, *Souls of Black Folk,* chap. 1.

52. See, e.g., A. W. Stockwell, "Problem of Superannuation in the Civil Service," *Putnam's* 7 (1910): 565–571; F. MacVeagh, "Civil Service Pensions for United States Employees," *Annals of the American Academy of Political Science* 38 (1911): 3–5; L. Roth, "Pension Funds for Public Service Employees," *Survey* 35 (October 30, 1915): 109–110; J. A. Fitch, "For Value Received: A Discussion of Industrial Pensions," *Survey* 40 (1918): 221–224; J. B. Andrews, "Old Age Pensions for Federal Employees," *Survey* 44 (May 22, 1920): 271; see also "Civil Pensions and Old Age Pensions," *Chatauquan* 57 (1910): 334–336.

53. Sheryl R. Tynes, *Turning Points in Social Security: From "Cruel Hoax" to "Sacred Entitlement"* (Stanford, Calif.: Stanford University Press, 1996), 42.

54. California Department of Social Welfare, *Old Age Dependency: A Study of the Care Given to Needy Aged in California* (Sacramento, Calif.: State Department of Social Welfare, 1928); Orloff, *Politics of Pensions,* 101–102.

55. *New York Times,* November 16, 1905, 5. For an official history, see Howard Savage, *Fruit of an Impulse: Forty-five Years of the Carnegie Foundation, 1905–1950* (New York: Harcourt Brace Jovanovich, 1953).

56. See Abraham Flexner (a social insurance advocate and medical educator), *Henry S. Pritchett: A Biography* (New York: Columbia University Press, 1943).

57. Henry Pritchett, "Moral Influence of a University Pension System," *Popular Science* 79 (1911): 509–510.

58. "Benefits and Dangers of a Centralized Endowment for Public Purposes," *Popular Science* 76 (April 10, 1910): 413–415.

59. Redding S. Sugg, *Motherteacher: The Feminization of American Education* (Charlottesville: University Press of Virginia, 1978), chaps. 3–4.

60. Thomas Dublin, *Transforming Women's Lives: New England Lives in the Industrial Revolution* (Ithaca: Cornell University Press, 1994).

61. David Tyack, *The One Best System: A History of American Urban Education* (Cambridge: Harvard University Press, 1974), 60–64.

62. Ibid., 66. See also William Graebner, *A History of Retirement* (New Haven: Yale University Press, 1980), 92–93.

63. *Mahon v. Board of Education of the City of New York.*

64. U.S. Bureau of Labor Statistics, *Public Service, Retirement Systems,* 4.

65. *Attorney General v. Connolly,* 193 Mich. 499 (1916); *State ex rel. Haig v. Hague,* 37 N.D. 583 (1917); *State ex rel. Dudgeon v. Levitan,* 181 Wis. 326 (1923).

66. Roy Lubove, *The Struggle for Social Security* (Pittsburgh: University of Pittsburgh Press, 1986), 91; Gordon, *Pitied,* chap. 6.

67. See also *Hammitt v. Gaynor,* 144 N.Y. Supp. 123 (1913).

68. *State ex rel. Jennison v. Rogers,* 87 Minn. 130 (1902); *State ex rel. Ward v. Hubbard,* 12 Ohio C.D. 87 (1901); *State ex rel. Jackson v. Kurtz,* 11 Ohio C.D. 705 (1901).

69. U.S. Bureau of Labor Statistics, *Public Service Retirement Systems,* 77.

70. *Hughes v. Traeger,* 264 Ill.612 (1914).

71. H. L. Wilgus, "Constitutionality of Teachers' Pensions (I), (II), (III)," *Michigan Law Review* 11 (May 1913): 451–477; 12 (November 1913): 27–49; 12: 105–123.

72. Wilgus, "Constitutionality (II)," 27.

73. Wilgus, "Constitutionality (I)," 467–469. For another discussion of education as a public service, see *Miller v. Korns,* 107 Ohio State 287 (1923).

74. U.S. Bureau of Labor Statistics, *Public Service Retirement Systems,* 77.

75. "Teachers' Pensions in New York City: Age of Retirement," *School Review*, 1914, 122–124.

76. Adolph Reed, "Du Bois's 'Double Consciousness': Race and Gender in Progressive Era American Thought," *Studies in American Political Development* 5, no. 2 (1992): 93–139.

77. U.S. Bureau of Labor Statistics, *Public Service Retirement Systems*, 76.

78. Ibid., 4, 45.

79. In 1911, at the same time that the Illinois state legislature was fighting over police pensions, the city of Chicago enacted contributory pensions for its civil servants. Edward Hughes, a stenographer for the city, complained; he did not want to pay the $2 per month deducted from his $80 per month salary. He lost in the Illinois Supreme Court in 1914; the law of office meant that he was not party to an employment contract. He had no property right in his salary. *Hughes v. Traeger.*

80. *New York Times*, November 3, 1913, 3.

81. Rodgers, *Atlantic Crossings*, 234–241.

82. See, e.g., *Journal of the House*, 1917 (New Hampshire), 75, 108, 401, 594, 687, 928.

83. Mr. Mason of Keene, *Journal of the Constitutional Convention of 1920* (New Hampshire), 341.

84. Mr. Barton of Newport, in ibid., 343.

85. Alice Kessler-Harris, *A Woman's Wage: Historical Meanings and Social Consequences* (Lexington: University Press of Kentucky, 1990), 8–9; Glickman, *Living Wage*, 42, 45, 75–76.

86. Mr. Pillsbury of Londonderry, *Journal of the Constitutional Convention of 1920*, 351.

87. "Teachers Urge Passage of Retirement Measure," *Manchester Union*, March 5, 1931, 12.

88. "Teachers' 'Pension' Killed," *Concord Daily Monitor and New Hampshire Patriot*, March 5, 1931, 1, 5.

89. Wilgus, "Constitutionality (II)."

90. *Bowler v. Nagel*, 1157.

91. Glickman, *Living Wage*, 52–53; Stanley, *Bondage*, 145–148.

92. *Bowler v. Nagel*, 1161.

93. U.S. Bureau of Labor Statistics, *Public Service Retirement Systems*, 56.

94. McCurdy, "Justice Field"; Kens, *Justice Stephen Field.*

95. Stanley Kutler, *Privilege and Creative Destruction* (New York: Norton, 1971), 61–63.

96. Orren, "Primacy of Labor," 377–388.

97. See, e.g., Joan Zimmerman, "The Jurisprudence of Equality: The Women's Minimum Wage, the First Equal Rights Amendment, and *Adkins v. Children's Hospital*, 1905–1923," *Journal of American History* 78 (June 1991): 188–225.

98. Gillman, *Constitution Besieged*, 61–100; Karen Orren, "Labor Regulation and Constitutional Theory in the United States and England," *Political Theory* 22, no. 1 (1994): 98–123.

99. William E. Forbath, *Law and the Shaping of the American Labor Movement* (Cambridge: Harvard University Press, 1991); Purcell, *Brandeis*, chap. 3.

100. Rodgers, *Atlantic Crossings*, 201.

101. Gillman, *Constitution Besieged*, 45–60; Cushman, *Rethinking*, 33–46.

102. Shklar, *American Citizenship*, chap. 2; Stanley, *Bondage*, 1–10, 98–114.

103. Orloff, *Politics of Pensions*, 275–276; Levine, *Poverty and Society*, 230–231.

104. Orloff, *Politics of Pensions*, 275–278; Graebner, *History of Retirement*, 60.

105. Steven Erie, *Rainbow's End* (Berkeley: University of California Press, 1989).

106. *Railroad Retirement Board v. Alton Railroad Co.*, 295 U.S. 330 (1934).

107. For the difficulty of demonstrating that one is doing a good job of what one is supposed to be doing, see John W. Meyer and Brian Rowan, "Institutionalized Organizations: Formal Structure as Myth and Ceremony," in *The New Institutionalism in Organizational Analysis*, ed. Walter W. Powell and Paul J. DiMaggio (Chicago: University of Chicago Press, 1991).

108. Novak, *People's Welfare*, 237, 245–248.

109. Alice Kessler-Harris, "Designing Women and Old Fools: The Construction of the Social Security Amendments of 1939," in Kerber, Kessler-Harris, and Sklar, *U.S. History as Women's History;* Mettler, *Dividing Citizens*, 212.

110. Martha F. Davis, *Brutal Need: Lawyers and the Welfare Rights Movement, 1960–1973* (New Haven: Yale University Press); Jill Quadagno, *The Color of Welfare: How Racism Undermined the War on Poverty* (New York: Oxford University Press, 1996).

III. Kessler-Harris, "Designing Women"; Mettler, *Dividing Citizens.*

112. Ann Shola Orloff, "Gender and the Social Rights of Citizenship: The Comparative Analysis of Gender Relations and Welfare States," *American Sociological Review* 58 (1993): 303–328; Susan Pedersen, *Family, Dependence, and the Origins of the Welfare State: Britain and France, 1914–1945* (Cambridge: Harvard University Press, 1993).

113. "Annotation: Constitutionality of Mothers' Pensions," *American Law Reports* 3 (1917): 1233; "Annotation: Constitutionality of Statutes Providing for Bounty or Pension for Soldiers," *American Law Reports* 7 (1920): 1636; "Annotation: Validity of Statute or Ordinance Providing for Pensions for Municipal Employees," *American Law Reports* 37 (1924): 1162–1166; "Annotation: Constitutionality of Old Age Pension or Assistance Acts," *American Law Reports* 37 (1924): 1524–1525.

6. Mothers' Pensions in the Courts

1. For a variety of perceptive analyses of how programs were instituted, see Ashford, *Emergence;* Crenson, *Building the Invisible Orphanage;* Gordon, *Pitied;* Katz, *In the Shadow;* Skocpol, *Protecting;* Orloff, *Politics of Pensions;* Rodgers, *Atlantic Crossings.*

2. Crenson, *Building the Invisible Orphanage,* 46–50.

3. Ibid. That practice has had implications for the care of children throughout the twentieth century. In New York, discretionary funding for private charities that cared for children in public foster care meant that charities housing white children received better funding than those housing black children. See Nina Bernstein, *The Lost Children of Wilder: The Epic Struggle to Change Foster Care* (New York: Pantheon, 2001).

4. See White, *Constitution,* chap. 4; Sterett, "Legality"; Sterett, "Constitutional Law," 587–610.

5. Kenneth Cmiel, *A Home of Another Kind: One Chicago Orphanage and the Tangle of Child Welfare* (Chicago: University of Chicago Press, 1995); Crenson, *Building the Invisible Orphanage,* 209–210; Katz, *In the Shadow,* 115–116.

6. Stephen O'Connor, *The Orphan Trains: Charles Loring Brace and the Children He Saved and Failed* (New York: Houghton Mifflin, 2001); Marilyn Holt, *Orphan Trains: Placing Out in America* (Lincoln: University of Nebraska Press, 1994).

7. Crenson, *Building the Invisible Orphanage,* 214–222.

8. "Child savers" was the contemporary term for the group of reformers in the early twentieth century who made improving the life of poor children their life's calling. See Anthony Platt, *The Child Savers: The Invention of Delinquency* (Chicago: University of Chicago Press, 1969), 3.

9. Katz, *In the Shadow,* 124–129.

10. Ibid., Crenson, *Building the Invisible Orphanage,* 246–283; Skocpol, *Protecting,* 426–428, 432–439.

11. Gordon, *Pitied,* 37–43; Skocpol, *Protecting,* 439–456; Sklar, *Florence Kelley.* Arguments that women earned their payments by raising children were continuous with those of women's rights advocates, who insisted in the late nineteenth century that women had a right to their earnings; both groups claimed that women could work apart from the tutelage of a man. See Siegel, "Home as Work," 1073; Stanley, *Bondage,* 175–217.

12. Gordon, *Pitied,* 56–64; Crenson, *Building the Invisible Orphanage,* 268–280.

13. Mark Leff, "Consensus for Reform: The Mothers' Pension Movement in the Progressive Era," *Social Service Review* 47, no. 3 (1973): 397–417.

14. Gordon, *Pitied,* 62–64.

15. See, e.g., Thomas Krainz, "Implementing Poor Relief: The Welfare State in Progressive Era Colorado" (Ph.D. diss., University of Colorado, Boulder, 2000).

16. Skocpol, *Protecting,* 424–428.

17. Ben B. Lindsey, "The Mothers' Compensation Law of Colorado," *Survey* 29 (February 15, 1913): 716.

18. Gordon, *Pitied,* chap. 6.

19. Edward T. Devine, "Central and Common Features of the Current Legislation," *American Labor Legislation Review* 3 (1913): 192; Gordon, *Pitied.*

20. Devine, "Central and Common Features," 197.

21. William Hard, "General Discussion," *American Labor Legislation Review* 3 (1913): 229–233.

22. Leff, "Consensus." For analysis of the advocates involved, see Goodwin, *Gender*, 101–115; Gordon, *Pitied*, chap. 4; Sonya Michel, "The Limits of Maternalism: Policies Toward American Wage-Earning Mothers during the Progressive Era," in Koven and Michel, *Mothers of a New World*, 292–303; Skocpol, *Protecting*, 321–350; Sklar, *Florence Kelley*.

23. Orren, *Belated Feudalism*, 4, 8, 20; Stanley, *Bondage*, chap. 5.

24. *Muller v. Oregon*, 208 U.S. 412 (1908). For a systematic discussion of the state and federal cases in which the courts overwhelmingly upheld protective labor legislation targeting women, see Julie Novkov, "Liberty, Protection, and Women's Work: Investigating the Boundaries between Public and Private," *Law and Social Inquiry* 22 (1997): 857–899.

25. Alice Kessler-Harris, *Woman's Wage*, 33–37; Novkov, "Liberty"; Zimmerman, "Jurisprudence of Equality."

26. Devine, "Central and Common Features," 198.

27. Gordon, *Pitied*, chap. 1.

28. Glickman, *Living Wage*, 40–44; Stanley, *Bondage*, 186–194; Gordon, *Pitied*, 126–138.

29. Gordon, *Pitied*, 160–167.

30. Quoted in Sherry Katz, "Socialist Women and Progressive Reform," in *California Progressivism Revisited*, ed. William Deverell and Tom Sutton (Berkeley: University of California Press), 127.

31. Skocpol, *Protecting*, 457. The reasons for the early adoption by western states is somewhat unclear. Theda Skocpol (456–465) has argued that the states that adopted programs early had a high rate of literacy, which meant many could read the articles urging the pensions in popular women's magazines. They were also the states in which women and children were less likely to work for wages. Western states also first granted women the vote and provided for referenda, allowing programs to be proposed outside the ordinary legislative track.

32. Crenson, *Building the Invisible Orphanage*, 59–60.

33. Cases appear in the court records of eleven of the twenty-eight states that enacted mothers' pensions between 1911 and 1915. Arizona: *State Board of Control of Arizona v. Buckstegge*, 18 Ariz. 277 (1916). Illinois: *People ex rel. Stuckart v. New Jersey Sandberg Co.*, 282 Ill. 245 (1918); *People ex rel. Stuckart v. Chicago*, 270 Ill. 477 (1915); *People ex rel. Stuckart v. Klee*, 282 Ill. 440 (1918). Iowa: *DeBrot v. Marion County*, 164 Iowa 208 (1914). Minnesota: *In re Koopman*, 146 Minn. 36 (1920); *State ex rel. Stearns County v. Klasen*, 143 N.W. 984 (1913). Montana: *State ex rel. Board of Commissioners v. District Court of Second Judicial District*, 204 Pac. 600 (1922). Nebraska: *In re Rumsey*, 102 Neb. 302 (1918). North Dakota: *Cass County v. Nixon*, 35 N.D. 601 (1917); *In re Walker*, 49 N.D. 682 (1923); *Pierce County v. Rugby, Pierce County*, 47 N.D. 301 (1921). Oregon: *Finley v. Marion County*, 81 Or. 294 (1916); *Buster v. Marion County*, 84 Or. 624 (1917); *Badura v. Multnomah County*, 87 Or. 466 (1918); *In re Sharp*, 88 Or. 594 (1918); *In re Wolfe*, 81 Or. 297 (1916); *Zachary v. Polk County Court*, 74 Or. 58 (1914). Pennsylvania: *Commonwealth ex rel. Mothers' Assistance Fund v. Powell*, 256 Pa. 470 (1917); *Commonwealth ex rel. Attorney General v. Schlager*, 18 Lackawanna Jurist 16 (1917); *State Supervisor, Mothers' Assistance Fund*, 28 Pa. Dist. Rep. 244 (1918); *Mothers' Pensions*, 28 Pa. Dist. Rep. 244 (1919). Utah: *Denver and Rio Grande Railroad Co. v. Grand County*, 170 Pac. 74 (1917); *Startup v. Harmon*, 59 Utah 329 (1921). Washington: *In re Snyder*, 93 Wash. 59 (1916).

34. *People ex rel. Stuckart v. New Jersey Sandberg Co.; People ex rel. Stuckart v. Chicago; People ex rel. Stuckart v. Klee; Denver and Rio Grande Railroad Co. v. Grand County*.

35. On the national context for the politics of municipal reform in the West, see Amy Bridges, "Winning the West to Municipal Reform," *Urban Affairs Quarterly* 27, no. 4 (1992): 494–518. On water, see Amy Bridges, *Morning Glories* (Princeton: Princeton University Press, 1997), 38–39. On the concern that welfare programs would have an endless foreign clientele, see Gwendolyn Mink, "The Lady and the Tramp: Gender, Race and the Origins of the American Welfare State," in Gordon, *Women, the State and Welfare*, 92–122.

36. Statute quoted in *State Board of Control of Arizona v. Buckstegge*, 278.

37. *Men and Women of Arizona: Past and Present* (Phoenix, Ariz.: Pioneer, 1940), 20; *History of Arizona* (New York: Lewis Historical Publishing, 1958), 3:93. I am grateful to Wendi Goen of the Arizona

State Library, Archives Division, for this information. At Fennemore Craig, now a large law firm in Phoenix, the archivist could not find any documentation concerning this case.

38. On corporate reorganization, see Robert Gordon, "Legal Thought and Legal Practice in the Age of American Enterprise, 1870–1920," in *Professions and Professional Ideologies in America*, ed. Gerald L. Geison (Chapel Hill: University of North Carolina Press, 1983), 101–110; and Berk, *Alternative Tracks*. On railroads and injuries, see Friedman and Ladinsky, "Social Change." On the Interstate Commerce Commission, see Stephen Skowronek, *Building a New American State: The Expansion of National Administrative Capacities, 1877–1920* (New York: Cambridge University Press, 1982), chaps. 5, 8. On the significance of the railroads in politics in California, see George Mowry, *The California Progressives* (Chicago: Quadrangle Books, 1951); and William Deverell, *Railroad Crossing: Californians and the Railroad, 1850–1910* (Berkeley: University of California Press, 1994), which notes the significance of lawyers to railroads (72–73; 87–88; 154–155).

39. Brief of Appellee, *State Board of Control of Arizona v. Buckstegge*, 5.

40. *Buckstegge v. State Board of Control of Arizona*, #8308, Superior Court of the State of Arizona in and for Maricopa County.

41. Gordon, *Pitied*, 26.

42. Brief of Appellant, *State Board of Control of Arizona v. Buckstegge*, 23.

43. Ibid., 10, 13, 15.

44. Brief of Appellee, *State Board of Control of Arizona v. Buckstegge*, 27.

45. *State ex rel. Heaven v. Ziegenhein; Mahon v. Board of Education.*

46. Of course, as has been often noted, advocates did see the new pensions as an opportunity to abolish the stigma attached to the old almshouses. Fennemore and Ryan quoted the pamphlets that had urged the measure to the electorate of Arizona; the language denigrated the almshouses and declared that "society owes [the pensioner] a living." Brief of Appellee, *State Board of Control of Arizona v. Buckstegge*, 76.

47. Ibid., 50, 51.

48. Ibid., 31.

49. Brief of Appellant, *State Board of Control of Arizona v. Buckstegge*, 17.

50. Ibid., 19.

51. Brief of Appellee, *State Board of Control of Arizona v. Buckstegge*, 24.

52. *State Board of Control of Arizona v. Buckstegge*, 288, 841–42.

53. "Rudely Drawn Pension Law without Life," *Arizona Republican*, July 2, 1916, 7.

54. "The Old Age Pensions Law," *Arizona Republican*, July 2, 1916, 4.

55. Ibid.

56. For a detailed discussion of the origins of mothers' pensions in Illinois, see Goodwin, *Gender*.

57. Ethel Cleland, "Pensions for Mothers," *American Political Science Review* 6 (1912): 96–98; Mary E. Richmond, "Motherhood and Pensions," *Survey* 29 (March 1, 1913); John M. Glenn, Lilian Brandt, and F. Emerson Andrews, *The Russell Sage Foundation* (New York: Russell Sage Foundation, 1947), 1:130; Goodwin, *Gender*.

58. Goodwin, *Gender*, 119–130; Molly Ladd-Taylor, *Mother-Work: Women, Child Welfare, and the State, 1890–1930* (Urbana: Univeristy of Illinois Press, 1994), 147–148.

59. *People ex rel. Stuckart v. New Jersey Sandberg Co.; People ex rel. Stuckart v. Chicago; People ex rel. Stuckart v. Klee; Denver and Rio Grande Railroad Co. v. Grand County.*

60. *Denver and Rio Grande Railroad v. Grand County*, 77.

61. Crenson, *Building the Invisible Orphanage*, 64.

62. *Denver and Rio Grande Railroad Company v. Grand County*, 76–77.

63. Virginia Sapiro, "The Gender Basis of American Social Policy," in Gordon, *Women, the State, and Welfare*.

64. Crenson, *Building the Invisible Orphanage*, 97–99; 118–121; 136–139; Katz, *In the Shadow*, 118–121. See also *State ex rel. Stearns County v. Klasen*.

65. Purcell, *Brandeis*, 39–46.

66. Goodnow, *Comparative Administrative Law*, 2:138.

67. Ibid., 1:230, 232.

68. See, e.g., *State ex rel. Stearns County v. Klasen.*

69. On centralization, see Hanson, "Federal State Building," 98–99.

70. *Mothers' Pensions.* For other cases in which the states read the mothers' pensions laws as creating statutory duties for counties, see *Startup v. Harmon*; 59; *In re Walker*; *Pierce County v. Rugby*; *In re Koopman.* Reading the law differently allowed for variability among the states.

71. White, *Constitution*, 99–108, argues that commentators offered extraconstitutional justifications for bureaucracies, then relied on procedures to control them.

72. Goodnow, *Comparative Administrative Law*, 1:21–23.

73. Eastwood, *Governing Rural England*, 133–134.

74. Paul Craig, "Dicey: Unitary, Self-Correcting Democracy and Public Law," *Law Quarterly Review* 106 (1990): 105.

75. For a discussion of the use of history in relation to the courts and the New Deal, see White, *Constitution*, chap. 1.

76. *Cass County v. Nixon*, 205.

77. Ibid., 206.

78. *Buster v. Marion County.*

79. *Badura v. Multnomah County; In re Sharp; Finley v. Marion County; Wolfe v. Marion County.* In *DeBrot v. Marion County*, Mrs. DeBrot could not get poor relief because her husband, who lived in Connecticut, owed child support. Whereas the Iowa court held that a husband owed support to his family, the Minnesota court in *In re Koopman* held that the state statute did allow payments to divorced women. The new mothers' pensions laws did unsettle the law of poor relief, allowing variable results across the states.

80. Some did, however. The court presented the applicant in *Zachary v. Polk County Court* as in desperate circumstances. She had four children, the oldest was fourteen, and her husband was in prison. She won.

81. For the variability of practices in Colorado, see Krainz, "Implementing Poor Relief."

82. *American Law Report* 3 (1917): 1233.

83. Kerber, *No Constitutional Right*, chap. 1. A woman's citizenship was derivative of her husband's from 1855 and remained so for some women until 1934. That is, women could gain or lose citizenship automatically depending on whether they married an American or alien man. Women's derivative citizenship appeared as an issue when a woman married across national boundaries. Bredbenner, *Nationality of Her Own*, 241.

84. *Denver and Rio Grande Railroad Co. v. Grand County*, 78.

85. *DeBrot v. Marion County.* The court refused a woman who was separated from her husband a pension because he was still legally obligated to support his family, though he lived in Connecticut, and she and the children lived in Iowa. Men might be permanently obligated to pay support, but people in the United States moved frequently, and no one could collect child support across state borders. Some men may have paid support anyway. Or, some men and women may well have colluded to present a woman as deserted in the few areas that *would* grant pensions to deserted women. All we can know from the case law is what was the most acceptable way to present one's case in court. On the ambiguities of desertion, see Linda Gordon, *Heroes of Their Own Lives* (New York: Viking Press, 1988), 90–91. For a thought-provoking discussion of the significance to laws of divorce and separation of the ability to move in the United States, or for what Hartog calls a culture of federalism, see Hartog, *Man and Wife*, 19–23.

86. Mary Frances Berry, *Why ERA Failed* (Bloomington: Indiana University Press, 1986), 30–44; Nancy Cott, *The Grounding of Modern Feminism* (New Haven: Yale University Press, 1987), chap. 1.

87. Siegel, "Home as Work," 1073; Stanley, *Bondage.*

88. See, e.g., Basch, *In the Eyes of the Law.*

89. Stanley, *Bondage*, 204–217.

90. Novkov, "Liberty"; Orren, *Belated Feudalism*; Zimmerman, "Jurisprudence of Equality."

91. See, e.g., Skocpol, *Protecting*, 477; Orloff, "Gender."

92. Carole Pateman, *The Disorder of Women* (Palo Alto, Calif.: Stanford University Press, 1989), 10; and Pateman, *The Sexual Contract* (Palo Alto, Calif.: Stanford University Press, 1988), 1–6.

93. Mink, "Lady and the Tramp," 94–101.

94. Graebner, *History of Retirement*, 88–91.

7. Pensions for the Blind and Workmen's Compensation

1. *Lucas County v. State,* 75 Ohio State 114 (1906), 132–133.
2. *State v. Edmondson,* 89 Ohio 351 (1913); Harry Best, *The Blind: Their Condition and the Work Being Done for Them in the United States* (New York: Macmillan, 1919), 554–562.
3. Robert B. Irwin and Evelyn C. McKay, *Blind Relief Laws: Their Theory and Practice* (New York: American Foundation for the Blind, 1929), 11.
4. Best, *The Blind,* 548.
5. Ibid., 557–564.
6. See Frances A. Koestler, *The Unseen Minority: A Social History of Blindness in America* (New York: David McKay, 1974), 13–24. The American Foundation for the Blind was organized in 1921.
7. Irwin and McKay, *Blind Relief Laws,* 38, 106–117.
8. Crystal Eastman, *Work Accidents and the Law* (New York: Survey Associates, 1980).
9. Friedman and Ladinsky, "Social Change"; Edward D. Berkowitz, *Disabled Policy: America's Programs for the Handicapped* (New York: Cambridge University Press, 1987), 15–43; Lubove, *Struggle for Social Security,* 45–65; Skocpol, *Protecting,* 287–293; Rodgers, *Atlantic Crossings,* 247–252. All sources but Lubove rely on Friedman and Ladinsky.
10. Guthrie, "Constitutional Morality," 167–170.
11. Friedman and Ladinsky, "Social Change," 274; Charles McCurdy, "The 'Liberty of Contract' Regime in American Law," in *The State and Freedom of Contract,* ed. Harry N. Scheiber (Stanford, Calif.: Stanford University Press, 1998), 184–186.
12. Rodgers, *Atlantic Crossings,* 247–250.
13. *Ives v. South Buffalo Railway,* 201 N.Y. 271 (1911).
14. Guthrie, "Constitutional Morality," 169.
15. Lubove, *Struggle for Social Security,* 57–58.
16. Skocpol, *Protecting,* 293–296.
17. *New York Central Railroad Co. v. White,* 243 U.S. 188 (1917), 207.
18. *Mountain Timber Co. v. Washington,* 243 U.S. 219 (1917), 224, citing *Lochner v. New York,* 198 U.S. 45 (1905).
19. *Mountain Timber Co. v. Washington,* 239.
20. McCurdy, " 'Liberty of Contract' Regime," 186–187, 178.
21. *Stertz v. Industrial Insurance Commission,* 91 Wash. 588 (1916), quoted in *Mountain Timber Co. v. Washington,* 240.
22. *Mountain Timber Co. v. Washington,* 239–240.
23. Purcell, *Brandeis,* 150–153.
24. *New York Central Railroad Co. v. White,* 206; see also McCurdy, " 'Liberty of Contract' Regime," 186–187.
25. Indeed, the broader implications of these decisions were evident to governments as well as to social insurance advocates such as Brandeis. The federal government instituted old age pensions for its employees in 1920, and the leading state court case allowed that program's extension to the states in 1924 (see chapter five).

8. Old Age Pensions

1. Graebner, *History of Retirement,* 90–91, 120–124.
2. Katz, *In the Shadow,* 22–35.
3. Goodnow, *Social Reform,* 31.
4. Ibid., 13, 357–358.
5. Ibid., 17.
6. Ibid., 300–304.
7. Goodnow, *Comparative Administrative Law,* 2:74–78.
8. Goodnow, *Social Reform,* 293–297, 299–300.

9. Ibid., 301.

10. Ibid., 309.

11. Ibid., 301–304; Goodnow, "The Constitutionality of Old Age Pensions," *American Political Science Review* 5 (1912): 200–204.

12. Goodnow, *Social Reform,* 25–32; Orloff, *Politics of Pensions,* 4–6; Gordon, *Pitied,* 145–157.

13. Howard McBain, "Taxation for a Private Purpose," *Political Science Quarterly* 29 (1914): 213.

14. See, e.g., *Chamberlin, Inc. v. Andrews,* 271 N.Y. 1 (1936).

15. Goodnow, *Social Reform,* 15.

16. Michael Kammen, *A Machine That Would Go of Itself* (New York: Vintage Books, 1986), 226–229.

17. Goodnow, *Social Reform,* 13, 17.

18. For an extended discussion of Howard McBain, *The Living Constitution* (New York: Worker's Education Bureau Press, 1927), see White, *Constitution,* 208–209. White argues that McBain and others who agreed with him were advocating not only a constitution that would accommodate new facts but a constitution with principles that could change as the world in which it operated changed.

19. The alternative to expanding "service" to include all the work that people did was to portray old age pensions as a replacement for poor relief; see F. S. Baldwin, "Old Age Pension Schemes: A Criticism and a Program," *Quarterly Journal of Economics* 24 (1910): 713–742.

20. Orloff, *Politics of Pensions,* 69.

21. Other states followed suit. Industrial Commission of Wisconsin, *Report on Old Age Relief* (Madison, Wis., 1915); Pennsylvania Commission on Old Age Pensions (PCOAP), *Report* (Harrisburg: J. L. L. Kuhn, 1919); Ohio Health and Old Age Insurance Commission, *Health, Health Insurance, Old Age Pensions: Report, Recommendations, Dissenting Opinions* (Columbus, Ohio: F. J. Heer, 1919); California State Department of Social Welfare, *Old Age Dependency: A Study of the Care Given to Needy Aged in California* (Sacramento: State Department of Social Welfare, 1928).

22. Ohio Health and Old Age Insurance Commission, *Health,* 271.

23. Industrial Commission of Wisconsin, *Report,* 18.

24. Kammen, *Machine,* 226–229; White, *Constitution,* 208–210.

25. PCOAP, *Report* (1919), 4, 212.

26. The justification for the much-discussed Carnegie Fund, which paid pensions to professors, was that it would prevent dependence in both professors and their widows. Henry S. Pritchett, "Moral Influence of a University Pension System," *Popular Science* 79 (1911): 502–513. Even judges cited the fund: *State ex rel. Dudgeon v. Levitan,* 181 Wis. 326 (1923).

27. PCOAP, *Report* (1919), 231.

28. In 1917 the state legislature of New Hampshire asked the state supreme court for an advisory opinion on the constitutionality of proposed old age pensions. The justices issued a firm "no" eight days later, on February 15; only service would make pensions legitimate and, under the state constitution, only for a year at a time: *In re Opinion of the Justices,* 100 A. 49 (1917). That decision received only the briefest mention in the newspapers; a bill to prohibit closed booths in restaurants compelled greater attention, since closed booths invited sexual misadventure: "Leighton Bill Dead," *Concord Evening Monitor,* February 20, 1917, 1. Old age pensions were not yet the subject of a mass movement, and policy elites' discussion of them seemed to have little connection with what newspapers thought their readers wanted to see. On the two days after the supreme court issued its opinion, the headlines in the *Manchester Union* told of the war against Germany, while the state news centered on a proposed bill for back pay and a local fire. The legislative journal has neither discussion of the pension bill nor any real discussion of the supreme court opinion, and the committee reports for the time have not been saved. Only the newspaper articles and the opinion itself provide much in the way of clues to the nature of the controversy. What is clear is that the state would continue to insist on indigence as a criterion and that the supreme court was playing on some concerns that state legislators shared.

29. Gillman, *Constitution Besieged,* 127, 129; Guthrie, "Constitutional Morality," 165.

30. Smith, *Civic Ideals,* chap. 10.

31. PCOAP, *Report* (Harrisburg: J. L. L. Kuhn, 1925), 48–49.

32. Orloff, *Politics of Pensions,* 116.

33. PCOAP, *Report* (1925), 19.

34. California State Department of Social Welfare, *Old Age Dependency*, 57, 58.

35. The overlapping problems people faced would worry economists who contemplated more general disability payments during the New Deal; they saw the demand for them as potentially endless, given that disability presses home more urgently when jobs are scarce. See Berkowitz, *Disabled Policy*, 43–49.

36. California State Department of Social Welfare, *Old Age Dependency*, 34.

37. Don Conger Sowers, "Old Age Pensions in Colorado," *Regents of the University of Colorado Bulletin* 38, no. 18, gen. ser. 422 (1938): 9–10. In more recent years, states have had to abolish residency requirements, leading to both concern and research about whether states with more generous welfare payments attract people from states with less generous payments. *Shapiro v. Thompson*, 394 U.S. 618 (1969).

38. Goodnow, *Social Reform*, 30.

39. Bridges, *Morning Glories*.

40. Ronen Shamir, *Managing Legal Uncertainty: Elite Lawyers in the New Deal* (Durham, N.C.: Duke University Press, 1995), 72–74.

41. Friedman, *History of American Law*, 587.

42. Frederic C. Howe, "New Constitution of Ohio," *Survey* 28 (September 21, 1912): 758.

43. New York Child Labor Committee Papers, box 9, folder 4, New York State Archives, Albany.

44. Schlegel, *American Legal Realism*, 266; White, *Constitution*, 185.

45. Susan Sterett, "Constitutionalism and Old Age Spending: Pennsylvania in the 1920s," *Studies in American Political Development* 4 (1990): 231–248; William Draper Lewis, "Constitutional Revision in Pennsylvania," *American Political Science Review* 15, no. 4 (1921): 558–565.

46. "Little Interest in Tomorrow's Election," *Philadelphia Inquirer*, November 8, 1921, 12.

47. Skocpol, *Protecting*, 457.

48. J. P. Chamberlain and Sterling Pierson, "Old Age Pension Legislation," *American Bar Association Journal* 10 (1924): 111.

49. *Busser v. Snyder*, 5 Pa. D. & C. 842 (1924), quoting *State v. Osawkee Township*, 14 Kan. 418 at 422 (1875).

50. Robert W. Bruere, "Unconstitutional and Void," *Survey* 53 (1924): 69 (cited in subsequent state reports concerning old age pensions).

51. PCOAP, *Report* (1925), 64.

52. Brief of Argument [of appellants], *Busser v. Snyder*, 282 Pa. 440 (1925), 19.

53. Ibid., 22.

54. Orloff, *Politics of Pensions*, chap. 9.

55. Argument (of appellants), *Busser v. Snyder* (1925), 15; Argument of appellees, 6–10.

56. *Busser v. Snyder* (1925).

57. Ibid., 454.

58. Ibid., 457.

59. Ibid., 454.

60. Supplemental Brief for Appellees, *Busser v. Snyder* (1925), 78 (bold type in original brief).

61. Pennsylvania Constitution, art. 44, sec. 1. See also Argument (of appellees), *Busser v. Snyder* (1925), 20–24. The limit on delegation presaged a conflict at the federal level over the New Deal, discussed in the next section.

62. Orren and Skowronek, "Beyond the Iconography of Order," 330.

63. "Fisher Again Hits Vare Pension Bill," *Philadelphia Evening Bulletin*, April 11, 1927, 1; "Fisher Gratified at Pension Defeat," *Philadelphia Evening Bulletin*, April 12, 1927, 1, 12; "Old Age Pensions Listed for Monday," *Philadelphia Inquirer*, April 8, 1927, 4.

64. Gordon, *Pitied*, 225–235.

65. Skocpol, *Protecting*, 44–50, 87–89.

66. Oscar Kraines, *The World and Ideas of Ernst Freund: The Search for General Principles of Legislation and Administrative Law* (University: University of Alabama Press, 1974), 64–65.

67. "Winant Comment on State Laws," *Manchester Union*, March 4, 1931, 3; but see Cynthia R. Fa-

rina, "Supreme Judicial Court Advisory Opinions: Two Centuries of Interbranch Dialogue," in *The Supreme Judicial Court of Massachusetts, 1692–1992,* ed. Russell K. Osgood (Boston: Judicial History Society of Massachusetts, 1993).

68. *In re Opinion of the Justices,* 154 A. 217, 223 (1931).

69. *Manchester Union,* March 4, 1931, 1.

70. "The Supreme Court Decisions," *Manchester Union,* March 4, 1931, 6.

71. "Old Age Pension Law Is Ruled Invalid by Court," *Manchester Union,* March 4, 1931, 2.

72. "Adams Signs Bill Dooming Poor Farms," *Rocky Mountain News,* March 4, 1931, 1. See also Orloff, *Politics of Pensions,* 69.

73. "Movement Begun to Abolish Poorhouses thruout Colorado," *Denver Post,* November 22, 1931, 12.

74. Alberta Pike, "Suit Will Test Law on Pensioning Aged," *Rocky Mountain News,* March 9, 1932, 1.

75. Ibid., 3.

76. Samuel R. Crawford, *The Old Age Pension Movement in Colorado* (Denver, Colo.: Samuel R. Crawford, 1939), 11. I am grateful to Marshall Quiat, Ira Quiat's son, for pointing out this connection.

77. Http://www.courts.state.co.us/district/12th/oldjudges/blickhahn.htm.

78. L. A. Chapin, "Old-Age Pension Law Is Upheld in Argument Filed in Test Case," *Denver Post,* December 16, 1932, 39.

79. Ibid.

80. Ibid.

81. *Denver v. Lynch,* 92 Colo. 102 (1932).

82. For a discussion, see "Annotation: Constitutionality of Old Age Pensions or Assistance Acts," *American Law Reports* 86 (1933): 912–913. Other state courts also relied upon the concern about unconstitutional delegation regarding old age pensions; see, for example, *Smithberger v. Banning,* 129 Neb. 651 (1935), which struck down the appropriation Nebraska had made in anticipation of the federal Social Security Act. As in the Busser case in Pennsylvania, the plaintiffs are described as taxpayers. It's unlikely that a lone individual brought the case, given the difficulties of pursuing a lawsuit. Small businesses often object to new taxes, and, indeed, the Nebraska Petroleum Marketers, an association of gasoline dealers, joined the suit. See "Annotation: Constitutionality of Old Age Pensions or Assistance Acts," *American Law Reports* 101 (1936): 1215–1216.

83. Carol Greenhouse, "Just in Time: Temporality and the Cultural Legitimation of Law," *Yale Law Journal* 98 (1989): 1631–1651.

84. Crawford, *Old Age Pension Movement,* 15–17.

85. "Increased Old-Age Pensions Payment Is Voted by Colorado," *Denver Post,* November 4, 1936, 1.

86. Fred S. Warren, "Showdown Due on Colorado Age Pensions," *Denver Post,* December 27, 1936.

87. Fred S. Warren, "Legal Battle Looms as Rogers Advises No Fund to Be Created," *Denver Post,* December 30, 1936, 1.

88. Fred S. Warren, "Court Will Get Pension Puzzle," *Denver Post,* January 10, 1937, 1; Robert L. Chase, "State Holds Up Pensions; Hands Dispute to Court," *Rocky Mountain News,* January 15, 1937, 1.

89. Fred S. Warren, "$45 Pensions Amendment Valid, Says High Court," *Denver Post,* January 26, 2937, 1; *In re Interrogatories of the Governor,* 99 Colo. 591 (1937).

90. Quoted in Sowers, *Old Age Pensions,* 8.

91. *Beeland Wholesale Co. v. Kaufman* [Alabama], 174 So. 516 (1937); *Board of Education v. City of Louisville* [Kentucky] 288 Ky. 656 (1941). California (art. 4, sec. 22a, 1930), Colorado (art. 24, 1937), Kansas (art. 7, sec. 5, 1936), and Arkansas (Amendment 31, 1940) all enacted constitutional amendments in the decade that saw passage of the 1935 Social Security Act that specifically enabled the state to pay old age and sometimes civil service pensions. For a challenge to the form taxation took for the programs under the new Social Security Act (a challenge that did not succeed), see *In re Hunter,* 97 Colo. 279 (1936).

92. Ann Shola Orloff's comprehensive analysis of old age pensions mentions the Pennsylvania and

Arizona constitutional cases as isolated incidents. In sequencing old age pensions in the United States, Orloff notes that Colorado enacted pensions in 1927, one of the earliest states to do so. But it took years for Colorado's pensions to go anywhere, partly because of constitutional politics, ignored in Orloff's analysis (*Politics of Pensions,* 69).

93. See, e.g., Bruce Ackerman, "Higher Lawmaking," in *Responding to Imperfection: The Theory and Practice of Constitutional Amendment,* ed. Sanford Levinson (Princeton: Princeton University Press, 1995); Peter H. Irons, *The New Deal Lawyers* (Princeton: Princeton University Press, 1982), 272–290.

94. California noted briefly that although a means-tested program might face the objection of being class legislation (a public purpose constitutional problem), a more generous program would both cost too much and draw more people into the state; it also noted that both Pennsylvania and Arizona courts had held their states' programs to be unconstitutional (California State Department of Welfare, *Old Age Dependency,* 10).

Conclusion

1. One of the most popular undergraduate textbooks in constitutional law tells this story: David M. O'Brien, *Constitutional Law and Politics,* vol. 1: *Struggles for Power and Governmental Accountability* (New York: Norton, 2000), chap. 6.

2. White, *Constitution,* chap. 1.

3. Ackerman, "Higher Lawmaking," 79–82.

4. Cushman, *Rethinking,* 33–43; Gillman, *Constitution Besieged,* 1–15; Novkov, *Constituting Workers;* Elizabeth L. Saunders, "Equal Protection, Class Legislation, and Colorblindness," *Michigan Law Review* 96 (November 1997): 245–337; White, *Constitution,* 1–4, 303–310.

5. Gillman, *Constitution Besieged,* 175–194.

6. Cushman, *Rethinking,* 66; Irons, *New Deal Lawyers,* 226–253.

7. Susan Sterett, " 'Entitled to Have a Hearing': Due Process in the 1890s," *Social and Legal Studies* 3, no. 1 (1994): 47–70; White, *Constitution,* 94–127; Skowronek, *Building,* chap. 8.

8. For a discussion of the importance of state constitutions and an overview of the tasks states have taken on through them, see Laura Langer, *Judicial Review in the State Courts* (Albany: State University of New York Press, 2002); G. Alan Tarr, *Understanding State Constitutions* (Princeton: Princeton University Press, 1998).

9. Gordon, *Pitied,* 62.

10. Mink, *Wages of Motherhood.*

11. Ladd-Taylor, *Mother-Work,* 17–42.

12. Goodwin, *Gender,* 57–156.

13. See Gordon, *Pitied;* Mettler, *Dividing Citizens;* Skocpol, *Protecting.*

14. For a useful discussion of how to understand gender analytically rather than as descriptive only of real men and women, see Joan Scott, *Gender and the Politics of History* (New York: Columbia University Press, 1987).

15. Fraser and Gordon, "Genealogy of *Dependency.*"

16. E.g., U.S. Works Progress Administration, *Analysis of Constitutional Provisions affecting Public Welfare in the State of Colorado* (Washington, D.C.: Government Printing Office, 1937); likewise the states of Delaware, Florida, Idaho, Maine, Montana, Ohio, Pennsylvania, Rhode Island, and Wyoming.

17. See, e.g., U.S. Works Progress Administration, *Migrant Families,* by John M. Webb and Malcolm Brown (Washington, D.C.: Government Printing Office, 1937).

18. See, e.g., Browning, *Development of Poor Relief Legislation,* 119; Kennedy, *Ohio Poor Law,* 110.

19. See Abbott, introductions to Browning, *Development of Poor Relief Legislation,* vii–viii, and to Kennedy, *Ohio Poor Law,* vii–ix. See also Breckinridge, introduction to Shaffer, Keefer, and Breckinridge, *Indiana Poor Law,* vii–viii.

20. Hanson, "Federal State Building."

21. Hanson notes this briefly: ibid., 109, 111.

22. Orloff, *Politics of Pensions*, 17, 269.

23. White, *Constitution*, 103–104, 106.

24. Goodnow, *Comparative Administrative Law*, 19–24.

25. White, *Constitution*, 107–108.

26. *Panama Refining Co. v. Ryan*, 293 U.S. 388 (1935); *Schechter Poultry Corp. v. United States*, 295 U.S. 495 (1935).

27. Irons, *New Deal Lawyers*, 17–54. Recent scholarship has emphasized that point; see Cushman, *Rethinking the New Deal Court;* White, *Constitution*, 103–114.

28. Goodnow, *Social Reform.*

29. Gordon, *Pitied*, 203–234.

30. On the Chinese, see Lucy E. Salyer, *Laws Harsh as Tigers* (Chapel Hill: University of North Carolina Press, 1995). On railroads, see Skowronek, *Building*, chaps. 5, 8. For discussion of the deployment of the language of due process, see Sterett, "Entitled."

31. Cushman, *Rethinking*, 33–39, 156–159. Cushman relies in part on Peter Irons, *New Deal Lawyers*, who offers evidence concerning the National Recovery Administration (chap. 2) and Agricultural Adjustment Administration (chap. 7) that supports this conclusion, though it is not what he argues.

32. White, *Constitution*, 36–37, 233–236.

33. Ludes, "Taxation."

34. See, e.g., *Milheim v. Moffat Tunnel Improvement District*, 72 Colo. 268 (1922); and 262 U.S. 710 (1923).

35. McBain, *Living Constitution.*

36. Orren, "Labor Regulation," 105–110.

37. Alexander Keyssar, *Out of Work: The First Century of Unemployment in Massachusetts* (New York: Cambridge University Press, 1986), 212–213.

38. *Chamberlin, Inc. v. Andrews*, 271 N.Y. 1 (1936); *Gillum v. Johnson*, 62 P. 2d. 1037 (1936); *Howes Bros. Co. v. Unemployment Compensation Commission of Massachusetts*, 5 N.E. 2d. 720 (1936); *Beeland Wholesale Co. v. Kaufman*. A divided Supreme Court affirmed the New York Court of Appeals's decision approving unemployment compensation: *Chamberlin, Inc. v. Andrews*, 299 U.S. 515 (1936).

39. *Carmichael v. Southern Coal and Coke Co.*, 301 U.S. 495 (1937), 514–515.

40. Ibid., 515–516.

41. Robert Jackson, *The Struggle for Judicial Supremacy* (New York: Vintage Books, 1941), 227.

42. *Helvering v. Davis*, 301 U.S. 619 (1937), 641–644.

43. Gordon, *Pitied*, 254, 256–260.

44. Martha Derthick, *Policymaking for Social Security* (Washington, D.C.: Brookings Institution, 1979), 31, 288.

Index

Page references in italics refer to illustrations